Absent-minded Imperialism

ABSENT-MINDED IMPERIALISM

Britain and the Expansion of Empire
in Nineteenth-century Brazil

PETER RIVIÈRE

Tauris Academic Studies
I.B. Tauris Publishers
LONDON · NEW YORK

Published in 1995 by
Tauris Academic Studies
an imprint of I.B.Tauris & Co Ltd
45 Bloomsbury Square
London WC1A 2HY

175 Fifth Avenue
New York NY 10010

In the United States of America
and in Canada distributed by
St Martin's Press
175 Fifth Avenue
New York NY 10010

Copyright © 1995 Peter Rivière

All rights reserved. Except for brief quotations in a review, this book, or any part thereof, may not be reproduced in any form without permission from the publisher.

A full CIP record for this book is available from the British Library

A full CIP record for this book is available from the Library of Congress

ISBN 1 85043 913 3

Library of Congress catalog card number 94–61500

Set in Monotype Bembo by
Ewan Smith, London E8

Printed and bound in Great Britain by
WBC Ltd, Bridgend, Mid Glamorgan

CONTENTS

	List of illustrations	vii
	Foreword	ix
	Map of the area	xiii
1	Introduction	1
2	First stages 1829–1837	10
3	The first mission at Pirara 1838	30
4	Retreat to Urwa 1839	50
5	Retreat to Waraputa 1840–41	75
6	The occupation of Pirara 1842	92
7	The withdrawal from Pirara 1842	122
8	The closing scenes 1842–43	139
9	The aftermath	161
10	Afterthoughts	169
	Appendix	178
	Bibliography	183
	Index	188

ILLUSTRATIONS

1 The boats of the boundary commission at Yupukarri inlet.
2 A temporary camp of the boundary commission.
3 Guards intercepting two mounted Brazilians carrying a letter from the fort commander, 15 February 1842.
4 Captain Leal, Senhora Libradiña and Friar José at the head of the column, 4 April 1842.
5 Pirara after the British occupation in 1842.
6 The quarters of the boundary commission at Pirara.
7 Fort New Guinea, the quarters of the detachment of the 1st West Indies Regiment outside Pirara.
8 The junction of the rivers Mahoo and Takutu.

We [the English] seem, as it were, to have conquered and peopled half the world in a fit of absence of mind.

J.R. Seeley

FOREWORD

This study deals with a dispute between Brazil and Great Britain in the middle of the last century over the boundary between the former and British Guiana. In outline the story is easy to tell. In 1838 a British missionary founded a mission in the interior, at a place called Pirara, which he assumed to be in British Guiana. This was contested by the Brazilians, who ordered him to leave. In reply the British government sent a detachment of troops on a month's journey to eject the Brazilians, which it duly did, and a boundary commission to survey the frontier. The two governments quickly decided that the question should be resolved by negotiation (although it was over sixty years before it was settled by arbitration) and the troops were recalled.

This boundary dispute has given rise to a vast literature, but this book is not designed as a contribution to that corpus. Nor has it anything to say on the matter of the boundary between British Guiana and Venezuela, a question that arose at the same time and that was also not settled until the end of the century. This study is narrowly focused on the events that occurred between 1838 and 1843 on the frontier between British Guiana and Brazil, and it concentrates almost exclusively on those who were directly involved. It is a study in micro-history. This is made possible because the sources are particularly rich; many of the individuals involved left behind eyewitness accounts in letters, reports and journals. The intentions, motivations and actions of these people are well displayed. The assorted bunch of characters includes explorers, soldiers, missionaries, officials, diplomats, cowboys and Indians.

The British sources are richer than the Brazilian, and the explanation for this is simply that on the Brazilian side, there is only one individual immediately involved who was likely to have produced a written account, whereas on the British side there are several such people. Furthermore there is no evidence that the Brazilian, a priest, ever did keep any personal record of the events and even if he had the chance of its survival are remote given the conditions under which he lived and finished his days. On the other hand numerous official communications penned by him are extant and, along with other such documents, do provide a Brazilian view of the affair. However, because of the imbalance in the nature of the material available the reader will inevitably find that this work has a British slant to it.

This position can be justified by one of the aims of this book, which is to examine a single example of the processes of empire building through the eyes of those physically involved. It will be seen that whereas decisions reached in London and Rio de Janeiro settled the matter, events were put in train in the first place by individuals taking actions, the consequences of which they either were unaware or chose to ignore. The politicians and officials at home were driven, often reluctantly, by events in the field.

The work is mainly based on documents in the archives of the Church Missionary Society at Birmingham University, the Public Record Office at Kew, the Archivo Histórico do Itamaraty, the Biblioteca Nacional and the Arquivo Nacional in Rio de Janeiro, and the National Archives of Guyana in Georgetown.

Many of the documents, either in whole or in part, were reproduced by the two sides to the boundary dispute in the cases they made when the matter went to arbitration in 1904. It was, however, felt necessary to go back to the originals as far as possible because the volumes of papers produced by the two sides in the boundary dispute have a very different purpose from that of the current study. What I have found interesting was often of little relevance to the boundary case and had thus been omitted from those volumes. Equally important have been the comments and minutes noted on these documents by various officials, as they provide insights that no reading between the lines would reveal. On the few occasions where I do cite the boundary case volumes it is because I have failed to locate the original of the particular document in question.

One of the most valuable sources has been the writings, the journal and letters, of Thomas Youd, the missionary who was not simply at the centre of the whole affair but whose actions triggered it off. This material has been little used before and I do not think there is any need to apologise for the inclusion of extensive verbatim quotations from it. In contrast, the best-known published account of the incident is undoubtedly that by Richard Schomburgk, originally published in German in 1847 and in an English translation in 1922. Richard Schomburgk was an eyewitness of the events but also to some extent a spectator not directly involved. However, it is necessary to treat his work with caution. He often gets his chronology of events wrong, frequently embroiders incidents and on occasion gives the impression of having observed something of which he only heard. An example of this is a case of revenge sorcery and the disposal of a young Indian's corpse which he expressly claims to have observed, whereas there is no doubt that it was described to him by Youd, who had witnessed the event the previous year. This position is supported by the writer of another journal who was present when Richard Schomburgk was (CW/O/100: 49; RS I: 253-4; Goodall 1962b: 47).

Despite these drawbacks Richard Schomburgk's descriptions are vivid and help to bring events to life; because of this I have not hesitated to cite his work at length. Indeed it is not only from Thomas Youd and Richard Schomburgk that I have cited extensively. I have to a large degree tried to leave those involved to speak for themselves wherever it is feasible for them to do so. This use of citation has as its aim to increase the emphasis placed on those most directly involved in the affair.

In order to sharpen further the focus on these actors I have also adopted another device in the construction of this work. This is to provide, where possible, some biographical and personal information about these people and virtually none about those less immediately involved. The purpose of this is gradually to blur the focus as one moves away from the action. Round the immediate periphery people are identified individually or by their title but as we shift still further away and towards the seats of government, even this personalization disappears and most of the time individuals are simply blended into their organizations, for example the British Colonial Office or the Brazilian Ministry of Foreign Affairs.

The main part of the work, the central eight chapters, is basically narrative. The construction of this narrative presented certain problems of a chronological nature. Because of the slowness of communication it was not unusual for some months to pass between the date at which some event occurred and news of it reaching the authorities and decisions being made (or not made, as was often the case). In order not to jump around too much from one place to another, although it has been impossible to avoid this completely, the action on the ground is used to provide the chronological framework and events elsewhere related to what was happening there. To help the reader, an outline chronology of the main events is provided in the Appendix.

I would like to acknowledge all the help and assistance that I received from many people during the course of preparing this book. In particular I would like to thank the various librarians and archivists on whose collections this work is mainly founded. Without permission from the Church Missionary Society to quote from its archives, this book would not have been the same and I am extremely grateful to it. I am indebted to the Hayter Fund and the Faculty Board of Anthropology and Geography of the University of Oxford whose financial support made possible a visit to Brazil and Guyana. Great gratitude is also due to the British Academy, which contributed both to my research in South America and to the publication of this work. The inclusion of Edward Goodall's coloured illustrations would not have been possible without a generous subvention from Booker Tate. Their presence has made all the difference to the book.

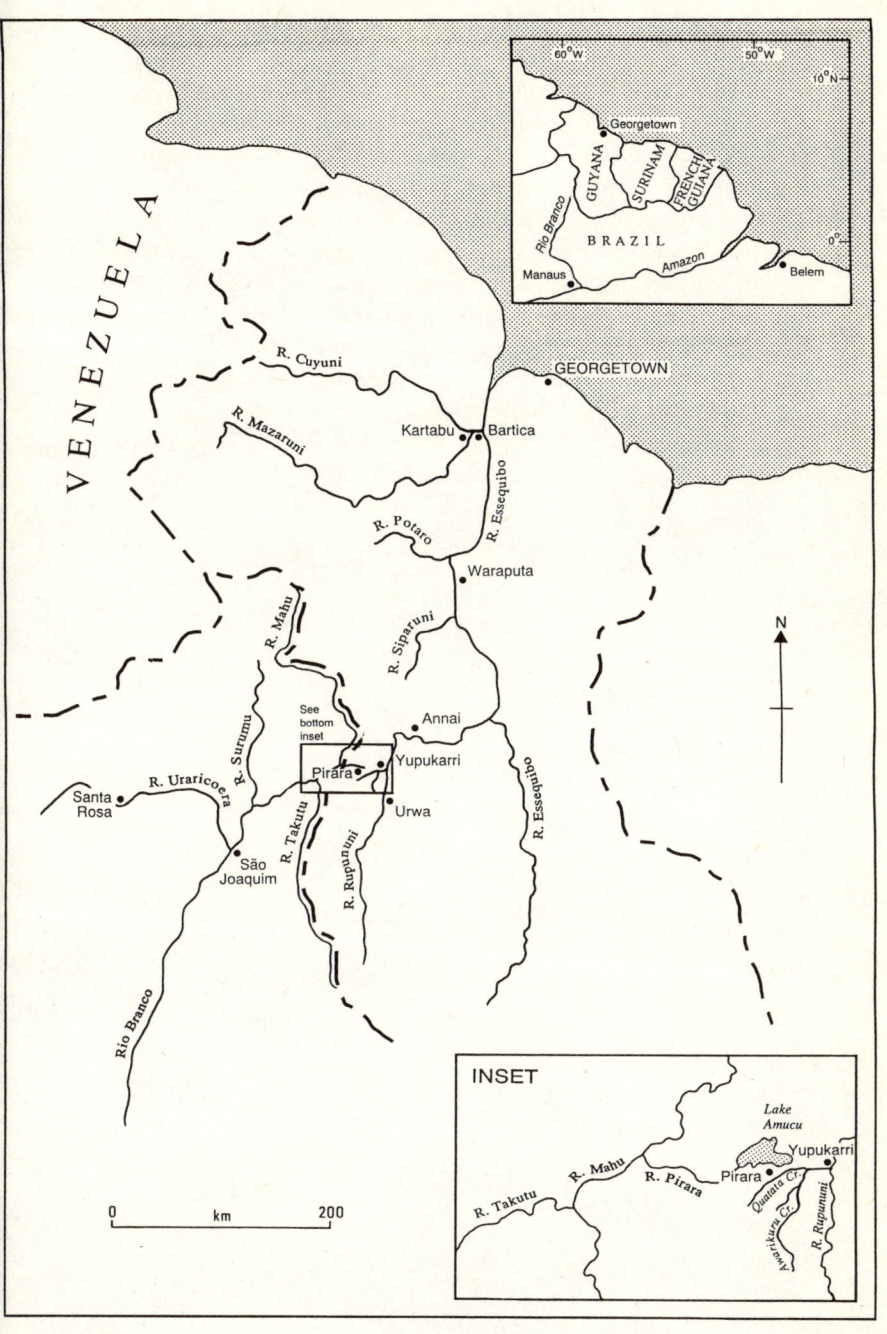

CHAPTER I
INTRODUCTION

Pirara is a creek, said to be named after a small red speckled fish with which its waters abound. In turn it gave its name in the past to an Indian village on its banks and today to a ranch. Briefly, during the period with which this book is concerned, it was the site of a mission and the locus of a frontier squabble between Brazil and Great Britain.

The Indian village of Pirara lay on open savannah in what is today Guyana, close to the point where the Pirara river leaves Lake Amucu to flow westwards to join the River Mahu or Ireng, the present-day frontier with Brazil. It does this at Pirara Mouth, not far above that river's confluence with the Takutu. To the east of Pirara is the Rupununi River, the major left-bank tributary of the Upper Essequibo. Pirara, therefore, lies on the flat watershed between rivers that form part of the Amazonian system and those that flow direct to the Atlantic Ocean. Whereas in the dry season the nearest navigable point on the latter river system is at Pirara Landing or Yupukarri Inlet, some five miles away, in the wet season it is possible to bring a canoe up the Awarikuru and Quatata creeks to within a few hundred yards of the village. Since it lies astride the portage connecting two major river systems, there is good reason to believe that Pirara was an important link in the extensive pre-Conquest aboriginal trade routes that covered South America.

The main disadvantages that the rivers here suffer from as highways for travel and commerce are two. Both the Rio Branco, which above its confluence with the Takutu is called the Uraricoera, and the Essequibo rise on the uplands of the Guiana Shield and as they flow off it their courses are broken by series of rapids, much worse in the latter case than the former, that greatly impede easy and safe communication. The difficulties that these rapids present to travellers are exacerbated by the second disadvantage; the great seasonal variation in water level. The difference in distance between Pirara and the nearest navigable point on the Rupununi River depending on the season has already been noted, but the problems are far more general than that. In the dry season (roughly September–March), and particularly at the height of it, the depth of water may be as little as a few inches, making it necessary to dig channels in the riverbeds along which to drag the canoes, while what are rapids at highwater represent walls of black rock. In the wet season, the force of the flood makes travel hazardous in both directions; going upstream was extremely hard work, especially when the only means of propulsion was human force. Canoes had to be manhandled through the rapids with the crews often up to their chests in the fast-flowing waters. On the Rio Branco during the wet season, the larger boats were literally hauled up the river by a rope and hook. The technique was for a light canoe to take the hook connected by rope to the boat and secure it to a tree. The boat was then pulled up to the hook and made fast, and the whole procedure repeated. In this way the journey from Manaus up the Rio Branco might take sixty days.

Crossing the savannahs during the dry season, especially if it is possible to avoid the midday heat, is a pleasant and pleasing experience. The scenery is beautiful, with the flat or rolling grasslands broken by patches of forest, strings of palms marking the beds of creeks and in the background hazy grey-blue mountains. Travel over the same terrain in the wet season is a misery, with much of the savannah a swampy flood, the creeks major obstacles and hordes of biting and blood-sucking insects.

At any season of the year, Pirara was remote but more so from the seats of power in Brazil than from Georgetown, capital of British Guiana. Whilst it often took longer, an individual travelling light at the right time of the year, could make the upstream journey from Georgetown to Pirara in under four weeks and the return trip in less than half that time. On the other hand, the Upper Rio Branco being in the Province of Pará, all important decisions had to be made in Belém at the mouth of the Amazon. This often meant a delay of months between reporting an event and the receipt of any response to it.

That Pirara formed an important junction in indigenous trade routes is witnessed by a report of Dutch manufactured goods finding their way into the hands of Amerindians on the Amazon as early as 1639. Europeans appear to have been aware of the portage at Pirara since the previous century, and the Dutch may have crossed it by 1660.[1] There is, however, no reason to think that the trade which continued over the centuries involved any direct contact between the Dutch and Portuguese, the latter being strongly opposed to it. It is far more likely that the exchange of goods and slaves was basically an Amerindian commerce, fuelled by Western goods.

The Portuguese had almost certainly penetrated into the Rio Branco during the seventeenth century and from the early years of the eighteenth century were making expeditions up that river and its tributaries to collect forest produce, and reduce or make alliances with Indians. There was a severe shortage of labour on the Rio Negro as elsewhere in Amazonia and the Rio Branco's population offered a relatively untapped source. At the same time there was a fundamental vagueness about the frontier between Portuguese and Spanish territory in South America, and being in *de facto* possession greatly strengthened any claim. Clearly the minute European population could not achieve this on its own and the policy was to use Indians for the purpose. Possession could be claimed by having one's 'own' Indians there; that is, Indians who could be persuaded to recognise Brazilian sovereignty.[2]

Towards the middle of the eighteenth century, as a result of increasing knowledge about the Rio Branco's connexion with the rivers of the Dutch colonies and of other incidents, the Portuguese began to consider a more secure and settled claim to the area than that provided by expeditions and Indian alliances. In 1752, a Royal Command ordered the construction of a fort on the Rio Branco, but through lack of resources this was commuted to regular patrols. While this did not prevent continued Dutch influence among the Amerindians of the Upper Rio Branco, it was not the Dutch but the Spanish who finally caused the Portuguese to take the occupation of the Rio Branco seriously. In 1775, a Dutch deserter arrived in Barcelos, capital of the *capitania* of São José do Rio Negro, and reported that Spaniards, coming from the Orinoco, had formed settlements on the Uraricoera. The Portuguese responded by sending an armed force which had little difficulty in overpowering the garrison on the Uraricoera and another force that had penetrated into the Takutu and perhaps as far as the Essequibo. The construction in 1775 and 1776 of Fort São Joaquim, overlooking the confluence of the Uraricoera and Takutu rivers, where the river becomes the Rio Branco, and the permanent presence of the Portuguese in the area were the direct outcome of the Spanish intrusion.

The next two decades were a period of considerable Portuguese activity in the Upper Rio Branco. A number of geographical and scientific expeditions visited the region and a policy of settling the Indians in villages was actively pursued. Attempts at this all ended in failure; the Indians revolted and deserted their villages in 1780–81, 1790 and again in 1798. These uprisings and the Portuguese response to them, including the transportation of many people to distant areas of Amazonas, meant that by the end of the eighteenth century the banks of the Rio Branco were virtually denuded of their native population.

At some point in the late 1780s or early 1790s,[3] cattle were introduced on to the Rio Branco savannahs. Initially there were three ranches, two in private hands and one state-owned. However, when the two private ranchers died, their properties were confiscated by the state, on an excuse of debt, so all three ranches came under state ownership. Despite or because of what appears to have been rather casual husbandry, the herds flourished, many animals running wild and spreading out across the tropical grasslands of the region. In the late 1830s, Robert Schomburgk (RGS/RHS: 1840c) was told that there were some 3,000 cattle under management, 5,000 running wild and 500 horses, but he considered these claims an exaggeration. Whatever their exact number there is no doubt that there were extensive herds of cattle on the savannahs, as most visitors to the area testify.

From 1800, after a quarter of a century of considerable attention and activity, the Rio Branco more or less reverted to being a backwater. Nor were things that much different in what had been the interior of the Dutch zone of influence, the colonies of Essequibo, Demerara and Berbice. The Dutch had shown considerable interest in the interior and its inhabitants, whose friendship they courted. Indeed political alliance with the Amerindians, in particular the Caribs, was an important part of their survival strategy. Friendly Indians not only enslaved other Amerindians and acted as a defence force against any intrusion by the Spanish from the Orinoco region, but were also a powerful deterrent against revolt or desertion by the African slaves who heavily outnumbered the Dutch colonists.[4]

During the Napoleonic wars, the Dutch colonies of Demerara, Essequibo and Berbice changed hands several times, and even if the British held *de facto* possession from 1803 onwards, this was not officially confirmed until a convention signed by Great Britain and the Netherlands in 1814. The three colonies were finally merged into the single colony of British Guiana in 1831. It cannot be said that the British authorities paid any great attention to the interior of their new colony; they mainly seemed happy in their ignorance of it and its inhabitants. Even so there were a number of expeditions into the interior. For example, the appearance in Georgetown in 1810 by a Carib 'chief', Manariwan or Mahanarva, who sought to reactivate an old alliance that he had with the Dutch, did result in an official expedition into the interior to assess the potential threat the Indian population represented, but this was an exception rather than the rule.[5]

Undoubtedly the best known of the handful of travellers who visited the area during the first three decades of the 19th century, for his eccentricities among other things, was Charles Waterton. He commented on how thinly inhabited the region seemed to be but does mention a white man who had fled to live among the Macushi Indians in order to avoid his creditors (1973: 21). On his first journey in 1812, he visited Pirara, a small Indian settlement, and made his way to Fort São Joaquim.[6] Waterton described the place in these terms:

> It has been much neglected; the floods of water have carried away the gate, and destroyed the wall on each side of it; but the present commander is putting it into thorough repair. When finished, it will mount six nine, and six twelve pounders.
> In a straight line with the fort, and within a few yards of the river, stand the commander's house, the barracks, the chapel, the father confessor's house, and two others, all at little intervals from each other; and these are the only buildings at Fort St. Joachim (1973: 29).

As we will see, the commander's plans to put the fort back into thorough repair came to nothing. Indeed the neglect of the region by both the Brazilian and British sides, and its resulting stagnation, continued into the 1830s.

At the beginning of the 1830s the only non-Amerindians, a bare handful, residing on the Rupununi savannahs were some escaped African slaves and at least one deserter from Brazil who has a part to play in this story. All of these had intermarried with Amerindians and were living as such. On the Rio Branco side the non-Amerindian population was rather larger and an 1840 census, if not necessarily accurate, gives an idea of its size. In the Upper Rio Branco, the area around São Joaquim, the census gives the population as consisting of ten whites and sixty mamelucos, which presumably constituted the garrison, ranchers and cowhands of the region (Araujo e Amazonas 1852).

This same census puts the Amerindian population on the Upper Rio Branco as 130. While this low figure may reflect the result of the reductions, revolts, massacres and deportations that occurred during the last twenty years of the eighteenth century, it may also indicate a continuing insecurity. Although it is difficult to estimate their frequency, as we shall see, there were still parties coming from the Rio Negro in search of Indian labour; expeditions described by the Brazilians as recruiters of Indian labour and by the British as slave-raiders. In fact the total Amerindian population of the whole savannah region, although difficult to estimate exactly, was much larger than this, perhaps numbering 5,000 Indians or more. Most of these were Carib-speaking Macushi and Arawak-speaking Wapishiana, although there are numerous references to other groups in the sources, including Atorai, Taruma, Caribs and Arecuna. All these people subsisted on an economy based on slash-and-burn cultivation, hunting, fishing and the collecting of wild produce. Their villages tended to be small, often with no more than thirty people, and were usually built on open savannah but with easy access to water and relatively close to the forest where their fields lay. Villages were not permanent sites but were relocated every few years. The population was also fairly mobile, moving easily from one village to another. Although the contemporary sources make frequent references to 'chiefs', in practice, unless supported by some external, non-Amerindian agent, they wielded little coercive power and what authority they had was mainly achieved through the exercise of personal influence.

It is wrong to think of this Amerindian population as being composed of uncontacted tribes. All of them had indirect links with non-Indian people and many of them had had direct contact and relationships of various sorts with Europeans for as much as two centuries. The Amerindians had long been reliant on manufactured goods, especially metal cutting tools, and obtaining possession of these was reason enough for maintaining contact. In the early 1830s there were certainly Macushi Indians trading down the Essequibo and across to the Demerara River. Even so the region round Pirara was a backwater that claimed little attention from either the Brazilian or the British side. The reason for this, other than its remoteness, inaccessibility and doubtful economic value, was that both sides had rather more serious matters on their hands.

In the case of Brazil these were the uprising during the 1830s known as the *cabanagem* and the border dispute with the French over Amapá. The *cabanagem*, a term reputedly derived from *cabana*, a rural thatched hut, basically involved the uprising of those who lived in such dwellings, those of Amerindian and mixed descent, against those of more immediate European, mainly Portuguese, origin. It was a revolt of the downtrodden and exploited against their oppressors. The uprising, which affected much of the Province of Pará, was at its fiercest in 1835–36 but it was not fully over until the end of the decade and fear of its revival in isolated parts of the province continued into the next. It was characterised by bloody massacres and its suppression by similar atrocities, leaving, it has been estimated, thirty thousand people, about a fifth of the province's population, dead.

The border dispute with the French, although peacefully settled, was also traumatic in its own way since it represented a threat to the territorial integrity of the province not far distant from the provincial capital, Belém. The French laid claim to a vast stretch of territory, today's state of Amapá, that would have extended the frontier of French Guiana to the north bank of the Amazon and given them part control over the river's mouth. This event certainly distracted attention from what was going on in the more remote regions of the province.

In British Guiana, the plantocrats, because of the colony's unusual constitution, which gave the final say in financial matters to the Combined Court on which they had a majority, were the *de facto* rulers of the colony.[7] In the 1830s they were much more worried about who was going to work their plantations following the abolition of slavery than with the remote and unremunerative interior which, as far as they were concerned (since Amerindians did not count), was to all intents and purposes unpopulated. A visitor in 1831 remarked that 'The merchants and planters on the coast ridicule the idea of expeditions into the interior, attended as they are with risk, discomfort and no profit' (Alexander 1833: 77). The plantocracy's confrontations with the colonial governor over the labour question and the civil list virtually brought the administration of the colony to a standstill at times.

It is also necessary to consider briefly the relations between Brazil and Great Britain at this time. They were not easy and the main bone of contention, as far as this study is concerned, was slavery and the slave trade. Slavery, and thus the slave trade, were an integral part of the Brazilian economy at that period. British attempts to persuade Brazil to abolish the trade began almost as soon as Brazil declared its independence in 1822. They became tied up with the negotiation for Britain's recognition of Brazilian sovereignty, and the treaty signed in 1826 that gave that recognition included the agreement that Brazil would abolish the slave trade in 1830. Although Brazil passed a law in 1831 making the slave trade illegal it proved totally ineffective, and by 1838 British ministers in Brazil reported that the Brazilian government, far from trying to suppress the trade, was protecting it. The effective suppression of the trade then fell to the Royal Navy, which up until 1839 was impeded by the limits on the action it could take. From that date Britain unilaterally extended its powers and the navy achieved considerable success. However, such success, especially when it involved captured slave ships being brought into Brazilian ports under a prize crew, ships being seized in Brazilian territorial waters, and landing parties operating on Brazilian soil, caused deep hostility towards Britain. It was this as much as anything that coloured Anglo-Brazilian relationships during the period with which this story is concerned.[8]

This was basically the situation in the 1830s, and it is not too surprising if the question of where the boundary between Brazil and British Guiana lay had not crossed anyone's mind. However, in 1838 this all changed as a result of one man's determination to found a mission among the Macushi Indians, at Pirara. This is where the story begins.

Notes

1. For an early history of the Pirara portage, see Bos (n.d.). The documentary sources referred to in that paper suggest that the Europeans were regular users of the Pirara portage by the eighteenth century, especially if one assumes that only a small proportion of the journeys made was documented.

2. For a detailed account of Portuguese Indian policy and practice during the seventeenth and eighteenth centuries, see Farage (1991). The title of her book, *As muralhas dos sertões*, is taken from a seventeenth-century description of the Indians as the 'bulwarks of the interior'. The following summary of events in the Rio Branco basin during the eighteenth century is taken from Farage (1991) and Hemming (1990a and 1990b). The former author is mainly concerned with Portuguese policy and treatment of the Amerindian population, whereas the latter provides more general accounts.

3. The exact date is uncertain but it is not before 1787 and it is known that cattle were there by 1793.

4. For an account of Dutch relations with the Amerindians, see Whitehead 1988; for the British Amerindian policy, see Menezes 1977a.

5. Richard Schomburgk (II: 346) gives an account of the Carib chief's visit to Georgetown and of the subsequent expedition into the interior led by Dr Hancock. Farage (1991: 169–73) provides an interesting commentary on the British treatment of Manariwan. Hancock and his companions (Van Sirtema and D.P. Simon) visited Fort São Joaquim and attempted to get permission to return to Demerara via the Amazon. The anxieties their visit gave rise to among the Brazilian authorities are well documented in an exchange of letters between the commandant of Fort São Joaquim and the governor of the Rio Negro. This correspondence is reproduced in part in Braz. M1, Ann 1. A more complete, if not complete, set of the correspondence is in the Biblioteca Nacional, Rio de Janeiro (Officios (quatro) dirigidos pelo governador da Capitania do Rio Negro: Ms 17, 4, 18).

6. Waterton found near Pirara some Indians and soldiers sent from Fort São Joaquim to make a canoe. A letter was despatched to the fort requesting permission to visit. The commander of Fort São Joaquim, Thomaz da Costa Teixeira, who had proved such an obstacle to Hancock's expedition the previous year, came to meet Waterton who, when they met, was suffering from a fever. The commandant is reported to have said: 'The orders I have received forbidding the admission of strangers, were never intended to be put in force against a sick English gentleman' (1973: 27–8). At the time of Hancock's visit there was also a party in the vicinity of Pirara making a canoe. In the Boundary Arbitration Brazil argued that this was evidence that at the time Pirara was occupied by Brazil.

7. For a summary description of the British Guiana constitution at the time and the problems it gave rise to see Menezes 1977a: 7–10 and Moore 1987: 52–5.

8. For a full account of the abolition of the Brazilian slave trade, see Bethell 1970.

CHAPTER 2

FIRST STAGES
1829–1837

In September 1829 John Armstrong, a catechist of the Church Missionary Society (henceforth Society), working among plantation labourers, proposed that a mission be founded to instruct the Amerindians. A month later he made a journey up the Essequibo River with the purpose of locating a site for such a mission. The place he chose was Bartica Point, the peninsula between the rivers Essequibo and Mazaruni. He received the go-ahead to found the mission in November 1830 and took up residence at Bartica Point between mid-March and mid-April 1831.[1] At the very end of that year, he sought permission for a visit to England during 1832, and was supported in his request by the Reverend Leonard Strong, Secretary of the Corresponding Committee of the Church Missionary Society (henceforth Committee) in Georgetown, who also asked for a replacement to be sent out (CW/O/14: 10, 11, 16, 17 and 19).[2]

Both requests were granted and just before Christmas 1832, Armstrong was joined by a young assistant catechist, Thomas Youd, recently arrived in British Guiana. He was a Liverpudlian who had attended the Society's college at Islington in North London. He was about 23 when he first arrived in British Guiana. The Reverend Strong described him as young and active but rather immature and wrote 'I should think Bunyan would say that he has not gone far on pilgrimage' (CW/M/2: 463).

Armstrong agreed that before he returned to England he would make a trip of twenty days' paddle into the interior. This he did between February and May 1833, accompanied, as interpreter, by a free coloured man who had been in the habit of trading with the Macushi (CW/O/81: 39).[3] He ascended the Rupununi River and made his headquarters at Pirara. Whilst there he endeavoured 'to obtain their [the Macushi Indians'] goodwill for a settlement of missionaries among them' (Brit C, Ann 2: 5). It is possible that there was a sizeable Amerindian village at Pirara in 1833, since we know that two years later it consisted of fourteen houses and 80–100 inhabitants (RHS 1836: 242). While there he wrote two letters (on 16 and 29 April) to the commandant of Fort São Joaquim. In the first he requested the commandant to put a stop to the depredations that the Portuguese slave-raiders were making on British subjects, by whom he meant the Amerindians of the area, and threatened to report the matter to the British Government 'who, I believe, will endeavour to protect their helpless subjects from being enslaved'. In the second he declined what appears to have been an invitation from the commandant to visit the fort (CW/O/14: 23).

Armstrong arrived back at Bartica on 18 May and soon after sailed back to England as planned. He did not return to British Guiana until April 1835. While in England he expressed a wish to set up a mission in the interior, and noted the Indians' keenness on the idea. However, he also commented on the expense and difficulties of the enterprise given the remoteness of the area and the fact that such a mission will need a staff of three (CW/O/14: 25 and 29; CW/O/100: 30).

In Armstrong's absence, Youd got on with the business of running the Bartica Mission. His daily and weekly schedules were very heavy. Not only were there divine services for Indians, Coloureds and slaves, and school for children and adults to be held at Bartica, but much of the week was occupied with journeys to settlements in the neighbourhood. In 1834, he founded a school on the Cuyuni, spent three days a week there and believed that if it were possible to hold divine service there on Sundays there would be a congregation of a hundred Indians. He administered medicine to sick Indians and learnt to pull teeth. He often had difficulty in recruiting adults to paddle his canoe and had to rely on children which, he complained, slowed down his work. This lack of help with many secular tasks was a frequent problem, and on one occasion, after having overexerted himself unloading supplies from his canoe, he remarked that it is 'an unsuitable station for a Gentlemanly Missionary' and that often he is no more than a common labourer. He later described his job as being that of 'schoolmaster, doctor, sick nurse, steward or provider, overseer and manager in cultivation, architect, boat builder, mason, blacksmith, etc.' (CW/O/100: 33, 34 and 39).

In March 1834, Youd decided to build himself a house at a place called Bartica Grove on the Essequibo side of the peninsula, a distance of about two miles from the site where Armstrong had settled and built a combined chapel and dwelling. He took up residence there in November 1834, but the decision had unforeseen repercussions. The reason he initially gave was that he would have easier access to the settlements there, but he later referred to the poor condition into which Armstrong's building had fallen and his unwillingness to repair it. He then went on to argue that the building had been badly designed, it was excessively hot during the day, and had injured his health (CW/O/100: 33, 34, 35 and 36).

From the start, various themes run through his journal and correspondence. Within six months of his arrival at Bartica, there are the first references to the fevers that were to afflict him continuously. Even earlier than that, we find Youd mentioning the importance of learning Carib; he devoted much time to this activity. Indeed, it was his desire to do this and to visit distant settlements of Indians that appears to underlie the wish, frequently expressed in his journal, for an assistant to teach school. This wish he fulfilled in August 1833, not long after Armstrong had departed for England. He visited Georgetown and on the 12th of that month employed on a trial basis John Doyce, a single coloured man, aged 24, a baker by trade who came with good recommendations. John Doyce, about whom we know little more, was to share many of Youd's hardships over the following years. A year later Youd was unexpectedly joined by his 16-year-old nephew, who visited the mission with the intention of working there for three or four months. In fact he ended up by assisting in the school and doing other chores for fifteen months, until his death there in December 1835 (CW/O/100: 31, 35 and 40).

In this first year we can also recognise some of Youd's other traits. One was his enthusiasm, verging on impetuosity, mixed with determination. He was determined to eradicate what he saw as the evils and wrongs in Indian life. These included, as might be expected, such practices as drinking, dancing and shamanism. On 9 June 1834 his journal records:

> On coming close to a party of Indians the other day, who were dancing ... they immediately stopped, as soon as they perceived me coming towards them from the bush, each one of the dancers fled, music was soon put aside; and feign would they have been clear of the fault they knew I should blame them for. I merely speak of this, to shew that we are gaining influence.
>
> Peïng [shamanism] is still, and will I think continue to be daily practised till an utter change comes. On Thursday night last, I was about laying down to sleep, when I heard an Indian using his

enchantment, I immediately rose, took corial and proceeded to the place, where I found the husband trying to cure his wife of a bowel complaint, I bid him to stop, told him the folly of it, and made known who it was that made men sick, and who gave health (CW/O/100: 34).

Youd's fervent sabbatarianism also revealed itself early, and it was not only Indians who were upbraided for going about their usual business on Sundays. On Sunday, 8 December 1833 he received a quantity of venison from the postholder,[4] to which he responded with the following letter:

> With all gratitude, I receive your kind present of such a quantity of fine venison, but permit me without offence to reprove you, for permitting your huntsman to exercise his abilities on the Lord's day (CW/O/100: 32).

Nor was he above admonishing a planter, who had offered him a day's hospitality when stranded by an adverse tide on a trip to Georgetown, for hiring 'negroes' to work on Sundays; he dismissed the excuse of necessity as a 'stale argument' (CW/O/100: 33).

Youd was also out to change other, rather less heinous activities. Before he had been there a year, he had taken upon himself to correct the way in which the Indians planted their yams (CW/O/100: 32) and a year later was interfering with the division of labour at planting time to make men do more of the work 'at [which] the women rejoice greatly, and laugh to see men performing that work at which they had long been bound to labour'(CW/O/100: 36).

The Society, doubtless pleased by Youd's efforts, at the same time needed to ensure that he knew his place. In his enthusiasm, he inadvertently referred in his journal to preaching against the evils mentioned (CW/O/100: 31), which produced two remarkably firm reprimands from the Society for overstepping the bounds of a catechist's duties by preaching, thus assuming the role of a minister (CW/L/1: 274 and 279).

While Youd was extremely busy he was also rather lonely. In September 1833, he wrote to the Society, apologising for not having brought up the matter before he left London, but asking whether it would be possible for a certain Miss Ann Davies to accompany Mr Armstrong when he returned in order for her to be his 'lawful companion'. He referred to the importance of a man having a wife in tropical climes and how she would be a help with his work. She could not only teach the Indian women to sew but would also have contact with them because 'it is notorious ... that the aged women or wives of the Indians are the chief rulers' (CW/O/100: 4). Youd was not alone in this fear of temptation, for hardly had Armstrong arrived at Bartica Point two years earlier than he mentioned the allure of the Indian women; the need to find a wife was one of the main reasons for his visit to England (CW/O/14: 18).

In January 1834, Youd repeated the request that Miss Davies be sent out in order to save him from the gossip that was flying about (CW/O/100: 6). A letter from Strong to the Society of 15 March enlightens us on this matter as it refers to Youd's reputation being imputed because unwisely he has had a young woman (one suspects as a housekeeper) about the house (CW/M/2: 544). However, the business of Miss Davies dragged on. At the end of June 1834 the Society gave permission for Youd to marry Miss Davies (CW/L/1: 299), but six months later Youd complained that he had not heard from her (CW/M/3: 86), and in March 1835 that there was still no news (CW/O/100: 10). By mid-July, he had assumed that Miss Davies had refused him and requested that he be allowed to marry 'a suitable devout local girl' if his choice was approved by the Corresponding Committee (CW/O/100: 12). There is then the indication that Miss Davies felt that Youd had slighted her (CW/L/2: 40–1) and the Society suggested that he return to England to sort matters out. Youd rejected this in March 1836, saying:

> I really do not understand being played with by young Ladies at all and as to come home for one, and to leave my work, is a thing I cannot do ... Miss Davies shall not have the opportunity of trying my patience much longer (CW/O/100: 50).

The following month the Society wrote to inform Youd that Miss Davies had declined his proposal, hinting that it was Youd's fault. When Youd learnt of this is not clear, but he did not acknowledge it until January of the following year, by which time he was already married (CW/L/2: 196; CW/O/100: 18).

It is difficult to judge the success of the mission at Bartica. Youd was delighted one Sunday in December 1833 with a congregation of about a hundred, of whom about half were Indians. This figure had grown to 120 by late February 1835, which seems to be about as large as it ever became. In October 1834 there had been a sudden influx of Indians, mainly Caribs and Akawaio, who settled at Bartica Grove. By the end of that year Youd put the number of Indians at the mission at seventy, and he had to insist that future settlers first cut fields and had a source of subsistence there before moving in as he could no longer afford to provide for them. At the same time there were those Indians who demonstrated some caution about moving to Bartica. A Carib chief from the Cuyuni River declined Youd's invitation to join the mission on the grounds that 'fever reigns on that place' – an accusation that Youd's frequent fevers barely allowed him to contradict except to say that he had moved to Bartica Grove, a more healthy site than Bartica Point. Inevitably these cautious Indians were proved wise: in July 1835 measles struck at Bartica Grove and many Indians died. This epidemic spread widely through the region and by September was reported among the Indians on the Cuyuni River. As a result many Indians left the mission and others who had planned to come did not do so. The mission was never fully to recover its Indian population and another missionary, Bernau, when he arrived there in 1837 described it variously as 'deserted' and 'crippled' (CW/O/100: 32, 36, 37 and 39; CW/O/18: 11 and 12).[5]

William Hilhouse, a controversial character in British Guiana but someone who was genuinely knowledgeable and concerned about the Indians, was more openly damning. His main complaints were the tendency of the missionaries to reduce the Indians' self-reliance and their failure to make proper provision for them, so that they starved.

> I found it, strange to say, the result of the Protestant Mission established at the confluence of the Massaroony with the Essequebo, whose first essay at conversion had this melancholy effect. ... as an Indian Mission the Bartika one is a total failure. The Indians of the vicinity are much more depraved than they were before the Mission was established (1896: 313, 324).

However, some of his criticism, almost certainly part of a general prejudicial response to missionaries, was misplaced because Youd had worried about subsistence for new settlers and its provision was a source of dispute between the missionaries at Bartica and the Corresponding Committee. On the other hand, Robert Schomburgk (to be introduced below), who was certainly not anti-missionary, remarked that up until the time Bernau arrived the mission had had little effect but that this situation was now expected to improve (CO111/150: 2977).

Armstrong's stay in England was much longer than expected and he did not arrive back at Bartica with his new wife until the end of April 1835. It was not, however, his search for a wife that was the reason for his delay but the question of his ordination. This had been the other main reason for his return to England, and had been a matter of concern to him for some years. As early as August 1830 he had lamented that as a catechist he was not sufficiently respected and it would help if he were ordained. This refrain reappears in many of his letters. Even so, he returned to British Guiana with this wish still unfulfilled. Youd, contemplating the difficulties that Armstrong was having, remarked 'I hope I shall get Orders in a snugger way than what he gets them or not at all' (CW/M/3: 92; CW/O/14: 16, 18 and 19).

The main problem was that the Corresponding Committee was unwilling to support Armstrong's ordination. Strong wrote to the Society in October 1834 saying that he was unable to sign a testimonial to the effect that Armstrong had not 'held, written or taught any thing contrary to the doctrines, and discipline of the Church of England' as he had heard him deny the king's supremacy in church matters and considered that he was against the union of church and state. It is not clear whether Armstrong was aware of this opposition to his ordination, but if he were it could well have been an underlying cause for the bitter rows that were shortly to ensue between him and the Committee. These concerned a range of matters, including the fact that on his return to Bartica Point his house was in an advanced state of disrepair, and he found that Youd had moved the mission to Bartica Grove without his approval. There were arguments about where a new chapel was to be built and who was to pay for it, and the question of how Indians coming to settle at the mission were to be fed and the food paid for became an issue. At one point in early 1836 the disagreement between Armstrong and the Committee got so bad that all the members of the latter resigned and had to be persuaded by the Society to take up their duties again (CW/O/14: 32, 33, 38; CW/O/81: 22, 23, 27; CW/L/2: 192; CW/M/3: 257, 328).

Despite the disagreement over the move from Bartica Point to Bartica Grove, Youd and Armstrong seem to have got along quite well and the former cleverly managed to distance himself from the dispute between Armstrong and the Corresponding Committee. Indeed he wrote to the Society on 31 December 1835: 'I fear their [sic] is something unpleasant going on with Mr Armstrong and the Corresponding Committee but I will have nothing to do with it for peace is happiness' (CW/O/100: 14). On the other side the

Reverend Strong was able to write in the middle of it all that Youd 'has grown much in spirituals' (CW/M/3: 96).

In the meantime, another central actor, Robert Hermann Schomburgk, appeared on the scene. Schomburgk's name will be forever associated with the exploration of British Guiana and the fixing of its boundaries. He was a Prussian by birth, born in Freiburg on 5 June 1804, son of a pastor. His early career was in business but he gave this up in 1830 to pursue the life of a naturalist. After completing a successful survey of the coast of Anegada in the Virgin Islands, he spent from 1835 to 1843 exploring in British Guiana, first on behalf of the Royal Geographical Society and then as the government-appointed Boundary Commissioner. He was knighted by patent in 1844, and served as British Consul in Santo Domingo and then in Bangkok. He retired from the latter post due to ill health in 1864 and died in Berlin on 11 March 1865 (DNB; Ojer 1969).[6]

In 1835 Robert Schomburgk, under the auspices of the Royal Geographical Society, undertook his first expedition into the interior of British Guiana. He ascended the Essequibo and Rupununi with two companions, Lieutenant James Haining of the 65th Regiment and Mr Robert Brotherson of Demerara. They stayed some weeks at the Amerindian village of Annai because many of the expedition's members were suffering from fever. At this time Schomburgk made his first contact with the Brazilians, which came about in the following way.[7] Brotherson being too ill to attempt the next stage of the expedition, the ascent of the Rupununi River, Schomburgk wished him to go to Fort São Joaquim to recuperate. As he wrote to Mr H.E.F. Young, secretary to the British Guiana Government, from Pirara on 5 December 1835:

> An excellent opportunity has offered itself for that purpose; on leaving Georgetown, I was requested to take charge of a letter to the Bishop at Para and to send it by an Indian to the Portuguese Fort; as I did not understand Portuguese I wrote to the Commandant in French requesting him to forward the letter with the first eligible opportunity, but the gentleman not understanding French conjectured that I wanted to come to Fort San Joaquim.

The commandant, Captain José Valente Cordeiro, replied that he had sent a sergeant, a canoe and seven horses to escort Schomburgk and his party to the fort. When the members of the expedition reached Pirara Landing they learnt that Cordeiro had himself come to meet them and had been at Pirara for seven days awaiting their arrival. He arrived with horses at Pirara Landing, and not wishing to offend him the expedition members all travelled with him to Pirara, where they were well entertained on fresh beef. The next day Brotherson left for the fort with Cordeiro and the expedition continued on its way. It is not without interest that Schomburgk noted that 'The Commandant has here [Pirara] an Indian hut of his own, and as Pirarárá is the entrepôt between the Rupununy and Branco, he sojourns here very frequently'[8] (RHS 1896: 132–50; RGS/RHS/Corr: 5/12/35; RGS/RHS/MS: 1836).

In March 1836, the Bishop of Barbados visited Bartica and was much impressed by the work being done and in particular by Youd, of whom he comments that 'he had scarcely met a young man so laborious, so sensible and so selfdenying' (CW/O/81: 29). He made plans for the ordination of both Youd and Armstrong, and told them to be prepared to be in Barbados for that purpose in June and July (CW/O/100: 15).

While the Bishop of Barbados was at Bartica the question of a mission to the Macushi was brought up. As we have seen, Armstrong had already expressed a wish to set up such a mission and had referred to the Indians' enthusiam for such a project. Schomburgk, returning downstream from his first expedition, was at Bartica at the same time as the bishop. He was aware of Armstrong's intention to found a mission station among the Macushi and supported the plan. He was later to write to Alexander von Humboldt:

> Pray do not regard it as a bit of superfluous brag on my part if I tell you that I have a small share in the negotiation of this desirable measure [the setting up of the mission]. ... If I took such an active share in this excellent and desirable institution before its inception was assured, how much greater then must this interest now be (O.A. Schomburgk 1931: 117).

In a letter dated 25 August 1838 to T.F. Buxton, president of the Aborigines Protection Society, he claimed not so much to have proposed the mission than as to have supported its location. Thus he wrote:

> in a conversation with the Lord Bishop of Barbados, after return from my first expedition, I took the liberty to recommend Pirara in particular as the site of a Mission, not only in consequence of its salubrity,

but as being likewise a central place between the Canuku and Pacaraima Mountains, both inhabited by the Macusi and Wapishana Indians (CO111/162: 3).

On another occasion Schomburgk was to say explicitly that it was the Indians themselves who had been responsible by inviting a missionary to come and live with them.

> Their [the Indians'] zeal stands perhaps unparallelled in the history of the missions for the propagation of the gospel; not only that the missionary was invited to come and settle among them, but long before it was decided whether the Church Missionary Society intended to maintain a mission among the Macusis they build not only a chapel but likewise a house for the missionary (RGS/RHS/MS: 1840c).

In other words Schomburgk himself did not claim to have done much more than to have supported an idea already proposed by Amstrong and eagerly taken over by Youd, as this passage from one of the latter's letters confirms:

> I may here state, that I introduced his Lordship [i.e. the Bishop of Barbados] to the latest traveller, Mr. Shumberg [*sic*] who has a few days come from his tour up the Essequibo, following the trails of Mr. Armstrong. ... Mr. Shumberg gives a splendid account of things, saying, that it is very desirable that a Missionary should go among them [the Macushi], for they are desirous of instruction, this information backing up what I had already stated to his Lordship, made still greater impression on the minds of our friends (CW/O/100: 50).

Certainly Richard Schomburgk (I: 72) is wrong when he states that Youd had been induced by his brother to found the Pirara Mission. However, this version of what happened has been accepted as true by Ojer, who can see the founding of the mission only as a political event. He is certainly wrong when he rashly writes:

> Without fear of being mistaken, we can fix the date of that suggestion to Youd in March 1836, when returning from his first expedition to Pirara he [Schomburgk] meets with the Anglican Bishop of Barbados, who is visiting Bartica. Then must have been decided the missionary occupation of Pirara with the sending of Youd (1969: 22).

As we have seen and as we will further find, this is not what happened at all.

There is a break here in Youd's correspondence and journal, but we learn from Armstrong's communications that on 19 May Youd was about to go to Barbados and on 19 July he was expected back from there. In the meantime, although still living at Bartica, Armstrong had resigned from the Church Missionary Society. Before doing so and not long after the Bishop of Barbados's visit to Bartica, he wrote to the Society in London supporting Youd's wish to found a mission among the Macushi. Then, following upon his ordination as a deacon in Bridgetown on 13 November 1836, the Bishop of Barbados sent him to look after the parish of Anguilla. At this point Armstrong fades out of the story (CW/O/14: 37, 40, 41 and 45).

Youd was admitted to the Order of Deacons on the same day as Armstrong, and four days later married Rachel Wolcott Adamson, who resided with her uncle, Dr William Adamson, proprietor of the Venture Estate, St John's. Youd admitted that his 'choice ... has been somewhat speedy' (CW/O/100: 42). The Society in London congratulated him on both accomplishments and took the opportunity to remind him that the 'most essential qualities in a faithful Minister & Missionary is a deep sense of his own inadequacy & unworthiness' (CW/L/2: 341–3, 356–8).

Mr and Mrs Youd returned to Bartica Grove, where they were joined in mid-January 1837 by a replacement for Armstrong, the Reverend John Bernau, a German who had already worked in British Guiana for a number of years. His name is to become intimately linked with Bartica Grove as he served there for fourteen years[9] and his book *Missionary Labours in British Guiana* (1847) stands along side those of the Reverend William Brett as the best-known accounts of nineteenth-century missionary work in the colony.[10]

In a letter dated 23 January 1837, the Society proposed some plans for the future of the Indian mission including the consolidation of the station at Bartica Grove and exploratory trips into the interior with a view to founding a station there. It was suggested that Bernau should be responsible for the latter (CW/L/2: 304–6). However, Youd wrote on the last day of March that he and Bernau had agreed a division of labour whereby the latter would mainly look after affairs at Bartica while the former would have responsibility for visiting the local outposts. He expressed the hope that permission would speedily be granted for setting up a mission in the interior. It had been agreed between Bernau and Youd that the latter would undertake this because of his greater experience of the Indian language and character. Youd said that he would go with Doyce and mentioned at this point that it was his aim 'more to settle than to go on a tour'. The following list of equipment that he claimed he would need clearly underlines his intention:

> four or five corials built suitably for the falls. A Tent, like the roof of a house, the sheet of which when spread flat on the ground will measure 40 feet by 20 & which when raised up will give a long square 40 feet by 14 as a shed. 2 Indian rubber cloaks coming down to the feet & two pairs of overalls, ½ doz of the largest size blankets. 3 doz small blankets 5 or 6 feet by four. 60 pieces of common Calico 7 yds each, of different patterns. 50 pieces of salempores 18 yds each. Hooks 4000 of three different sizes ... ten barrels of common biscuits, 12 canisters of fine ones. 60 yds of summer-cloth ... 10 gall of sperm oil. a complete Box of Joiners tools well tempered. Two double barrelled guns & two Rifles. 12 common guns. 50 lbs of no 1 shot or the coarsest shot. 50 lbs of powder & two hundred bullets suitable for the Rifles that we may supply ourselves with beef from the vast herds of wild cattle in the savannah. Two Saddles and Bridles as also one ladies saddle and bridle as horses can be bought for a gun and will be very useful in travelling about. 50 small tooth combs & 50 long combs suitable for combing out a woman's hair. One Bugle. 8 boxes of common washing soap. two hundred yds of cotton shirting suitable for the Missionaries. One keg of ten penny & one of sixpenny nails & a ½ of 20 penny nails. 3 doz pair of strong H L Hinges. two small hand travelling compasses. One sextant Quadrant, two lamps one corn mill. One portable forge & tools suitable. 4 doz pair of mens white cotton stockings. One crosscut & fretwork saw with suitable files. One pair of kitchen bellows two cold chisels. 50 yds of baby flannel, two hundred fathoms of inch rope for hawling up the falls, 12 doz of knives with white handles ... 20 yds of check. For the other necessary articles the Committee [i.e. Society] will authorise the Corresponding Committee to grant the request of the Missionary (CW/O/100: 16).

Many of these items, he noted, were needed for barter as money was of no use in the interior.

After Armstrong's visit to the interior in 1833, there had been regular if intermittent contact between the missionaries and the Indians. On several occasions Youd refers in his journal to Indians, mainly Caribs, coming from or going to Macushi country, and in one case there is mention of a chief from there wanting to settle at Bartica Grove. At the very end of January 1836 Youd mentions a congregation composed of Macushi and Akawaio Indians at Hipaia, the last settlement of coloured people up the Essequibo, about a day's paddle from Bartica Grove. Then, in early March 1837, there is reference to a Macushi interpreter with whom he was spending a lot of time and the hint that work on that language had been underway for awhile (CW/O/100: 33, 38, 41 and 44).

On 11 March, on one of his routine visits to the settlement at Hipaia Youd found a newly arrived group of Macushi there. The next day he recorded:

> The Macushe Indians came to me early this morning who appeared much pleased when I told them that they might soon expect to see a minister amongst them. During the service the Macushe stood at the outside of the Chapel witnessing our devotions with apparent surprise. One asked me, saying will you come to teach us? I said I long to come but I cannot, unless the Gentlemen in England send me. But, I said some one will I fully expect soon be sent to teach you therefore have hope (CW/O/100: 42).

It would appear that the Macushis' expectations were quite high and that they had made plans already for the arrival of a missionary, although it is not clear how these were initiated. Youd's journal entry for 5 June 1837 reads:

> Our Macushe interpreter who with several others returned last week from a tour to the Macushe country, came to see me, in company with Avaristo[11] son-in-law to the principle chief of the Macushe tribe, whose settlement is at Perârâ in the Macushe country, or the Southern Border of the English territory in British Guianâ. He stated that the Chief [Basiko], his father in law had heard that Domine Youd or some other Domine was about to come & reside amongst them, to teach them the great things of God. From firm belief in this, his father in law had ordered a large & strong shed to be erected as a church; at the end of which was a large room for the minister to live in for the present, which was just finished as they came away. – that a large house was erecting for the company who should bring up the minister to live in – and moreover that two fields of yams and a third of plantains had been made & was growing quickly, for the supply of the missionary & people: this have we done by way of preparation & I am sent down to convey yourself at the beginning of the dry season (September) if you or any other are going. We hope not to be disappointed for my father says if someone does not come, he will order the house to be burned. Domine Armstrong came to see us, he shewed us the books, & told us it was God's word, then put them into his box again & went away and we have see no one since, but as we heard of your coming we have prepared for you. We do not want any one to come & look at us, and then leave us, and therefore if you come, come to stay for the Macushe wish to learn & be instructed like other nations. I then enquired of our Macushe interpreter if he had seen the Chapel; he said 'Yes, for I slept in it and

so did Mr Waterton the white Gentleman with whom we went up.[12] The yams are yet young in the field, but the plantains will soon be ripe. The house for the people will be finished by this time, and they are waiting for you or some other to go up to live there'. I enquired of a third person by the name of Laurumai father of our four youths who also went up, and he confirmed the whole naritive [sic]. My answer to the Deputy, or at least the sum & substance of it was, that as far as I was concerned I was ready to go, but that I was waiting to hear from gentlemen [the Committee] at home to whom I had already sent off a letter and that I believed something would be agreed upon by them, and that either I or some other would soon come to dwell amongst them (CW/O/100: 43).

At its meeting on 18 July the Corresponding Committee agreed to an 'exploratory excursion' by Youd to the Macushi, but it hoped that a reply from the Society to Youd's request would be received before his proposed departure. Youd awaited the Society's reply impatiently and twice in the next two months (28 August and 4 September) expressed his anxiety about knowing whether he would be allowed to go among the Macushi. At the beginning of October he had a meeting with members of the Committee, who declined to authorise the £150 he required to cover the expenses of the expedition. Towards the end of the same month he complained that he had still heard nothing and that the travelling season for the year would soon be over (CW/M/4: 340, 342-5; CW/O/100: 44).

At this point various events occurred that might have disrupted the plans of a less determined man. On 2 December, Mrs Youd gave birth to a daughter, who only survived seven weeks. Soon after the birth, Mrs Youd was also taken ill and in February, after she had nearly died at the end of January, Youd took her to Barbados to recuperate. Before doing so he had finally got the Corresponding Committee at its meeting on 28 December to agree to his making an exploratory trip into the interior in order to collect authentic information about the different tribes. The Committee was not entirely happy about this, since it had still not received any firm directions from London. At the meeting a letter from Bernau was read out in which it was affirmed that plans had been made for Youd's absence and that operations at Bartica would not be disrupted. In the end, because Youd was anxious to go and had promised the Macushi that he would visit them, the Committee relented, granted permission and promised assistance. However, they asked him to provide a plan of his intentions and a list of the articles that he would need. It was also proposed that, in order to save expense, the

Macushi Alfred, educated by the Society, should proceed to Pirara to raise an Indian crew to transport Youd upriver (CW/M/4: 342-5).

During the eleven days Youd spent on Barbados (11-22 February), he was admitted into the Order of Priests on the 18th. When he left to return to British Guiana and the mission to the interior, his wife was still too weak to walk (CW/O/100: 20). On 4 April, on the eve of leaving for the interior, he heard that his wife had died:

> I received a letter from Barbados two days ago, which announced the death of my dear wife. Of course my spirits are low, and I feel myself destitute indeed. But what should I say? He who gave has taken away: blessed be his holy name (CW/O/100: 21).

On reading his journal and letters, one is left with a feeling that Youd regarded his wife's sickness as an obstacle to his aims. At one point, he wrote that he was obliged to leave her, and this can only have resulted from what he regarded as his commitment to the Macushi because there was no pressure on him from his missionary organization. However, this cannot be taken to mean that he did not hold his wife in affection and esteem, and on the Sunday after he heard of her death he wrote:

> Today my dear wife's place was vacant, to my inward grief though accompanied with holy longings to be where she is. Keen feelings caused a few tears to flow, although I fain would have hidden them (CW/O/100: 45).

Of Rachel Youd we know very little. There are few references to her in Youd's journal. She had on occasion accompanied him to the Cuyuni River and other places but most of the entries refer to her being sick or otherwise upset, as this account of 9 September 1837 shows:

> This evening a strange & drunk Indian ran into Mrs Youds room in a very ferocious manner stamping on the floor & terrified her much. During the night she dreamt of him & dreamed aloud & could scarce be pacified for ½ an hour (CW/O/100: 44).

The only description I have found of her is that of Bernau who wrote:

> Mrs Y is gone to her rest. She was of a delicate & weakly constitution, and apparently disappointed in her expectations as a Mission's wife. She suffered much in mind and body yet was she resigned to the will of God, and towards her latter end enabled to rest her hope on Jesus (CW/O/18: 14).

FIRST STAGES

Youd's intentions and the plans of both the Society in London and the Committee in Georgetown were rather different. Youd's object was to set up a mission station, and he never tried to conceal this fact. Some of his statements are quite explicit on this, and the list of the equipment that he drew up could not have more plainly indicated his aim. On the other side, although the Society repeatedly expressed interest in founding a mission in the interior, it never seemed able to commit itself to such a venture. It was not until 8 March 1838, virtually on the eve of Youd's departure, that the Society wrote to the Committee rejecting, for the time being, Youd's proposal for the founding of a mission in the interior, on the grounds that such an enterprise was too extensive and expensive for the moment. What was needed were exploratory trips to collect information and only then for activities to be extended as appropriate and circumstances allowed (CW/L/2: 433-4). Letters of 16 July and 1 December to Youd himself repeat this position; in the latter it is doubted whether 'such information has at present been sufficiently obtained to warrant your safely deciding the point' and this despite the fact that Youd by that date had been operating the mission at Pirara since the previous May. The Society was certain on one point, which was that any mission must be located within the known limits of British territory. Pirara was therefore out, and in general anywhere near to the frontier was regarded as unadvisable (CW/L/2: 442-4, 510-12). Nearly a year later, November 1839, the Society wrote twice again on the matter, on these occasions to the Committee, stating that no undertaking of the sort entered into by Youd should be allowed without the express approval of the Committee and that what had occurred at Pirara showed 'how unsafe and improper it is to act hastily' (CW/L/3: 8-11, 23-5).

This position was faithfully echoed by the Committee which, although it had given Youd permission at its meeting on 28 December 1837 for an exploratory trip, declined to authorise anything more (CW/M/4: 342-5). At its meeting on 14 March 1838, after Youd's return from Barbados, the Committee minuted its regret at hearing the bad news about Mrs Youd (this presumably relates to her poor state of health, since it was before her death) and stated that:

> Under the circumstances of the case they conceived it to be a duty incumbent upon them to submit it to Mr Youd's consideration, whether, after the distressing intelligence he had lately received from Barbados, he ought still to prosecute his journey at this season into the interior.

However, correctly appreciating that his wife's condition was unlikely to act as a deterrent to Youd, the Committee reaffirmed its position, and noted that the equipment required by him suggested that he had mistaken the purpose of the journey. The minute of the meeting records:

> Mr Youd's intention at once to enter upon the establishment of a new Mission among the Macushe Indians, which the meeting thought a precipitate step and not in accordance with the express wishes of the Parent Society. ... It is foreign to the wishes of the Corr Com^{ee} to damp the zeal of any of the Missionaries, they are alike anxious that the glad tidings of Salvation should be conveyed, through the instrumentality of the Church Missionary Society, to the poor benighted Indians; but they would affectionately remind Mr Youd that his sanguine expectations drawn from Indian statements have on former occasions been disappointed, & therefore in the present case they wish to impress upon his mind that nature of his expedition, in prosecuting which, they recommend that all expenditure be made upon the most economical scale consistent with its object.

He was voted £100 to cover all the costs of the expedition (CW/M/4: 345–7). If, however, the Committee thought it could curtail Youd's activities any better by economic sanctions than by an emotional appeal, it was sadly mistaken. Youd, while expressing his gratitude to the Committee, remarked to the Society that £100 was not enough to cover the costs of the expedition and that he supposed the additional expenses would have to fall on his shoulders (CW/O/100: 20).

It is a matter of doubt whether Youd ever entertained any intention of restricting himself to an exploratory journey. Indeed the death of his wife, as the Reverend Strong noted, 'seemed a stimulant to Mr Youd's proceedings' (CW/M/4: 320–3). Early in his journey into the interior Youd wrote to the Society:

> The Lord has brought me so low by the various trials I have had, that now I really feel myself a pilgrim on earth; rather wishing to depart soon, if my work should be finished. At present I do desire, & have for a long time, that I may end my days, whether many or few, in the Interior (CW/O/100: 21).

Two months later he wrote from Pirara: 'I purpose to spend a good part (if not all) my future days in this or a more distant wilderness in the cause of our adorable redeemer.'

At the same time he stated that he did not plan to be in Georgetown until the end of January 1839; he would return to the interior the following month. He told the inhabitants of Pirara on his arrival there that his 'mind is to remain amongst them' (CW/O/100: 45). In other words, Youd made no effort to hide the fact that his intention was to set up a mission station, and thus to ignore the instructions of both the Society and the Committee. The curious and significant thing is how little control either of those bodies seemed to be able to exercise in the face of Youd's determination. However, the important point to make is that what Youd did was on his own volition, without sanction or permission from any third party.

Interestingly enough, the Committee failed initially to take into any consideration the question of territorial possession. Nor is there any evidence that the colonial government showed any interest in the project, although it is very unlikely, given the size of Georgetown, that it was unaware of what was going on.[13] It was left for Bernau to raise the question and he, on the basis of what he knew (probably derived from Schomburgk), considered Pirara to lie in Brazil. However, such a suspicion was no deterrent to Youd, and Bernau observed in a letter to the Society of June 1838 that 'Mr Y is sanguine enough to suppose that even if this were the case, there could not possibly any obstacle be thrown in the way.' There is also an indication in the same letter that there had been some disagreement, perhaps over what Youd was doing, between the two missionaries. Bernau wrote:

> Oh for watchfulness to quench the seeds of discord, and to mortify every thing that is not becoming in Brethren. I have freely opened my mind in a letter to Mr. Youd, to which circumstances did not give him time to return an answer as yet. It may have wounded, the Lord grant also that it may pour balm into the parts affected thereby (CW/O/18: 14).

Notes

1. There is a letter dated 14 March 1831 stating that Armstrong is about to leave for the interior, and another of 16 April saying that he is there. In Armstrong's first letter from Bartica Point, dated 11 August 1831, he states that his work was held up by ill health (CW/O/14: 18; CW/O/81: 11 and 12). A number of sources (e.g. Brett 1851) gives 1829 as the date of the mission's founding, which is too early. Richard Schomburgk (I: 72) gives the date of the founding as 1833, which is too late.

2. The Corresponding Committee was composed of local churchmen,

planters and others. Its task was to oversee the day-to-day affairs of the local missionaries and report to the Society in London.

3. Armstrong was in Georgetown on 8 February and arrived back at Bartica from the Rupununi on 18 May. This suggests that the longest he could have spent in the interior would have been two months.

4. A postholder, a title retained from the Dutch colonial era, was the local official charged with the care of the Indians. For a discussion of the office and its development at this time see Menezes 1977a.

5. When, a couple of years later, Youd was recruiting Indian labour to help build a chapel at Kartabu, the point between the Mazaruni and Cuyuni Rivers, one group of Caribs refused to join him on the grounds that 'that paper which the domine has is to get us as soldiers to catch the slaves, & if we learn we shall get sick' (CW/O/100/44: 3).

6. It is difficult to get an idea of what Robert Schomburgk was like from his published articles. These suggest that he was a rather austere man with little concern for those who accompanied him on his expeditions. This view is wrong, however, as the manuscript copies of these articles in the Royal Geographical Society reveal. These contain numerous allusions to his companions, but the editor removed most of them in preparation for publication. Furthermore, there are occasions when the editor has added words or sentences which make Schomburgk out to be far more jingoistic than he actually was. His letters are mainly formal and factual but on occasions he expressed strong feelings about what he considered to be the failure of those more comfortably situated to appreciate the deprivations that he and his men were undergoing. A rare example of personal feelings is to be found in a letter of 29 August 1842 from Pirara to Government Secretary Young, in which he asks the addressee to convey a note to the Governor's wife and a 'box of curiosities' to his daughter (NAG/MBD). The descriptions of him by those who were involved with him in British Guiana are not always flattering. They will be introduced at the appropriate places. On the other hand, the pictures we have of him represent him as a rather handsome and dashing young man. Robert Schomburgk has not received the attention he deserves and I plan to rectify this omission. I am presently engaged on a biography of him.

7. In the boundary dispute there was some disagreement about what happened on this occasion. The misunderstanding mainly results from the fact that due to editorial interference the account of the incident became garbled in the published report of the expedition. According to that version, when the expedition reached Pirara Landing it heard that the commandant of Fort São Joaquim, Captain Cordeiro, was at Pirara. Schomburgk sent a message to Cordeiro, who came, with horses, to meet the expedition. They all travelled to Pirara and one member of the expedition (Brotherson, although not identified in this source) went to recuperate at the fort (1836: 242). Schomburgk's original manuscript and two letters give a fuller and what sounds like a more accurate account of what happened.

8. This important detail in support of their case was apparently overlooked by the Brazilians, who tried to show that the Brazilians regularly

occupied Pirara. It only appears in a single source — RGS/RHS/Corr: 5/12/35. The fact that Schomburgk refers to Pirara as an unusually large and populous village also suggests some sort of external, non-Amerindian agency at work.

9. He was at Bartica Grove from 1837 to 1848 and again from 1850 to 1853. Ill health accounts for the two-year break, and was also the reason for his final retirement.

10. However, as we will see, Bernau is not an entirely reliable reporter of events.

11. Evaristo José Teixeira is a Brazilian who appears at regular intervals throughout the story. He will be fully introduced later.

12. Whoever this was it certainly could not have been Waterton. Nor can it be have been Schomburgk, because the timing is wrong. Schomburgk was not in Pirara between January 1836 and March 1838.

13. The governor at the time was Major-General Sir James Carmichael Smyth, who had held the office since June 1833. He died suddenly in March 1838. The colony was then under the administration of two military officers, first Major W.N. Orange and then Colonel Thomas Bunbury, until his replacement, Sir Henry Light, arrived in June that year.

CHAPTER 3

THE FIRST MISSION AT PIRARA: 1838

Before Youd accompanied his wife to Barbados in February 1838, he had, as proposed by the Committee, dispatched Alfred, his Macushi teacher and interpreter at Bartica, to Pirara requesting that canoes be sent down to collect him (CW/O/81: 33).[1] Thus it was that in March 1838, Schomburgk, then on his third expedition, met three canoes on their way from Pirara to Bartica Grove to collect Youd. The crews of these canoes included 'a Macusi and a Carib; [who] had both been trained at the Mission Station at Bartika Point'. When Schomburgk reached Pirara he found the missionary's house finished and men, women and children engaged in building a chapel. The village had grown to thirty Indian houses (RHS 1841a: 172; O.A. Schomburgk 1931: 117).

Youd left Bartica for the interior on 5 April, having heard only the previous day that his wife had died. 'My mind is quite unhinged; yet as all things are now ready, and my Company waiting upon me, I must proceed for the Interior,' he wrote on the day of his departure. His journey, which he described as 'eventful', took place in particularly bad weather, and he worried that he would be censured for exposing his men to dangers. However, he argued: 'I deem it well to see the interior in its worst condition, that both the rough and smooth of missionary exertion, may be correctly ascertained' (CW/O/100: 45).

He arrived at Pirara on 15 May 1838, and described the setting of the place in these words:

> The village of Perarara is situated on a rising ground, amidst a vast extent of almost clear savannah, with here and there a single shrub, which in no way obstructs the sight. A range of mountains run betwixt Perarara and Annie, and form a sort of boundary to the view that presents itself from the village, running northwest at a distance of twenty miles. Betwixt Perarara and the above mountains is a fine

plane [sic] on which immense herds may be seen feeding, that long ago have strayed from the Portuguese Cattle farm (CW/O/100: 45).

He found most of what he had been told about the preparations made for him to be true, and although no field had been cut for him there was a ready-made mission station. There was a chapel 40 ft × 36 ft and his house was 26 ft × 21 ft, with wattle and red clay walls 6 in. thick and 9 ft high. Youd hoped that the Indians' 'reward would be great benefit, which they will receive by being instructed in the things of God'. He was also welcomed by numerous presents of food, but noted that 'almost every present is connected with a requisition of a present in return' (CW/O/100: 45).

Youd described his first Sunday service at Pirara on 20 May as follows:

> I need not to say that the sight in the Chapel was somewhat strange. All parties excepting the Chief were well painted on the forehead, face, arms and legs. Some with cutlasses, others with bow and arrows having come from far, one with a monkey on the back, others with wreaths and crowns of feathers: others with belts of wild hog's teeth hanging from the top of the shoulder, crossing the breast and back and falling on the hips on the opposite side: others with knives, sticks and many other things. Some engaged in cutting their nails or small sticks: others picking the lice from their children's heads: some with their side to me and some with their back: others leant against the posts and gave me one eyed looks: in fact the whole event to me seemed like a fanciful dream instead of a reality. To see the monkey passing his judgment on the female's breasts and laying hold of first one and then the other to suck, with all the antic motions of which his tribe is capable, was enough to make a dying man to laugh. Of course I found it necessary to keep my eyes off such an unworthy object on such a sacred occasion or I could not have conducted the service (CW/O/100: 45).

Youd had asked that Doyce, his assistant at Bartica, be allowed to come to Pirara to take up the duties of schoolmaster whenever he and Alfred, his Macushi interpreter and assistant schoolmaster, were away. Bernau, who did not approve of Doyce or of his performance, disapproved of the idea but left the choice to Doyce, who decided not to go. Later the Society explicitly rejected the request on the grounds that Doyce was needed at Bartica until some other teacher had arrived there. Alfred, of whom Youd, in June, had held out the greatest hopes, did not last long and before the end of September Youd was forced first to dismiss him because he had 'grievously fallen in several instances' and then to ask him to leave the mission because of his 'perseverance in an evil course with females' (CW/O/18: 15; CW/L/2: 510–12; CW/O/100: 46).

Youd also expressed fears about loneliness as soon as the coloured men who had accompanied him had returned downstream and Schomburgk had left (CW/O/100: 45). Strong, Secretary to the Committee, was not, however, too concerned about Youd's plight and remarked:

> He [Youd] must be very lonely in the wilderness without a single Brother in Christ, but Mr Youd seems to love solitude ie from his compeers, he is certainly very active and persevering, but I think if ever you associate another with him he will remove (CW/O/81: 33).

There were, however, more serious matters on the horizon. On 19 June, Schomburgk wrote of Youd's arrival at Pirara that it was 'a circumstance which cannot be sufficiently hailed by every Christian and Philanthropist, and though he has been here only a few weeks the fruits of his zeal are already observable.' In the same letter he raised, perhaps for the first time, the question of the boundary, and commented that if Pirara lay in Brazil, 'the first information brought to the authorities at Para of the existence of a Protestant Mission in their territory will be its death-knell.' He continued with a note on the importance of Pirara, which 'commands the Savannah, and if the colony should continue to prosper and civilization extend, in a political point of view it will become of great importance' (CO111/159: 3350). At almost exactly the same date, Youd also raised the matter of in whose territory Pirara was located, but sanguinely expected it to 'fall to the English' (CW/O/100: 45).

This sudden concern about the boundary coincided with the arrival at Pirara of the new commandant of Fort São Joaquim, Lieutenant Manoel Affonço Gatto. However, there is no particular reason to associate these two events, because Schomburgk had written in mid-April to the commandant asking permission to spend the wet season at the fort. The commandant had replied that he could not grant such a request but would pass it on to his superior officer in Manaus, the military commander of Upper Amazonas, Captain Ambrosio Pedro Ayres. The commandant arrived in June after Ayres's reply that Schomburgk and his party were welcome to spend the wet season at São Joaquim and that he was sending his brother, Pedro Joaquim Ayres, to look after them. The warmth of this response was the result of a letter from the Foreign Office in

THE FIRST MISSION AT PIRARA 33

London requesting that the Brazilian authorities extend to Schomburgk every assistance in the course of his scientific expeditions. This request was duly passed via the president of Pará to the commander of Upper Amazonas. The Brazilians, however, were already suspicious about the expedition, fearing that its purported scientific nature was merely a pretext for more sinister intentions. Accordingly orders were given that, without causing any embarrassment, an eye was to be kept on Schomburgk's activities (AHI 308/4/1/; Braz M2, Ann 1: 2-5; CO111/178: 1367).[2]

It is worth pausing in the narrative here to take a slightly closer look at the Ayres brothers, because they are not unimportant in the later unfolding of the story. Ambrosio Ayres, who took the nickname Bararoá after the place (later Tomar) where he lived, had had a mysterious past. According to some he was of German descent, to others he was a banished refugee from Lima, but the most likely thing is that he was a Pernambucan exiled to the Amazon for anti-monarchist activity. During the bloody disturbance known as the *cabanagem*, which wracked Pará during the 1830s, he became a military leader and made a name for himself by the ruthlessness with which he suppressed the uprising around Manaus. His position as commander of Upper Amazonas seems to have been the formal recognition of a *de facto* situation. Some writers claim that his political ambitions gave rise to opposition within his own side which he had plans to crush when, on 7 August 1838 while on a military expedition against the Cabanos, he was captured, tortured and killed by Mura Indians (Araujo e Amazonas 1852: 67, 280; ANB/IG[1]10; Hurley 1936: 167; Reis 1931: 164-5; Souza 1873: 21-2).[3]

Pedro Ayres is given an equally shady background in many Brazilian sources and, as we shall see, he forms with Schomburgk and Youd part of the demonology of the whole incident. Indeed it was even claimed that he was not Ambrosio's brother, but an officer of the US navy on a scientific expedition who had arrived in Brazil via Lima and the Andes. In due course numerous accusations were made against him of betraying Brazil and allying himself with the English. He is said to have flown the English flag at Fort São Joaquim, and to have wasted gunpowder in saluting it with salvos (Araujo e Amazonas 1852: 280).[4]

Youd described Pedro Ayres as:

> a young man, of about twenty eight years, rather thin, and stands about five feet ten inches high: of pretty extensive reading, and has

travelled on the Continent a good deal, and the northern parts of South America, speaks English tolerably well, a Brazilian by birth; a Roman Catholic in religious profession, but inveighs bitterly against the Conduct of the generality of the Padres and heads of their Church; of lively spirits and restless nature: excellent company, and very obliging, even to an extreme; of many good parts; soon moved to pity; in judgement, offhand, from the impulse of the moment, and strong in assertion; in difficulties most persevering, a friend when a friend, but whether to be relied on a better and longer acquaintance alone will tell the sacred tale (CW/O/100: 46).

Ayres also claimed to have had a Protestant mother, and supposed that he had sucked in a little of that religion with her milk (CW/O/100: 46).

Schomburgk's party, together with Youd, reached the fort on 30 June and were received by Pedro Ayres, who had recently arrived there. Schomburgk and party were provided with two comfortable houses outside the fort while Youd, who was only on a brief visit, lodged in the fort. Schomburgk describes the fort as being constructed of red sandstone with fourteen embrasures and eight ninepounders 'in tolerable condition'. The garrison consisted of the commandant and ten privates of the provincial militia. The associated village was composed of five houses and a small chapel. A priest visited the outpost every two or three years (1841a: 179–80). Youd depicted the chapel as small, filthy and dark, the vestry as being in the possession of a company of bats, and the cross outside as a perch for vultures (CW/O/100: 46).

On the day after their arrival, Sunday 1 July, occurred an event, the accounts of which were to become gravely distorted in the telling and the basis for ill-founded accusations against Youd. It had been suggested on the Saturday evening that a ride across the savannah should be taken on the following day, but Youd objected on the grounds that it would be the sabbath and instead obtained permission to hold divine service. When it came to it, there was a disagreement about where the service should be held. Ayres wanted it held in the mess room of the fort, the commandant and the people proposed the chapel, and Youd declared that under a shady tree would suit him fine. In the event two services were held in the chapel. Youd commented on the small size of the congregations, and surmised that it resulted from either the shame the Indians felt about their nakedness or fear of 'the censure of their priest' (CW/

THE FIRST MISSION AT PIRARA

O/100: 46). Youd was later to be accused of entering the chapel by force and desecrating it.

The following day Youd crossed the Rio Branco with Pedro Ayres to spend the day with the administrator or head herdsman, presumably at the National Fazenda of São Marcos. He bought a mare and foal for £4, to be delivered to Pirara at the beginning of the dry season, and was presented with two large baskets of fresh beef. He and Ayres got into a discussion about the frontier. The latter thought that according to the Treaty of Utrecht the Rupununi River represented the boundary although, as far as he knew, no boundary marks or posts had ever been set up. Youd suggested that the most natural boundary would be a line from the head of the Mazaruni River, crossing the end of the Pacaraima Mountains, following the course of the Mahu and then across the savannah to the head of the Essequibo.

The wild cattle had possession of the savannahs and there was no evidence that any formal Brazilian occupation of the territory had ever taken place. Further, Youd wondered whether, even if the site of Pirara were found to lie in Brazilian territory, the Brazilians would object to a Protestant mission there since it was such 'a worthless out away place to them'. Ayres doubted that such permission would be forthcoming because 'the Brazilian Government is altogether under the power of the Padres, who were not very tolerant in their nature'. Nor was it just a matter of the few Indians at Pirara, for the mission would attract the Indian population from all around. Youd's response to this was that all he would have to do would be to withdraw the short distance to British territory and the Indians would join him there. Ayres agreed to write to his brother for clarification; a ruling should be known by September. In the meantime, and as far as he was concerned, Youd could remain at Pirara and continue with his work of preaching and schooling, for 'there can be no harm in doing good'. He also gave Youd permission to kill for meat as many wild cattle as he was in need of at five dollars a head (CW/O/100: 46).

Pedro Ayres did write to his brother, who received the communication not long before his death. Although this dispatch has not been seen it is possible to deduce some of its contents from the letter Ambrosio Ayres wrote to his superior officer, the military commander of the Lower and Upper Amazon at Santarém, Lt.-Col. Joaquim José Luis de Souza, on 1 August. There is reference in his letter to the Indians being converted and refusing to work at Fort São Joaquim. He refers to the arrival of Schomburgk's expedition and comments that the English do not seem well acquainted with the line of the frontier or have chosen to ignore it (AHI/308/4/1).

Perhaps as a result of his death a week later, Ambrosio Ayres's original letter went astray and it was not until October that the events on the Upper Rio Branco were officially reported in Santarém. From Ambrosio Ayres's letter, we learn that on receipt of the news about the mission, he had acted immediately. He had commissioned Captain Antonio dos Barros Leal of the 3rd Regiment of the National Guard to proceed to the Rio Branco to confirm the line of the boundary and, if he was certain that the mission had been located on Brazilian soil, to draw the intruders' attention to it with due politeness (AHI/308/4/1).

Captain Leal was to play an important part in the ensuing events but the information we have about him is limited. Robert Schomburgk stated that he was a man of 'violent temper' and with a 'hatred of the English' (CO111/195: 1836), and Richard Schomburgk gives us the following description of him (I: 311):

> a gaunt man of medium size with dark complexion and black piercing eyes. In the fateful years of Brazil he had served under the Cabanos, but later on had changed over to the Royalists, and still carried in his left cheek a musket ball: during some fight this had struck the right side of his face where by knocking some teeth out it had gone through his mouth and remained imbedded in the fleshy part of his left cheek. Although a simple incision would easily have effected its removal, he nevertheless did not seem to be able to part company with it.

It is not impossible that he changed sides during the *cabanagem* because many people did so, but having done so he clearly acquitted himself well. His name appears amongst a list of those who served the emperor with particular distinction during the uprising, and when, in due course, he was appointed commandant of Fort São Joaquim and administrator of the national ranches it was said to be in recognition of this service (ANB/IJJ[9]111).

On Tuesday, 2 July, after a visit to another *fazenda*, Youd set off in the evening back to Pirara with the intention of arriving in time to preach on the following Sunday. Progress was slow and it was after sunset on Sunday that he reached Pirara, despite which he held divine service. He then settled in for the misery of the wet season

THE FIRST MISSION AT PIRARA

on the savannahs, when biting insects and mosquitoes are at their worst. Thus he wrote on Thursday, 26 July:

> For three afternoons past we have not been able to hold any lectures on account of the mosquitos: they are truly dreadful towards evening, and when night comes on there is no comfort remaining out of doors nor yet in the house unless there be good fires, or a bed with mosquito netting. If I read at all at night it is under mosquito netting, and even there these savannah rangers find me out, and slyly rob me of a little blood (CW/O/100: 46).

The population of the mission grew greatly during these months, although the numbers fluctuated as groups came and went to their distant fields. A census that Youd took on 21 August showed there to be 513 Indians present, although, as we will see, this crowd was to some extent the result of events other than the missionary's presence.

Youd returned from São Joaquim worried about the territorial status of Pirara. He explained this to the Indians, who then held a meeting and informed Youd of their decision:

> That we will wait until you hear further, and if it be that you have to move, we will soon follow, wherever you go; whether it be amongst the Wapishana or Attorei Nations, or even higher if it should be thought good; for after we have had the trouble to fetch you, and you have come, and we like you, therefore we will go to, for it will not do to give up all after so much trouble, so we will wait to see what the Portuguese will do, we do not want their Padres here. This we say for the present (CW/O/100: 46).

On the last day of July Youd set off on a trip to visit the Macushi villages in the Kanuku Mountains, but his journey was interrupted on 8 August when Indians brought news of the arrival of Brazilian slavers at São Joaquim; information that was confirmed next day by a letter.[5] Youd hurried back to Pirara and found the population in a state of alarm.

> On coming to Pirara I found the people much agitated in mind, and the first thing they asked was what they should do – whether they should betake themselves to the mountains, or stand by each other? I advised them by all means to remain together, and promised them that in case the expedition did come against them I would endeavour to prevent their being taken, and as it was would surely represent their case to the Governor that they might not much longer be under the apprehension of being taken and enslaved (CO111/162: 3).

By 12 August Indians were flocking into the mission from all directions 'with provisions and implements of war'.[6] Youd was impressed by the way the Indians turned out for military exercises and by the dexterity with which they handled their arms. A certain amount of panic ensued and the noise of gunfire at night, which usually turned out to be the arrival of new groups of Indians, did not help to calm matters. Nor were things helped by rumours that *cabanos* rebels were within a few days of the fort and had murdered fifty families (CO111/162: 3).

Even so, Youd was able to see in these events the goodness of God:

> The Lord will bring good out of this awful evil to his own glory. The Indians will see the necessity of dwelling more together as a body and in such a place as is better adapted for cultivation which will also tend to the furtherance of a Mission (CW/O/100: 46).

This episode of the Brazilian pressgang deserves closer inspection, because it was to have far-reaching implications. On 1 August Schomburgk witnessed the arrival at São Joaquim of a party of what he describes as slavers, although they claimed to be officially recruiting labour for the navy.[7] He suspected that their target was the populous village of Pirara, and persuaded Pedro Ayres, with threats of reporting the matter to the Brazilian secretary of foreign affairs, to stop the slavers from attacking the mission. Schomburgk then left (together with Ayres) to explore the mountain range, Serra Grande, to the south of Fort São Joaquim, near where, on 17 August, he found the slavers' canoes where they had been left while the gang proceeded overland. Three days later the pressgang returned with their captives and to Schomburgk's horror he saw that 'out of the 40 slaves there were only nine men, three of whom were upwards of 60 years old, and that the rest consisted of thirteen women, and eighteen children under 12 years, six of them infants'. They were Wapishiana and Atorai from the right bank of the Takutu. The slavers claimed that the Indians had come voluntarily, but the latter told Schomburgk that their village had been raided in the middle of the night, their houses set on fire and their possessions stolen, and that they had been marched away with their hands tied behind their backs. He remonstrated with Pedro Ayres, who exhibited indifference to these events about this behaviour. Ayres was of the opinion 'that the inferior officers wished to use the pressing of Indians for the navy as an excuse to procure young and old, in order to sell those

THE FIRST MISSION AT PIRARA

who were not fit for that purpose to their allies'. He promised to inform his brother and felt certain that as a result only those who could genuinely serve in the navy would be selected, and that the old men, women and children would be returned to their village. On 25 August, the expedition, which Schomburgk described as bearing 'the stamp of the most barbarous kidnapping, only worthy of a Government of the darker ages', departed downstream with 'their spoil of human merchandise'. Schomburgk, as a result of this incident, was later to write:

> The system of the Brazilians of hunting the Indians for slaves exists to this day in all its atrocities. These slaving expeditions, or descimentos, from political motives are always directed towards the contested boundaries. ... These abominable proceedings were carried on under the warrant of the district authorities (RHS 1841a: 183-90; 1840: 512; CO111/162: 3; RGS/RHS/MS: 1840d).

The incident again brought to the fore the question of where the boundary lay and on whose territory Pirara was located. Indeed, it appears to have been this occurrence which brought home to Schomburgk the need to define the boundary if such raids were to be prevented in future. Youd was of like mind and wrote to Sir Henry Light, governor of British Guiana,[8] stressing the importance of fixing the boundary in order to protect the Indians because:

> The Portuguese, or Brazilians I should say, still continue to harass the minds of the Indians, and to seize them as captives, as on former occasions, the which practice I lately thought had completely ceased; but alas it is not so (CO111/162: 3).

While at Fort São Joaquim, Youd had expressed 'a high opinion' of Pirara as a 'fine healthy' place at the centre of Macushi country, but his doubts developed and once again he discussed with the Indians where to go if they were forced to leave. The Indians proposed a 'place on the other side of Rupununy in the English Territory as being excellent for cultivation, and a place where there's plenty of game and fish. I expect to visit the said place shortly' (CW/O/100: 46).

The place concerned was Urwa Rapids, a short distance up the Rupununi River from Pirara Landing. Youd visited the site and had just returned from there when on Thursday, 27 September Schomburgk arrived back in Pirara from his winter quarters at Fort São Joaquim. The latter's party had left the fort on 20 September to the sound of a seven-gun salute and the best wishes of their 'friends', Ayres and the commandant. During their journey, the news of Ambrosio Ayres's death was brought to them (RHS 1841b: 191–3).

On 8 October 1838 Schomburgk departed on his journey, which was to take him to Esmeralda on the Orinoco, through the Casiquiare Canal to the Rio Negro and back to Pirara via the Rio Branco. Before leaving São Joaquim Schomburgk had written to Governor Light informing him of his planned journey, and offering him any information that he had collected that might be useful in settling the boundary question. In transmitting this communication to the Colonial Office, together with Schomburgk's report to the Aborigines' Protection Society, on 17 December, Governor Light also stressed for the first time the need to define the boundary because of the 'unprotected state of our mission'. Schomburgk did not wait to hear whether Light would like any information, but wrote again from near Roraima in mid-November proposing certain natural features that should form the boundaries of British Guiana. He suggested that the southwestern frontier should be formed by the rivers Takutu and Surumu (also called Cotinga), a line much further west than ever previously proposed which was to become known as the 'Schomburgk Line' (CO111/162: 3; 26).

On the same day that Schomburgk departed Youd is said to have left to visit the Taruma Indians on the Upper Rupununi (RHS 1841b: 194–5), but he appears to have postponed his journey. He wrote that day to Governor Light stating that a Captain Leal, sent by the Brazilian authorities to confirm the boundary line, was due in Pirara.[9] In a postscript to the same letter, dated 3 November, he reported that Leal and party had arrived, and in a letter of 5 November to the Society said that the Brazilian party had departed that morning for the Siparuni River, a tributary of the Essequibo which the Brazilians claimed marked the limits of their territory (CW/O/100: 22; CO111/162: 3).[10]

There happened to be another Englishman, James Spencer, in the region at that time, and his journal provides a rather different, even improbable, picture of Youd. Spencer claims that his first meeting with Youd was on 3 November in a small Indian settlement near Pirara Landing. Spencer found Youd at midday fast asleep 'in a dirty Indian hammock'. Because he had a letter for him Spencer woke him. Youd first muttered a few 'unintelligible words' and then, when he tried to get up, staggered and fell back into his hammock. Spencer enquired whether he was unwell, but when he saw that

THE FIRST MISSION AT PIRARA   41

Youd was unable to hold the letter he became convinced that Youd was completely drunk. On the same day Spencer reached Pirara, where he found Leal with a party of Indians and soldiers. Leal claimed to have already met Youd at the same settlement as Spencer. Youd was back in Pirara by the following day and held Sunday school. Two days later Leal and Spencer left Pirara together, the former bound for the Siparuni and the latter for the Indian village of Curassawaka, higher up the Rupununi (FO13/165: 44).[11]

Leal, according to Youd, showed no liking for the Indians, saying of them that 'being taught ... they are like horses, of no understanding'. Leal also threatened to fetch back any Indians that moved to English territory. This led Youd to make the following plea to the governor:

> I do in great feeling cry out to the English Government, and to Your Excellency, and say, O friends of humanity, use your power, and save these my brethren, yea, speedily make them British subjects (CO111/162: 3).

Governor Light, in forwarding Youd's letter to the Colonial Office on 9 January 1839, commented that Youd seemed to have convinced the Indians that the British government was disposed to protect them and reported that he had written to Youd telling him to encourage the Indians' confidence in British protection. He also sought permission to communicate directly with the British minister in Rio de Janeiro concerning the status of Pirara and the whole matter of the boundary. In March the Colonial Office replied, sharing Light's anxiety over the Indians and giving permission for direct communication with the minister in Rio. It was, however, doubted whether it was worth opening negotiations with Brazil on the undefined boundary without some evidence on the matter and requested copies of any appropriate documentation available in British Guiana, if the governor thought it desirable to proceed (CO111/162: 3; CO112/21: 11).

Leal descended as far as the confluence of the Essequibo and Siparuni Rivers, where he claimed to have found the remains of the boundary marker set up by the Brazilian Boundary Commission of 1780–83. Schomburgk dismissed Leal's claim and declared that the so-called boundary marker had roots (Brit C, 3: 89).[12] It seems unlikely that Schomburgk himself saw it but Youd certainly claims to have done so. He describes the marker, which he 'had the curiosity to examine' as having 'three sturdy roots' and the engravings to be 'natural knotty projections, on which the bark had curiously split' (CW/O/100: 23). However, there is some niggling doubt about this statement because, if Spencer is to be believed, it is not clear on what occasion Youd could have seen it. According to Spencer, Leal arrived at Curassawaka from the Siparuni on 23 November and they travelled together to Pirara two days later. Youd was not there and both Leal and Spencer left almost immediately for Fort São Joaquim (FO13/165: 44).

Youd's movements during November and December 1838, for which months there is no journal, are uncertain. He mentions in his letter of 5 November to the Society that he planned to resume his tour to the south and southeast in two days' time and at a later date he mentions having done just that. He also reported to Light in March 1839 that he had visited the Atorai and Taruma but not the Waiwai (all of the Upper Essequibo) through lack of time. We have just noted that Spencer claimed that Youd was not at Pirara on 25 November, and it is likely that he was away on his tour at that date. He was back in Pirara at some date in December, since he reported that he had had news of Indians selling slaves in the Macushi village of Awara, and had been there to stop it. Bernau reported that Youd was back at Bartica Grove by 10 January 1839 (Brit C, Ann 2: 12–13, 15; CW/O/18: 18; CW/O/100: 22).

According to Richard Schomburgk, Youd had at this time set up a branch mission at Urwa, which he visited once a week from Pirara in order to conduct divine service (I: 305). It is doubtful that this is correct for various reasons, including the fact there does not appear to have been any Amerindian village there at the time since there was no more than the 'skeleton of a shed' when Youd arrived there the following year. He may, however, during this period, have started to prepare for the move of the mission to Urwa by cutting fields there and if he did do this it could only have been during November and December 1838.

As has been noted, Captain Leal was sent to check on the boundary by Ambrosio Ayres just before the latter's death, whereas the communication he sent to his superior reporting the happenings on the Upper Rio Branco went missing. It was not until Leal was carrying out his commission that a copy of Ambrosio Ayres's original letter finally reached the Military Commander of the Amazon Expedition at Santarém, Joaquim José Luis de Sousa, and it was forwarded to the president of Pará on 8 October.

By this time, Pedro Ayres had returned downstream and was at Santarém. On 13 November Pedro Ayres wrote two reports for Luis de Sousa on the events in the Upper Rio Branco. In the first he states that Youd was sent to evangelise the Indians of the Essequibo and Rupununi by the Colonial Government of Demerara. Youd, having found no converts in the Essequibo, crossed into Brazil, built a school and chapel at Pirara, and was converting Brazilian Indians. The *descimentos* that took place in the region in August had caused many Indians to flee to the mission. Further, because of certain Brazilian malfactors who had deserted to Pirara and because the Indians had armed themselves against further *descimentos*, the situation had become dangerous. Pedro Ayres adds that he had learnt that further missions and colonies were planned for the headwaters of the Courantyne and Berbice Rivers, near the Trombetas River (AHI/308/4/1).

In the second report of the same date Pedro Ayres responded to a request for information about Schomburgk's activities. He stated that he, Pedro Ayres, had been about to make a scientific expedition to the Rio Branco when his brother asked him to keep an eye on Schomburgk and to offer him hospitality. He reported that Schomburgk had shown him proof of his identity and his instructions from the Royal Geographical Society. Whilst Schomburgk and his party were at Fort São Joaquim they were engaged in astronomical observations and in making natural history collections. He also referred again to the plans of the British Guiana government to missionize the most populous and colonize the most fertile parts of the frontier. Pedro Ayres also handed over a letter from Schomburgk, written in August, in which the latter formally requested the loan of six Indians and a Brazilian interpreter for his Orinoco trip of which he provided details. Schomburgk also gave thanks for his good treatment and for all the help that had been provided (AHI/308/4/1).

The military commander, Luis de Sousa, in forwarding this correspondence to the president of Pará on 22 November, expressed worries about the intentions of the British Guiana government and referred to the need to send missionaries, furnished with presents, to instruct the Indians in the religion of the state and thus make known to them that they belong to the 'Brazilian Family'. He also considered it necessary to send a boundary commission to erect markers. He further informed the president that he had expressly ordered the new military commandant of the Upper Amazon, João

Ignacio Rodrigues do Carmo, to prohibit all recruitment of Indians for national service, not because recruiting itself was wrong but because of the 'irritating' way in which it was done (AHI/308/4/1).

The president of Pará acknowledged receipt of the military commander's report of 8 October on 22 November. He saw the mission at Pirara as a threat to the integrity of the empire and to the principles of the Roman Catholic religion. Accordingly he had ordered the military commander to send a reliable officer with a large enough escort to oversee the withdrawal of the missionary to the English side of the frontier, although this had to be done as gently and as courteously as possible. On 24 November the president wrote to the minister of foreign affairs in Rio de Janeiro to inform him of the English mission. He worried about the lack of experienced officers and soldiers to man the frontier, and commented that the English, friends of humanity, having sought the abolition of Negro slavery now sought to save other souls, occupying Brazilian territory in order to do so (AHI/308/4/1).

Luis de Sousa had already reacted to Youd's intrusion. He wrote to him on 11 November pointing out that he had established his mission on Brazilian territory and suborned 500 Indians who owed obedience and service to the imperial government. He asked Youd to recognise the frontiers of Brazil, to close the mission at Pirara and to stop sheltering criminals, including the deserter and murderer Evaristo (AHI/308/4/1).

This is an appropiate moment at which to introduce Evaristo more fully. He was a Brazilian soldier, stationed at Fort São Joaquim, who had murdered his commanding officer, Antonio José Bragança. He had then fled eastward into Macusi country, where he had married the daughter of the Macusi chief, Basiko. Robert Schomburgk had first met him in the Macusi village of Annai in 1835 and, as we noted earlier, in 1837 he had accompanied the Macusi delegation to Bartica that requested Youd to settle among them. He changed sides with great frequency and in the end was the only person involved in the whole incident to meet a violent death.

On 7 January 1839, the president sent to Rio de Janeiro copies of Pedro Ayres's letters and the comments of Luis de Sousa. The latter, he noted, had recommended that a priest be sent to the area but he doubted that this could be done as there were not enough people in the province and they tended to be men of the worst conduct and the most revolutionary (AHI/308/4/1).

By March 1839, Leal had reported on his trip to examine the

boundaries, but his report had not reached Belém by 8 April when the outgoing president, Francisco José de Souza Soares d'Andrea, gave his annual account of the state of the province. In this the president referred only in general terms to the grave offence against the peace caused by an English mission converting Brazilian Indian subjects and reported that action had been taken and a reply was awaited (ANB/040.0.79).

Leal had procured two documents in English, one definitely from Youd and the other presumably from the same source. The latter was the minutes of the meeting of the Corresponding Committee of 14 March 1838, which were to become seriously distorted in the course of translation. The former was a letter from Youd to Leal of 6 November 1838, in response to the latter's demand that the missionary justify in writing his presence at Pirara. In this letter Youd states that there is no clear evidence to support the claim that Pirara is on Brazilian territory, that the matter will be sorted out by the respective governments and that 'all this has nothing to do with his objective since his mission is entirely religious and not at all political'. He trusts that, whatever Leal's findings about the frontier, the Brazilians will continue to allow him to preach 'to the poor abandoned souls, so that they may know Him who spilt his blood for them'. Spencer, who was shown this letter by Leal, gave its author 'poor credit for prudence or sagacity' and described its contents as being 'little calculated to promote good feeling' (AHI/308/4/1; FO13/165: 44).

In transmitting these communications to the president of Pará on 27 March, Luis de Sousa added some comments on Leal's report.[13] According to Leal, Youd had persuaded himself that he was in British Guiana and accordingly would continue to convert the Indians to the Anglican faith. Leal further claimed that, although the boundary marks set up by the commissions of the previous century were obvious, Youd proposed to stay on Brazilian soil. The Indians whom he was converting were baptised Roman Catholics, had for many years provided help for the garrison at the fort, and traded with the Brazilians on the Rio Branco. Brazilian cattle grazed on the Rupununi savannahs. If the Macushi traded with Georgetown it was only to obtain firearms and ammunition that were not made in Brazil. Luis de Sousa concluded that unless this question was settled it might be a matter of great future trouble and prejudice to Brazil (AHI/308/4/1).

The new president of Pará, Bernardo de Souza Franco, received these communications soon after taking up office and forwarded them to the minister of foreign affairs on 29 April. In a covering letter he increased the number of Indians at Youd's mission to 700 and showed that he had misread the minutes of the Corresponding Committee's meeting of 14 March. In particular the two clauses of the sentence 'The Meeting regretted to hear such bad accounts of Mrs Youd, and were sorry that the journey to Barbados had not produced that beneficial effect hoped for' were separated, and the latter part taken to mean that Youd had undertaken a mission to Barbados that had proved unproductive. Accordingly the missionary had turned his attention to the interior of British Guiana. Further, the minute was taken to say that, while the missionary society would contribute £100 because the costs of Youd's mission would be very great, the Indians ought themselves to pay them since the evangelisation was for their own benefit. In fact what the Committee was doing was merely repeating previous injunctions that:

> They think it has an injurious tendency to pay persons (besides feeding them) for every service they may render to a Mission which has been established with an exclusive reference to their benefit, the duty of contributing to the support of the Mission should be inculcated upon the Indians & coloured people around, who obtain instruction from the Missionaries, & none should be allowed to retain the idea, that it would appear some have taken up, that the Mission was established to support them (CW/M/4: 345–7).

The president, in order to combat the threat represented by Youd, aimed to try and call the Indians to settle closer to the fort, to enlarge the garrison there and to send a Catholic missionary who might counteract the Protestant danger and return the Indians to the Catholic faith. However, he concluded, these things needed means and money which were not available to him (AHI/308/4/1).

This information formed the basis of the president's speech on 15 August. He reported that a missionary society had sent a representative on to Brazilian soil to convert the Indians to the religion of Luther. The missionary had gathered together about 600 Indians whom he was teaching to read and write. The missionary had expressed his doubts that he was on Brazilian soil, wished the decision on the matter to be settled by the British government, and had declared that since his mission was purely religious it did not matter whose territory it was on. The president stated that he had no reason to suppose that the British government was involved in

THE FIRST MISSION AT PIRARA 47

the usurpation of Brazilian territory. He did, however, note that what he called the 'thoughtless' ordering of Indians to serve in the navy – Indians who were immediately returned to their villages – had given rise in Georgetown to accusations of bad treatment and persecution of the Indians by Brazilians. He had recently heard that the English missionary had retired to the east bank of the Rupununi, but even before this news had arrived he had given orders for the garrison of Fort São Joaquim to be augmented and had asked the ecclesiastical authorities to appoint a priest to the newly created mission of São Joaquim do Rio Branco. The duties of the latter would be to combat the heresies taught to the Indians, to bring them back into the fold of the Roman Catholic religion and to re-establish them as subjects of the emperor (ANB/040.0.79).

A few days later he wrote to the minister of foreign affairs acknowledging the latter's communication of 3 July, in which he was ordered to remove the English missionary from Pirara by 'kind and conciliatory means'. He informed the minister that by a dispatch of 19 July from the military commander at Santarém he had heard that the missionary had retired across the Rupununi and that the reinforcements were on their way to the Rio Branco, as was the priest who had been appointed (AHI/308/4/1).

At this point we have got slightly ahead of what was happening near Pirara; we shall return in the next chapter to pick up the story in early 1839.

Notes

1. It is not clear whether this interpreter, Alfred, is the same person as the Macushi interpreter whom Youd refers to several times at earlier dates but without mentioning a name.
2. Schomburgk had planned as early as March 1837 to spend the 1838 wet season at Fort São Joaquim. While on the Upper Demarara during his second expedition he had written to the Royal Geographical Society saying that he wished to use Fort São Joaquim as his base for the exploration of the Pacaraima Mountains and the Orinoco. He asked the RGS to arrange the necessary passport (RGS/RHS/corr: 4-3-37).
3. Bararoá appears as an improbable hero in Francisco Gomes de Amorim's historical novel *Os selvagens* (1875).
4. This is difficult to accept at face value, but may well be an example of the distortion through which the accounts of events go due to their remoteness in time and space. In this case, it probably had its base in an incident recorded by Youd. He recorded that Schomburgk, on approaching the fort to winter there in 1838, hoisted both the British and Portuguese

colours and fired a salvo (CW/O/100: 46). There are many more examples of this happening in this story and it is still a feature of the area today. Accounts of events rapidly become distorted and elaborated as they are passed along, so that the actions or words of one person become attributed to another.

5. This letter is presumably that from Pedro Ayres to which Youd refers in his journal where he states that he has sent it together with a copy of his response to Governor Light. This correspondence has not been traced. Schomburgk also wrote to inform Youd of the events at São Joaquim (CW/O/100: 46). There are two accounts of these events by Robert Schomburgk, and they are rather different in tone. There is a letter to the Aborigines' Protection Society (CO111/162: 3) that contains a good deal of emotional and rhetorical language and his published article (1841a), which gives a more austere account of the incident.

6. Although how these differ from hunting weapons is not clear. The Trio Indians of Surinam once told me that the point of an arrow designed for shooting people is fixed at a different angle from that intended for shooting animals. The difference has to do with the ease of entry between the ribs; because of their different postures human ribs are horizontal and animal ribs vertical.

7. What this means is to act as paddlers for official canoes.

8. Sir Henry Light had only recently arrived in the colony as the new governor. He was governor from June 1838 until May 1848, and his period of office was marked by running disputes between the plantocracy and the British government. Youd's letter appears to be the first formal contact between the missionary and the colonial government concerning the founding of a mission in the interior.

9. In the British Case (76) it is stated that it was the person in charge of the slave-raiding party who made the claim that Pirara lay within Brazilian territory and was thus responsible for the investigation of the boundary and for encouraging Brazilian occupation of the place. However, no evidence is provided to support this claim and anyway we know that Ambrosio Ayres, as a result of his brother's letter, had given orders to Leal to investigate the frontier by 1 August, the date on which Schomburgk first reported the presence of the slave raiders on the Upper Rio Branco.

Bernau (1847: 120) refers to a Roman Catholic priest appearing at Pirara to make a survey soon after Youd's arrival there. It is possible that one of Leal's companions was a priest, but Youd makes no mention of one, nor do any of the other sources. Bernau is frequently wrong on such matters.

10. In the same letter he acknowledges receipt of the Society's letter of 31 August of the previous year (CW/L/2: 356), which had taken thirteen months to reach him. He regrets that he is unable to do what is requested in that letter, which was to ask Mrs Youd to write to the Society giving an account of her feelings about the mission, and her views on things and people around her, especially Indian women.

11. It is much more likely that Youd was ill than drunk, for he suffered from fever much of the time. As we will see, Spencer was to make a serious

THE FIRST MISSION AT PIRARA 49

attempt to discredit Youd in the eyes of the British authorities. Youd was not, however, an abstainer. He did keep drink in his house, for there is a reference to his providing port for visitors. There is also this description of a convivial evening at Pirara a few years later: 'After dinner the young officers, Mr. Richard Schomburgk, Mr. Fryer and myself formed quite a conspiracy against the poor parson every one of us asking, as soon as we saw his wine-glass empty, to have the pleasure of a glass of wine with him, and the consequence was quite merry and talked the most horrible nonsense' (Goodall 1962b: 52).

12. It is difficult to understand Schomburgk's mockery, given that a few years later he was to carve boundary markers on trees.

13. Neither Youd's letter nor Leal's report has been found, and their contents have been deduced from the comments made on them.

CHAPTER 4

RETREAT TO URWA
1839

In March 1839, Youd was in Georgetown and wrote to Governor Light, on the 6th of that month, proposing to move his mission to Urwa because he did not think that there would be 'any possibility of bringing the Indians lower down than the above place at present'. The reason he gave for wanting to move was because of:

> [the] jealous eye some of the Brazilians look upon me as a Protestant missionary, fearing that all their capturing expeditions will have to come to an end, and that they will finally lose some of their fancied possessions.

He requested from the governor some favours and future guidance. He wanted a letter of protection (together with a Portuguese translation of it) giving him authority to work among the Indians living at Pirara and nearby; permission to form a mission at Urwa with 'as many ... Indians as may choose to settle on the station for the purpose of bringing them into our body in order (under God) to further their temporal as well as their spiritual welfare'; permission to stop the slaving among Indians; and finally guidance on what he should say to Indians from around Pirara (which he describes as a 'neutral place') who wished to settle at Urwa. 'May I receive them or not? and will they be protected by your Excellency from being assaulted or taken back by the Brazilians or any other power?' (Brit C, Ann 2: 12–13). From the same letter we learn that Youd planned to return shortly ('next Tuesday') to the interior. In fact, he left on the afternoon of Wednesday 13 March, having that morning married his second wife, Jane Ann Ross, another Barbadian (CW/O/100: 47).

On their way upriver, they stayed at Bartica Grove for nearly two weeks. While they were there news came that the Pirara Mission had been occupied by the Brazilians, who had seized Youd's possessions and were waiting to take him prisoner, and that all the Indians had fled. Youd, however, discounted this, stating that it was his intention anyway to settle at Urwa and that the Indians were great inventors of the truth. It was thus that when, in the previous October, Leal had visited Pirara, the rumour had spread down to the coast that Youd had been taken captive and removed to Fort São Joaquim, where 'nothing but death might be expected' (CW/O/100: 47).

The Youds left Bartica for the interior on 27 March accompanied by Youd's assistant, Doyce. On this occasion Bernau had agreed to his going, for although he still held a poor opinion of him as a teacher he believed he could be of some material assistance to Youd (CW/O/18: 18).

The Youds' journey into the interior, interrupted by illness and accidents, proved long and hazardous, and one can only wonder at what his new bride made of it. An accident at one of the falls on the Lower Essequibo meant the loss of a canoe and many of their supplies. A few days later, the failure to moor a canoe properly at night resulted in its sinking with a further loss of goods. The damage sustained was exacerbated by Youd's respect for the sabbath, as the following entry in his journal testifies:

> This morning the sun broke out in his usual brightness, and seemed in every way to invite us to use our exertion in getting our books and clothing etc in some measure dry. As to the propriety of so doing or otherwise, on the Lord's day, became a matter of much concern to me, nor could I satisfy my mind, as to the right or wrong of it, even after I had put out a few of the things to dry. On a subsequent occasion, we found that our hired canoe had sunk with a greater part of its load, early on a sabbath morning, near a sand beach, where we had come to, purposing to rest during the sunday. Most of our valuable articles, salt etc were in her, which we dragged out of the water (well saturated as may be supposed) and laid them on the beach, and there let them remain untouched during the sabbath; making it a matter of conscience, not to open out the boxes until monday. The little salt that remained, I did put over the fire, but for the rest nothing of importance was done. I should much like to have the opinion of our parent Committee as to the propriety or impropriety of opening out articles on the sabbath to dry when under such circumstances as we were placed (CW/O/100: 47).[1]

It was not until 17 May that they reached the vicinity of Pirara, having taken, as a result of the low level of the river, some seven weeks for a journey which normally took four.

While the Youds were struggling upriver, Schomburgk had arrived back at Pirara on 1 May after his long journey to Esmeralda, the Casiquiare Canal and the Rio Negro. During the last leg, up the Rio Branco, he had found at the village of Santa Maria some of the Indians whom he had seen being forcibly transported downstream the previous year. It turned out that Pedro Ayres's prediction that the Brazilian authorities would order the release of those not suitable for work in the navy had proved partly correct; sixteen of them were making their way home (RHS 1841c: 263).[2]

At Pirara, Schomburgk found that most of the Indians had dispersed and that a detachment of the 1st Battalion of the Brazilian National Guards, consisting of a sergeant, a cadet and six privates under the command of Pedro Ayres was stationed there. This detachment was presumably the one that the president of Pará had ordered to be sent the previous November, although no document has been found commissioning Ayres for this duty. Schomburgk commented that it was not for him to question by what right the Brazilians had done this, but he reported that the former chapel had been converted into a barracks 'and the building where the first seeds of Christianity had been sown among the benighted Indians, became the theatre of obscene language and nightly revels'. On 17 June, during his journey downriver to Georgetown, he chanced once again to find the Bishop of Barbados at Bartica Grove and reported to him the sad demise of the mission (1841c: 263-6; CW/O/18: 18).

On 17 May Youd set out to walk across the savannah to Pirara, since he had heard that Pedro Ayres and Robert Schomburgk wished to see him. He arrived after dark that same day and was received with 'every shew of gladness and hospitality'. He left again the next day, but the canoes had been delayed and it was not until Thursday, 23 May that he finally reached Urwa. It consisted of little more than the remains of a shed in a small clearing (CW/O/100: 47).

Whilst Youd was at Pirara, Pedro Ayres handed him a letter from the military commander at Santarém which he put aside to deal with later. There is here a slight discrepancy between the journal and the correspondence. There is a gap in the former until August, whereas in the latter Youd says that he returned to Pirara from Urwa on 29 May and claims that it was on this occasion that he received the letter from Joaquim José Luis de Sousa, military commander at Santarém (CW/O/100: 23). In fact, what seems likely is that Youd returned to Pirara to get Ayres to translate the letter (there is a copy of the translation among the CMS papers) although, in fact, he had already prepared a reply on the basis of his own, apparently adequate, reading of the document.

Luis de Sousa's letter, dated 14 November 1838, accused Youd of setting up a mission on Brazilian territory, of having persuaded 500 Indians, Brazilian subjects, to withdraw from their obedience and duty to the imperial government, and of harbouring criminals and employing one of them, Evaristo, as an interpreter. Luis de Sousa asked Youd to recognise the imperial boundaries and to withdraw. Youd replied to the military commander to the effect that Evaristo had been living at Pirara for four years before he arrived there and had only occasionally been used as an interpreter when the usual interpreter was not available. The question of the location of the boundary was being dealt with by the governor of British Guiana, who had communicated with the British envoy in Rio de Janeiro on this matter. Until a decision was reached he had, for the time being, ceased his work at Pirara (AHI/308/4/1; CW/O/100: 23).

These documents were enclosed with a letter from Urwa to the Society, dated 25 September. In the letter Youd, in an accusatory tone, identified Pedro Ayres as responsible, through his brother, of drawing the military commander's attention to the mission's presence at Pirara. This seems less than honest given that Youd had agreed the previous July that Ayres should do just that. Youd continued:

> Indeed, I believe that the cause of his [Ayres's] coming to Pirara at all, had been that of overstating matters in his first report which had led to the sending of the Governor of Santarem's letter to me and his temporary appointment to Pirara. It appears further that the Brazilian authorities think they have acted unadvisably in sending the said letter, and in appointing Pedro Ayres to come to Pirara at all, and that they fear they will finally loose [sic] Pirara altogether (CW/O/100: 23).[3]

Ayres left Pirara at the end of June, having received neither supplies nor further orders, and 'having heard that all things were not well respecting him'. Youd later learnt from Ignacio, the chief Brazilian herdsman, who had recently come from Manaus and visited Youd at Urwa, that Ayres had fled to the 'Spanish settlements', i.e. Venezuela (CW/O/100: 23).[4] The reason why Pedro Ayres fled is that he had been branded a traitor in league with Schomburgk and the British, although why and how he suffered this fate is not certain. The accusations against him focused on his dealings with Schomburgk during the wet season of 1838 at Fort São Joaquim. It could be that after he had lost a powerful protector on the death of his brother, the latter's political opponents took the opportunity of getting their own back. However, as we will see, his departure from Brazil by no means signalled the end of his presence in the incident since he remained in the background as a threatening bogeyman.

Bernau's views on the whole venture of the interior mission oscillated. In December 1838 he had recommended that Youd be allowed to stay in the interior until the Society had reached a definite decision about a mission there. In June 1839, despite the relocation of the mission to the east bank of the Rupununi, Bernau expressed concern about its proximity to the frontier and noted the alarm that the Portuguese had taken. He would prefer to see the mission sited lower down the Essequibo, but because of 'Mr Y's sanguine expectations with regard to success' decided to say nothing at present (CW/O/18: 18).

Three months later, Bernau elaborated on this. He was worried that the mission was 'too near upon the boundary of a lawless people' and thus exposed to further depredations. He also wondered how the citizenship of the Indians was to be recognised. He noted how alarmed the Brazilians had become and how they had occupied Pirara 'on the ground that the Missionary lately arrived in that quarter were contemplating an attack upon the fort'. He thought it was a mistake on the part of Youd, at the time when slave raiders were in the vicinity, to have allowed Evaristo to drill the Indians, an activity that must have looked very suspicious to the Brazilians. The Indians, he thought, should have been persuaded to disperse, but in his opinion Youd did not anticipate the baseness of the Brazilians. He summarised the reasons why Urwa should be abandoned and the mission relocated downstream, and recommended a place called Waraputa. Bernau, however, concluded by stressing that this was his view and said that he would not be disappointed if Youd, whose opinion must be heard, remained where he was (CW/O/18: 19).

Youd, however, was equally certain that he was in the right place and given the Indians' desire for instruction, he could not leave. He was convinced that what he was doing was right both spiritually:

> I firmly believe now, as at first, that the Lord's time for calling out some of those wary wanderers to a knowledge of himself, *is come.*

and politically:

> Surely we cannot do wrong in forming a Mission here for British Indian subjects, that are now, and were settled in the British territory

when I first visited them. As to the Brazilians, I would say, fear them not, yet act wisely and cautiously respecting them, and if possible give no offence, either in language or manners, and use hospitality towards them when they come to pay a visit, not forgetting to allow them a few links of forbearance for boasting, of which they seem rather fond; for (poor destitute creatures) many of them know no better, never having gone beyond their leaf-like world, or Amazon stream (CW/O/100: 23).

It was not, however, only about the Brazilians that Youd had to worry. Light wrote to Youd in August saying that a Frenchman, a certain M. Rouillon, had complained that Youd had armed the Indians against the Brazilians and supplied them with guns. Youd replied in October, hotly denying such allegations, and Light, in reporting the matter to the Colonial Office, discredited Rouillon's word on the grounds that he was a refugee who formerly kept a low eating-house and cook-shop in Georgetown (Brit C, Ann 2: 17; CO111/171: 94).[5]

Youd's optimism was gradually rewarded and by the end of 1839 he painted a relatively glowing picture of a thriving community at Urwa, which was very different from the uninhabited small clearing that it had been earlier in the year. However, it is noticeable that he often refers to the place as 'temporary', which suggests some doubts about its long-term viability. The population gradually grew; whereas to begin with the Sunday congregation consisted of about forty Indians, by the last Sunday of the year the figure had reached 138 people from many different groups. Some Indians, however, just attended for the service, and there were numerous casual visitors, most of whom came out of curiosity. If some said that they would come to live at the mission, few seem to have done so. There was some reluctance on the part of many Indians to live at Urwa because they regarded the place as naturally unhealthy. Youd noted in August that there was a lot of fever about, but he attributed this to the change of season (wet to dry) and the unhealthy state of Urwa to the small size of the clearing, which did not allow for the proper circulation of air. Nor were Youd's efforts helped by strict instructions that he was not to incur any expenses whatever because the Church Mission Society's finances were in a very poor way, having had a shortfall of £21,000 during the previous year (CW/O/100: 23; 47; 48).

In mid-August a group of Indians from Pirara told him that many people were expected there because they had heard that Youd intended to visit. Although not recovered from a recent bout of fever, he travelled there on 20 August and arrived so exhausted and ill that he had to cut short 'the usual tedious salutations'. He found the place almost deserted and in a lamentable condition, overrun with grass and vines, with the chapel being used to stable the horses that Pedro Ayres had left behind. He stayed only three days before moving on to the village of Awara to the south. There, on the following Sunday, Youd preached to 160 Indians who had gathered from neighbouring villages, although by this time he was so weak that he had to do so sitting in his hammock. By next day the fever was so bad that Alfred, his former Macushi interpreter, now accepted back into the fold, 'shewed much concern, and now and then wept, supposing I should not recover, nor could I conceive myself, what the will of the Lord was concerning me'. On Tuesday he was well enough to make it back to Pirara, and after a further attack of fever on Wednesday he was able to cover the nine miles to where the canoes were on the Rupununi River. He described the final stretch of his journey home thus:

> About cock crow we started again, being anxious to reach Urwa, our temporary home, before ten a.m. the time when I might expect a return of fever. Through God's mercy, and by his gracious help we got to Urwa about nine a.m. No sooner had I entered our rude sort of cottage than the fever came on, however, I felt thankful that we had found the place, we so much desired, in due time to escape being laid down by the ague at the bottom of our small canoe, which is far from being desirable (CW/O/100: 47).

At the end of September Youd said of himself: 'I am able to creep about a little now, and to perform my duties, but am far from being strong.' By this time the supplies of quinine and Peruvian bark were exhausted and Doyce was sent to Georgetown in early October to obtain more (CW/O/100: 23; 47).

There are no journal entries for October and November 1839, but this is not too surprising when one learns that from early October onwards the attacks of fever became much worse. For three weeks on alternate days and then for two months everyday, his daily routine was:

> Each morning, as soon as the cock crew, the ague came on and remained until eight or nine, ... then came on the hot fever and continued until eleven a.m. and sometimes until midday. This left me quite low and with severe headache, until the perspiration came on,

which left me about three P.M. In the evening, I chiefly endeavoured to accompany my dear wife to the Chapel to meet overanxious people, and to preach the word, sometimes in a leaning, sometimes a sitting position (CW/O/100: 24).

He nearly died twice, and news of his death reached Georgetown. Bernau did not believe it, because if it were true then Mrs Youd would have descended the river long ago (CW/O/18: 20). In fact it was Mrs Youd who died. During Youd's illness, her health had been relatively good and she had got 'very stout', which was a source of 'great comfort' to her husband. Youd put her final illness down to her over-exerting herself. On Christmas morning, they went to bathe in the Rupununi but 'the walk seemed to be rather too much for her, being with child'. Her death was sudden. On 30 December both she and her husband were down with fever and he noted in his journal 'we could not help observing to each other what poor frail creatures we were, yet, our consolation being in the Lord, we had inward comforts which the world can neither give nor take away'. In the afternoon of the following day Mrs Youd came down with a burning fever, her breathing became increasingly difficult and she died early on New Year's Day 1840 (CW/O/100: 24; 48).

Youd's reaction to this personal calamity was characteristic. He wrote in his journal:

> I am as one that is struck dumb or speechless. I know not what to say, I am greatly amazed, but it is the Lord's doing, let him act as seemeth him best, for I hope shortly myself to go and see Jesus face to face, and to rejoice, because of the goodness and infinite wisdom in which the Lord has acted towards me and mine, although it be, that at present, the cloud of an adverse providence seems to hang over my head (CW/O/100: 48).

After his wife's death, Youd continued his work at Urwa. Doyce returned on 5 January,[6] and the month passed in a routine way with Indians coming and going and Youd continuing weak and ill, but buoyed up by his faith. Twice he commented that he would go downriver to recuperate at Bartica Grove, a place he considered to be as healthy as any in the colony, as soon as it was convenient. However, he expressed the fear that if he did so the doctor would recommend that he go to Barbados or England for the sake of his health, which he did not want to do because for the present he felt perfectly happy where he was (CW/O/100: 48).

On 30 January, an Indian brought the news that Captain Leal

(newly appointed as commandant of Fort São Joaquim and administrator of the national ranches) and several militia men had arrived at Pirara on horseback, and that three or four canoes were also heading there. Then on Saturday, 1 February, Samuel Naripo, a faithful Macushi from Pirara, came with an introductory letter from the Roman Catholic priest who had arrived to establish a mission at Pirara. The priest requested Youd to come and see him, and apologized for not visiting him but he had a bad toe – at which point in his journal Youd parenthically comments 'perhaps the gout'. Further news was that Leal and the soldiers were to retire the following week and no troops were to be stationed at Pirara. Youd decided to go, and sent a message to Leal asking for two horses to be available next Wednesday morning, 5 February, at Pirara Landing, where he arrived on Tuesday evening and spent the night. Early next morning Captain Leal, in full uniform, arrived with the horses and by ten o'clock they were at Pirara. There Youd was greeted by the hoisting of the Brazilian flag, several rounds of musket fire and the ringing of the mission bells. The padre, in his robes, gave him a hearty welcome, invited him into what was Youd's former residence and extended to him every respect and courtesy (CW/O/100: 48).

The padre was the discalced Carmelite Friar, José dos Santos Innocentes, who was to take a leading role in the events that followed. He had had an unusual career. A Paraense by birth, he had been a missionary on the Rio Negro for some years. He had been in Manaus in 1832 and had played an influential part in the uprising of that year in support of Amazonas's independence from Pará. He had attempted to reach the Imperial Court by way of the Rio Madeira in order to plead Amazonas's case, but was turned back in Matto Gross as a result of becoming involved in certain local problems. He was not long after this vicar in Manaus (Reis 1832: 55–63; 1935: 72).

It has been claimed that his presence on the Rio Branco was a form of exile, resulting from his involvement in the 1832 uprising, but this is doubtful given that he was not apparently the first to be offered the job; another priest had declined the post. There is also the question of whether Fr. José was attached to the Brazilian army in any way. It is variously claimed that he held or had held the rank of lieutenant-colonel or major in the Brazilian army or that he had been an army chaplain. Whereas this is possible, it might equally have been a courtesy title. Schomburgk is regularly referred to as lieutenant-colonel in the Brazilian sources and on occasion even Youd is given the same rank (AHI/308/4/1/; CO111/195: 1813; Hemming 1987: 340; RS, I: 311).

According to J.W. de Mattos (1856: 125) the mission in the Upper Rio Branco was created by a provincial law of 29 September 1839, and whilst this may be formally correct we have noted that five weeks before that date the president of Pará had reported to Rio de Janeiro that a missionary for the Upper Rio Branco had been nominated. Almost certainly wrong is de Mattos's claim that Fr. José set up his first base there in 1839. Fr. José, in a letter from Pirara dated 14 February 1840, states that he had only arrived there on the 30th of the previous month. It is true that Richard Schomburgk claims that his brother had become well acquainted with him while staying at São Joaquim during the wet season of 1838. This, however, is flatly contradicted by Robert Schomburgk in April 1841, when he says that he had never met him before (CO111/178: 1367; AHI/ 308/4/1; RS I: 311).

There are various descriptions of Fr. José. Goodall twice refers to him as 'old' (1962b: 53); Robert Schomburgk mentions his 'age and weak constitution' (CO111/204: 493), and Richard Schomburgk describes him as 'pale and gaunt' (I: 311). He himself complained of his chronic illnesses and advanced age (de Mattos 1979: 150). Governor Light, who, as far as we know, never met him and probably depended on Robert Schomburgk's views, wrote of him as 'an inoffensive well-meaning man, who benefits by his connection with the English, carrying on from time to time a trade with Georgetown'. Light also supposed that 'the cares of his flock do not occupy much of his time' (CO111/195: 1813). Alfred Russell Wallace, the British naturalist, who met Fr. José at Guia on the Rio Negro in 1850, has left some comments about him which are worth quoting at length:

> Frei Jozé dos Santos Innocentos was a tall, thin, prematurely old man, thoroughly worn out by every kind of debauchery, his hands crippled, and his body ulcerated; yet he still delighted in recounting the feats of his youth, and was celebrated as the most original and amusing story-teller in the province of Pará. ... I ... was always much amused with his inexhaustible fund of anecdotes: he seemed to know everybody and everything in the Province, and had always something humorous to tell about them. His stories were, most of them, disgustingly coarse; but so cleverly told, in such quaint and expressive language, and with such amusing imitations of voice and manner,

that they were irresistibly ludicrous. ... He had been a soldier, then a friar in a convent, and afterwards a parish priest: he told tales of his convent life, just like what we read in Chaucer of their doings in his time. Don Juan was an innocent compared with Frei Jozé; but he told us he had a great respect for his cloth, and never did anything disreputable – *during the day!* (1889: 157).

However, when they met again in September 1851, and Fr. José told him how he had solved the problem of some warlike Indians in Bolivia some years earlier by leaving smallpox-infected clothes for them, Wallace 'could hardly help a shudder at this cool account of such a cold-blooded massacre, but said nothing, consoling myself with the idea that it was probably one of the ingenious fabrications of Frei Jozé's fertile brain' (1889: 225).

On the other hand, from the Brazilian side he was much applauded as his patriotic and energetic actions were seen as having obstructed the British imperialist designs. Furthermore he appears to be the only person involved in the whole affair to have had a street named after him, as there is in Manaus.

There are two reports of what happened next, that of Youd and that of Fr. José, and whereas they do not differ substantially, there are some significant variations in emphasis. Youd's account of the events is contained in his journal. First a statement from the president of Pará was read to him in which the land to the east of the Rupununi River was claimed for Brazil, and accordingly Youd was teaching the doctrines of Luther to Brazilian Indians. The two missionaries discussed the problem and the location of the boundary and did so with 'great calmness', aware that it was not up to them but to their respective governments to resolve the issue (CW/O/100: 48).

Youd claimed that his mission was on British territory and that he had Governor Light's authority to be there. (He was not, however, too certain about his claim and wondered to himself whether it was the consequence of what he and Schomburgk had concluded on the best information available.) If the Brazilians were going to dispute the claim, he stated, he would have no alternative except to go to Georgetown to make representations to the governor. Fr. José amicably agreed that until the two governments had come to an understanding, Youd might remain at Urwa and teach the Indians from the east bank of the Rupununi while he taught those from the west side and from the neighbourhood of Pirara. Youd should probably have accepted this arrangement but went on to ask whether there would be any objection if Indians from around Pirara came to visit him and stayed over for the sabbath. Fr. José found no difficulty with that but Youd, pushing his luck further, asked whether there would be any objection to such Indians joining the various classes and learning English, as they had been doing up until then. Fr. José:

> immediately said, 'that I cannot allow', they may hear you preach, but you must not teach them English. I then told him, that if any came and joined the classes, as would be natural for them to do, I could not tell them to shut their books.

On that note, discussion of the topic ended for the day and was replaced by more general chat (CW/O/100: 48).

The following day, the tone had changed. Fr. José informed Youd that he had orders from the president of Pará to bid him to leave Urwa and all Brazilian territory, and that included the east bank of the Rupununi and most of the Upper Essequibo. Youd expressed the opinion that the British government would never accept such a claim. At this Leal 'got a little angry', saying that 'the eyes of the English were too big', and inveighing against the territorial encroachments of the English, French and Spanish. Youd agreed, despite his doubts, to obey the Brazilian demand, but only on condition that it was put in writing. Leal, however, would not issue the order there and then because Youd had been invited to Pirara as a friend. Instead the order would be served on him when he was back at Urwa (CW/O/100: 48).

Youd found the whole affair rather strange, given that on the previous day Fr. José had been willing to let him stay at Urwa and now was ordering his evacuation of the place. He was suspicious of some double dealing and felt that 'the whole design' was against him (CW/O/100: 48).[7]

During the next day, Friday, further points emerged. Youd was told that the president of Pará was very angry with him because Youd had never contacted the British consul at Pará about his presence on Brazilian territory, which was a very grave offence. Youd reasonably rejoined that since he believed himself to be on British territory, he had seen no reason for being in touch with the consul. Fr. José also told him that as a result of the president's reading in a newspaper a statement by Youd concerning the enslaving and maltreatment of Indians by Brazilians, he had instructed the authorities to prevent such practices. Indeed, he had sent Fr. José to Pirara to teach the Indians and to protect them from further molestations. At this news Youd thanked God that he had 'at all been a means of getting an end put to the Indian enslaving business'. Finally, Youd learnt that the Brazilians had got hold of a letter to him from either the Corresponding Committee or the Society. This was said to contain the information that he had been sent by a small body of men for the purpose of recruiting Indians to work on the coastal plantations. He vehemently denied this accusation, and explained that the objectives of the Church Missionary Society were purely evangelical (CW/O/100: 48).[8]

Youd extended his stay until the following Monday, 10 February, and at Fr. José's invitation attended Mass on the Sunday. He was horrified to discover that the service was in Latin and baptism was given without instruction. Despite these outrages against his 'protestant principles', Youd was grateful for all the respect and attention he received from Captain Leal and Fr. José. Indeed, despite their very obvious differences, they seem to have got along well. On the Monday, Leal accompanied Youd to the banks of the Rupununi, and the latter reached his mission station the following evening. The next day the Indians assembled and Youd explained the situation, assuring them that he would do everything he could to help them and would immediately go to visit the governor. The Indians, in their turn, rejected any attempts by the Brazilians to impose their authority, stating that they had been happy under British law, having no fear of being kidnapped (CW/O/100: 48).

Fr. José's account of these events is contained in a letter of 14 February addressed to the administrator of the provincial treasury, in which he gives a general report of his activities. He had arrived at Pirara on 30 January and had made a speech to the Indians in which he said that he had been sent by the president of Pará to found a mission. The place belonged to Brazil, the English missionary did not belong there and no credence should be given to what he said. The next day he sent a message to Youd asking him to visit him. The description he provides of their discussions does not differ greatly from that given by Youd, although he mentions the Englishman's obstinacy in refusing to accept that he was on Brazilian soil and his insistence that he had permission from the governor of British Guiana to be where he was. However, Fr. José claims that in the end his persuasiveness won and Youd agreed to leave (AHI/308/4/1).

In the same letter Fr. José wrote that Youd had gathered under his command 800 Indians who were well instructed in his wrong doctrine. He was teaching them so that they would go with him and was telling them that the Brazilians wished to enslave them. It was hard for him to combat this but he was gradually succeeding, and could have done nothing if he had not recruited the services of the deserter, Evaristo, who knew the Indian language and was worthy of esteem because of his good behaviour. He sought a pardon for Evaristo. The real problem, however, was all the presents that Youd had made to the Indians. Unless he also gave the Indians presents he would be unable to get anywhere; he asked that they be sent as quickly as possible.

Fr. José then continued about how important the mission was to the interests of the province because of the large number of Indians in the territory. He would need help to stop the Indians going over to the English and asked for two more priests and four experienced Indian women[9] who would make manioc flour and undertake other duties, such as spinning cotton, and help to accustom the Indian women to such service. Finally he needed manioc flour to sustain the Indians for he was only given 60 alqueires (about 780 litres) of which 22 had been used on the journey. This letter is not untypical of those written by Fr. José in its listing of all the problems and difficulties he was facing, referring to his success in overcoming them and at the same time his need for material and human assistance if he was fully to succeed (AHI/308/4/1).

There is another document, a report to the president of Pará, which gives another account of the happenings in February that year, but which stresses Youd's lack of concern about political and territorial questions. Youd is reported to have said:

> that the Nature of His Mission was this that he mearly [sic] came in that part of Brazilian Dominions to instruct the Indians in Reading & writing and that he did not come to dispute about the land or Boundery [sic] but to preach & instruct those that would follow him (NAG/MBD: 5).[10]

On 29 February, Youd was visited at Urwa by Captain Leal and a Major de Freitas,[11] who served him with the order to leave. They told him that the Indians who were to accompany him to Georgetown must obtain passports from the Brazilian authorities before they did so and that these should be collected at Pirara by Youd. Youd said he would do no such thing because so far as he was concerned the Indians were not Brazilian citizens (CW/O/100: 27; CO111/171: 94).

The visit of the Brazilians to Urwa is not covered in Youd's journal, although a report to Governor Light fills in some of the detail. It would appear that Youd left Urwa fairly soon after the visit because when the journal entries resumed on Saturday, 7 March he was on his way downstream, having left 'Pirara water' that day. It is possible that he had visited Pirara again, because two days later he refers to the loss of 'a keg of newly salted meat for our journey (a present from the Roman Catholic Missionary at Pirara)'. If he went to Pirara on this occasion we do not know why he did so, but it seems unlikely that it was to fulfil the condition laid down by Leal that any Indians accompanying him downriver must first call at Pirara in order for them to obtain passes. It would have been out of character for Youd to have accepted such a condition and thus tacitly to have acknowledged the Brazilian citizenship of the Indians (CW/O/100: 48).

Leal backed up his expulsion of Youd with a letter to Governor Light in which he accused Youd and his assistant not only of having encroached on Brazilian territory but also of having encouraged Portuguese labourers to desert, harboured refugees from Brazilian justice, alienated 500 Macushi Indians and armed some of them against the Brazilian authorities, ordered the slaughter of cattle belonging to His Imperial Majesty and caused 'a great riot and disturbance' on the Rio Branco. He ended with the assurance that 'none will quit the Rio Branco under my command for Your Colony without being provided with their Passport'. Youd wrote to Light on 14 April denying all these charges. He admitted to having killed four head of cattle in 1838 but claims that he had permission to do so and had paid the Brazilian head herdsman for them. He explained in some detail the events surrounding the so-called deserters, who were back with the Brazilians as he had seen them with Leal at Pirara. He could not see how he could have caused a disturbance on the Rio Branco when he was a hundred miles away from there, and at no time had he ever supplied arms to the Indians. Finally, he pointed out that neither Leal nor Fr. José were witnesses of the actions of which they accused him; they had only learnt of them by hearsay (CO111/171: 94).

Before Youd left Urwa, he wrote to Governor Light concerned about the fate of the Indians if the British did not counter the Brazilian claims. He reported that on the Sunday after his return from Pirara:

> Several of the principal men of the different tribes came before me and stated in very strong language their entire disapprobation of my leaving them, especially under such unfavourable circumstances saying they considered my going in the light of running away now that trouble had come.

A properly demarcated boundary, he argued, would set at rest 2,000 greatly agitated Indians. On his journey down to Georgetown he had further evidence of this agitation and his journal records many instances of Indians expressing dismay at his departure and a wish for British protection and trade in the future:

> Here, also, I found the Indians much disturbed in mind respecting the said Brazilian boundary, being determined to quit, if the English do not take up the land. They came shewing their clothes, and spoke of their guns, powder, shot, cutlasses, hoes etc., saying they did not get them from the Portuguese; they wanted nothing from the Portuguese, nor would they have them to rule over them (CW/O/ 100: 48).

Youd, accompanied by thirty-nine Indians, was in Georgetown in April to petition Governor Light about the British taking some action with reference to the Brazilian threat to the interior of the colony. The governor was not overly sympathetic. He gave the Indians a present of $70 but warned them not to expect any more in future. He ordered Youd not to enter into any negotiations concerning the territory in dispute, to locate himself within the certain limits of British Guiana, and to give:

> instruction only to such Indians as seek it from you within these territorial limits, and taking care most distinctly to impress upon the Indians the impossibility of affording them any effectual protection either to their persons or their property unless they abandon the remote parts of the Country & place themselves in the Neighbourhood of our Magistrates & Police.

The governor also reprimanded Youd for his stubbornnesss in attempting to found a mission in the interior. Youd's comment on this was that it was the best thing he had done in the colony. He wrote to the Society expressing the opinion that the government could not ignore the Indians' requests for protection. He argued:

> Shall our Government allow of this. D.V. I may yet live to hear whether two thousand Indians are much or little thought of by our nobles at home, seeing they have by myself or other deputies sought

for English protection. The land itself is but of little value, but the souls thereon are (CW/O/100: 24; NAG/GSO/LB).

Just as Youd was being forced to retreat from Urwa, things were at last beginning to move on a wider front. Schomburgk, soon after his arrival back in Georgetown on 20 June 1839, had given news of the occupation of Pirara and prepared a lengthy report for Light on matters in the interior. He stressed the urgent need to fix the boundary between Brazil and the British colony. He advanced three reasons, in the following order of importance. The first, to which most space and rhetoric is devoted, concerns the future of the Indians.

> If the Indians who inhabit these regions are to be rendered useful subjects, the uncertainty of our boundary claims the particular attention of Her Britannic Majesty's Government. ... Terrified by the threats of the Brazilians and their commands not to attend to the instructions of the missionary they wander among haunts as are only known to themselves and the wild beasts of the forests, and the work of civilization, which began with such fine prospects, has been unfortunately checked. ... Although the Indians' dread of the Brazilians knows no bounds they are still so attached to the regions of their birth and to those territories which they know from tradition to have been held in possession by their ancesters for ages, that every attempt to induce them to settle on our coast regions would for the present prove abortive.[12]

Second, it was important to secure the Pirara portage, as it was the key to an immense system of inland navigation and thus invaluable to the development of commerce. Third, the Rupununi River was a rich fishing ground and an asset to the colony. Schomburgk's recommendations were that the Brazilian detachment be asked to withdraw, the disputed territory be declared a neutral zone and that a survey be conducted with the setting up of durable boundary markers (CO111/164: 111). In August Schomburgk sailed for England, arriving there in September.

Governor Light, in transmitting the information to the Colonial Office on 15 July 1839, wrote:

> The Brazilian Government is on the alert to extend the limits of the Empire ... a large number of the Aborigines would thereby be subject to the reckless rule of masters who have not yet learnt to consider them as human beings.

He further reported that there were no archives relating to the frontiers in British Guiana, strongly urged that some immediate action be taken on the question, and recommended that Robert Schomburgk be employed as boundary commissioner (CO111/164: 111).

It was not until February 1840 that the Colonial Office acted, partly, it would appear, because the aforementioned memorandum prepared by Schomburgk had been mislaid. An internal minute of the 11th expressed the view that there was no longer any reason to delay consideration of the boundary question and went on:

> Motives of humanity & the obligations which this country may be considered to have contracted towards the Aborigines, w^d seem to urge very strongly the duty of extending to the Indians as far as we have any right to extend it, the protection of British territory.

The first view had been that it would be better for the Indians to move downstream, and this had been Schomburgk's opinion in 1837 when he had recommended that the Macushi and Wapishiana be induced to settle among the colonists, for whom they could provide labour while learning to reap the benefits from contact with 'civilization and religion' (CO111/150: 2977). Whereas the report of 1837 obviously forms the basis of his *Description of British Guiana* (1840), by the time he came to write it his views on this matter had changed. We have noted this change in the report he made to Light in July 1839. There was no longer a question of persuading the Indians to settle among the colonists. In fact, his thinking was now the reverse, and he argued that only the introduction of 'religion, civilization and industrious habits' would induce future generations of Indians to come and settle among the colonists. In keeping with this new advice the Colonial Office discarded its earlier policy as unrealistic, for 'nothing will induce Indians to leave their homes'. Accordingly it would be 'extremely desirable for motives of humanity & also with a view to support the efforts of the missionary ... [to] give them all the protection we can where they are'. 'The Indians are the only parties who have any just or natural claim to them [territories]', but their lack of power made such a claim nugatory and therefore it fell to Great Britain, in whom the Indians had confidence, to protect them. Pirara lay a long way inland but it was thought that Brazil might not be 'tenacious of this wilderness' (CO111/162: 26).

A memorandum along these lines was sent to the Foreign Office and the response of the Foreign Secretary, Lord Palmerston, on 18 March was to propose that Britain should proceed in the following highhanded manner: that a map be drawn according to the boundaries described by Robert Schomburgk and copies of it be sent to the three countries adjoining British Guiana (Brazil, the Netherlands and Venezuela) as a statement of the British claim, and if any of the three governments objected:

> It would then rest with each of the three governments above mentioned to make any objections which they might have to bring forward against these boundaries and to state the reasons upon which such objections might be founded, and Her Majesty's Government would then give such answers thereto as might appear proper and just.

In the meantime commissioners should proceed with the erection of *permanent* markers along boundaries claimed by Britain. Palmerston further considered that 'it would be expedient that the Brazilian detachment should be required to withdraw from Pirara' (CO111/164: 111).

In April Robert Schomburgk was duly appointed boundary commissioner and he began making plans for the survey. He wrote to the Colonial Office saying that it was essential to have high quality survey instruments and assistants. The Colonial Office immediately started getting cold feet about the cost of the whole business. A minute to Schomburgk's letter reads:

> It was orignally supposed that on the writer's journey he would be able to accomplish this business with but little trouble to himself and little expence to the Public. But the fact is obviously otherwise.

It was also suggested that the expense of the boundary survey be equally divided between the home country and British Guiana and this proposal was conveyed to Light (CO111/175: 988; CO112/21: 111).

During the summer of 1840 there was a regular flow of correspondence between Schomburgk and the Colonial Office. Much of it had to do with the arrangements for personnel and equipment for the boundary survey, but there were also other matters. In July, Schomburgk reported that the three Indians who had travelled with him to England the previous year and had been part of the exhibition he had mounted were shortly to return home.[13] Schomburgk was 'most anxious that they should be able to carry with them the assurance to their brethren, that H.M. Government intends to secure them against Brazilian aggressions' (CO111/175: 988). The Colonial Office turned to advice from Schomburgk on news emanating from British Guiana. On the report of the Indians who accompanied Youd following his withdrawal from Urwa, Schomburgk wrote:

> These tribes have claimed British protection, and their choice is substantially confirmed by the deputation of fifty individuals, consisting of chiefs and their families, who ... craved his Excellency's protection, and appear anxious as rightful owners to the soil, to cede Sovereignty to Her Britannic Majesty (CO111/175: 1586).

On the Brazilian order to Youd to withdraw downriver, he remarked that it had no more authority than if Youd had ordered the Brazilians to evacuate Fort São Joaquim, and he hoped that Youd had ignored it (CO111/175: 1586).

In the meantime Youd's standing *vis-à-vis* the Brazilians had not been helped by the actions of the British consul in Belém, H. August Cowper. Soon after his arrival, in August 1839, and in response to the president's report of that month already referred to, Cowper had written to the Foreign Office in these terms:

> I am sorry to say my Lord, that some religious fanatic of our nation, has caused considerable ill feeling towards us in general, by attempting the conversion from the Catholic faith, of some Indians upon the Demerara frontier.

He went on to say that he had assured the president of Pará that the missionary was not authorised in any way by the British government (FO13/156: 38).

In late December of that year or early in January of the next, Cowper received a letter from James Spencer, who, it has been noted, was in the vicinity of Pirara in November 1838 and had reached Manaus in March 1839, from where he was now writing.[14] In his letter he claimed to be a former land owner in Essequibo who, having abandoned his estate following the emancipation of the slaves, had made a scientific journey into the interior of British Guiana. He wrote to the consul on two scores; first he raised the question of profitable commerce between the colony and Brazil, and second he suggested that the British government should take action against Youd who, by his behaviour, had caused much ill-feeling towards Great Britain. In support of the second proposal, Spencer enclosed extracts from his journal relating to his experience of Youd, including his claim that Youd was drunk on their first meeting. He also accused Youd of a number of other things, including invective against the British Guianese government for not preventing Brazilian slave raiding, hypocrisy and uncharitableness. He reported that the Macushi headman at Pirara had told him that Youd claimed to be the Son of God and that he could bring down fire to burn the people and their houses. Youd had been appropriating Brazilian cattle and exercising the Indians with guns and poisoned arrows to resist the Brazilians (FO13/165: 44).

Cowper sent these communications on to the Foreign Office on 14 January 1840, stating that the story of Indians being enslaved could not be true as 'no Indian can be a slave in Brazil', and that he was writing to the governor of British Guiana raising the matter of trade between Pará and that colony and requesting Youd's removal as he was clearly an 'unworthy person' (FO13/165: 44). The latter he did on 24 January, but was informed in a reply of 21 March that Spencer was 'of notoriously bad character'. Accordingly, whereas Light was keen to foster trade with Pará, he did not regard it as appropriate to do it through the agency of Spencer. On the question of Youd, Light recommended Cowper to extend to him 'friendly and official notice and protection' for he is an 'exemplary and intelligent Minister in whom you may place implicit confidence'. The behaviour in the interior of both Spencer and Rouillon had already been brought to his notice by both Youd and Schomburgk and was 'calculated to throw discredit on the British name amongst the Indians Tribes' (CO111/171: 94). The British consul did not listen to Light for, as we shall see, he was involved in a further incident concerning Youd later in the year.

Fr. José's letter of 14 February concerning his discussion with Youd reached the president of Pará (now João Antonio de Miranda) by May, and he forwarded a copy of it together with a covering letter to the Ministry of Foreign Affairs on the 21st of that month. The president called attention to the success achieved by Fr. José in bringing 800 Indians back into the fold of the true religion, and to the important contribution to this made by Evaristo, to whom he has issued a pardon. He pointed out that it was the heretic missionary's generosity with presents that had been the reason for his success. However, it was not clear from Fr. José's letter whether the English missionary had left Brazilian territory, but even if he had not there was nothing more that the Englishman could do. The president ended by requesting help in the provision of presents since this was a matter not simply of religion but of the defence and security of Brazil's frontiers (AHI/308/4/1).

The president provided an even more up-beat version of the events at Pirara in the annual state-of-the-province speech delivered on 15 August 1840:

> The missionary [Fr. José] sent to the Rio Branco by my predecessor with the object not only of defending the principles of our Holy Religion against the inroads of the reformed religion of Luther but also the rights of the Empire against Father T. Youd, who on Brazilian territory preached his damned doctrines, supported by a Missionary Society of Demerara, has obtained the most happy results. Our envoy had an interview with that heretic, and by reason and persuasion succeeded in forcing him to withdraw and give up his high pretensions. More than 800 Amerindians[15] have been restored to the bosom of our Religion, which continues to obtain the most considerable triumphs. Father Youd, in the spot in which he located himself, tried recently to recruit some of our converts, who had abandoned him, however his final attempts have been unsuccessful (ANB/040.0.79).

The president noted in the same speech that Fr. José had requested the help of two more priests, but said he thought the needs of other missions had first call if any priests were available, which they were not (ANB/040.0.79).

At this point, the authorities in Belém seem to have felt the matter was resolved, and for the following year little attention was paid to what was going on in the Upper Rio Branco. However, the president's address of August 1840 did give rise to some events that are worth considering briefly.

The president sent the British consul a copy of his address, which the latter duly forwarded to the Foreign Office together with a copy of a letter he had written to the president. In the latter the consul states that 'I have done all in my Power to get him [Youd] removed' and denies that the missionary was any way supported by the British Government. In September he informed the Foreign Office that the president had copies of letters from the Demerara Missionary Society in which Youd was urged to proceed into Brazilian territory. In fact, what had come into the hands of the Pará authorities, as has already been noted, was a copy of the minutes of the Corresponding Committee's meeting of 14 March 1838 at which the Committee had authorised a £100 grant towards the cost of Youd's exploratory trip into the interior (CO111/174: 2176; AHI/308/4/1).

These dispatches from Belém were forwarded by the Foreign Office to the Colonial Office for comment, of which one reads:

> I suppose the missionary has violated the law of Brazil, and if so I do not perceive how his Govt. could support or countenance him. But on the other hand I cannot think that it is the duty of this country to take any measures for rendering effectual the law of a Foreign State having for its object to prevent the Propogation there, of what we regard as truth. If the Missionary has the spirit and is willing to sustain the burdens of a martyr, it seems to me that he should at least be left to do so. If not, Great Britain w^d be actively engaged in arresting the diffusion of Protestantism. But I surmise that the fact really is that the Missionary has addressed himself to those whom we claim as British Subjects and that there is indirectly in debate here the question which Mr. Schomburgk is about to investigate (CO111/174: 2176).

Lord John Russell, Secretary of State, more abruptly remarked: 'Have no observations for L Palmerston except that his consul had much better not have interfered' (CO111/174: 2176). Finally the Foreign Office replied to the consul on 4 December, pointing out that Youd had been operating on British terrritory, and that anyhow it was not the concern of the British Government if private individuals and societies wished to preach on Brazilian territory, although they would clearly be liable to Brazilian law (CO111/174: 2402).

Meanwhile the Colonial Office had transmitted to Governor Light Palmerston's recommendation, and mentioned that the latest intelligence from Robert Schomburgk was that the Brazilians had withdrawn from Pirara.[16] If this were the case there was no need for action, but watch must be kept for further intrusion or aggression against Indians within the Schomburgk line (CO112/21: 71). In June, Governor Light responded cautiously to this dispatch, pointing out that the Brazilians did not have the troops to take possession and that he could not recommend 'any military movements' on the part of the British (CO111/171: 94). The Colonial Office's answer to this was that whatever measures necessary should be taken to prevent British claims to the disputed territory from being prejudiced while the boundary survey was under way (Co112/21: 115). Three months later, the Colonial Office repeated this injunction:

> Pending the Settlement of these Boundaries it will be your duty to resist any encroachment upon Pirara or upon the Territories near the

Frontier which have been hitherto occupied by Independent Indians Tribes (CO112/24: 146).

Notes

1. He did not question the propriety of dragging the items from the water on the sabbath. To have been consistent he should have left the supplies in the river until Monday. On the other hand it would not have been too difficult to have found biblical justification for taking some action: 'Which of you shall have an ass or an ox fallen into a pit, and will not straightway pull him out on the sabbath day?' (St Luke, 14: 5).

2. Three years later Schomburgk, on meeting these Indians again, wrote of them 'whom I released from Brazilian captivity' (CO111/195: 1710).

3. In the boundary dispute documents the British argued that 'the idea that they [the Brazilians] had some claim to occupy Pirara seems to have been suggested to the Brazilian authorities by the person in charge of a slave-raiding expedition' (Brit C: 76). There is no evidence for such a claim and, as we have seen, Ambrosio Ayres received his brother's report of Youd's presence at Pirara on 1 August, the same date as the slavers arrived at São Joaquim.

4. The missionary W.H. Brett met on the Pomeroon River in 1841 two strangers, apparently on their way to Venezuela. The elder was thought to be 'Señhor Ayres, the commander of the Brazilian force which had destroyed the Pirara mission two years before' (1868: 114). Although this is certainly possible, the evidence adduced for this identification is very weak.

5. This Rouillon was the companion of Spencer, the man who had written so disparagingly of Youd. They had reached Manaus together, from where he was sent back to Demerara by Spencer with a load of sasparilla. He arrived in Georgetown in June or July 1839 (CO111/171: 94; FO13/165: 44).

6. Youd complained in his journal that there was no news either from the Corresponding Committee or the Parent Committee. The journal has been later annotated with the remark that Doyce had forgotten the letters.

7. If one were to hazard a guess one would see here the hand of Leal. From what we know of Fr. José and Leal, the former would have been quite happy to have let Youd stay at Urwa, but not the latter. Leal quite possibly got at Fr. José over Wednesday night and persuaded him to take a harder line.

8. It is not at all clear what letter is being referred to. If it is the minutes of the Corresponding Committee's meeting of 14 March 1838 that we know had reached Brazilian hands, then they have undergone even further distortion.

9. The actual words are *Indias ladinas*. There is no simple translation of the term *ladina*, but it means an Indian who is accustomed to working for Brazilians, probably speaks some Portuguese, has an understanding of Christianity and has some technical skill.

10. The provenance of this document is not certain. The original Portuguese, together with a copy of the English translation, is in the Public Record Office and there is another copy of the English translation in the National Archives of Guyana. It is entitled 'A Statement of fact for His Excellency the President of Pará with Respect to the Mission of Pirara in the Rio Branco Station'. It is undated but enclosed with a letter from Fr. José to Youd of 26 February 1840. It has been copied for transmission with the originals on 24 June 1840. The author is unidentified, but Fr. José or Leal is the most likely candidate although the handwriting does not appear to belong to either of them.

11. I have not noticed any other references to this officer in the material I have gone through and know nothing more about him. It is possible that he is the author of the document discussed in the previous note.

12. A point that, as we have just seen, was ignored by Light the following April when he told the Indians that they might only expect British protection if they settled downstream.

13. The exhibition was mounted at 209 Regent Street. The Indians seem to have had a fairly miserable time of it: 'The Indians were dressed in tight-fitting clothes painted with roucou, to give the appearance of nature but notwithstanding their partial covering they were stated to have cowered over a fire, shivering with cold' (Rodway 1889: 10).

14. Spencer had collected together a load of sasparilla and sent his French companion Rouillon back to Demerara with it. He had heard nothing more of him. His non-appearance is explainable because when he got back to Georgetown, Light refused to give him a permit to return to the interior. Spencer himself arrived back in Georgetown in April 1840 (CO111/171: 94; FO13/164: 44).

15. This figure swells to 'close to a thousand' later in the speech. João Wilkens de Mattos (1856: 125) brings the figure up to 2,000 Indians.

16. It is not at all clear where Robert Schomburgk, back in Europe, obtained this information.

CHAPTER 5

RETREAT TO WARAPUTA
1840–1841

Youd, after the deputation with the Indians to Governor Light, remained feeling responsible for the state of perturbation into which the Indians had been thrown by the withdrawal of the mission from Urwa and the apparent domination, in their view, by the Brazilians. Almost immediately, in May 1840, he returned to the middle Essequibo with Doyce, to found a mission at Waraputa below Siparuni Mouth. It was hoped that the mission, so located as to be irrefutably on British soil but still accessible to Indians from the interior, would thrive (CW/O/18: 21; CW/O/100: 24).

During his early months at Waraputa Youd took the opportunity to cross by the trail to the Demerara River and reported to the governor on the need to set up a mission there. In the same report, dated October 1840, he mentions that William Crichton, Inspector-General of Police, had recently visited him and he was pleased to learn that the British government had determined 'to take in the disputed territory'. However, the conditions under which he had been living for so long seem finally to have got to him and in an undated letter from the same period he wrote to the Society requesting permission to return to England during June and July the following year in order to recuperate because he was still suffering from fevers. Further, he said that his father, aged 72, had written 'again and again' wishing to see him before he died and Youd felt bound to obey. He would, however, be happy after that to return to British Guiana and end his days in the mission field (CW/O/ 100: 25; 28).

A postscript to the above letter written in Georgetown and dated 11 December mentions that he had been detained in town by the attorney-general to act as an interpreter in a case against the Demerara postholder, charged with enslaving Macushi Indians. Otherwise we know very little about the first year that Youd spent at Waraputa, as there is no journal for the period from March 1840 until April 1841. On the other hand his last journal, covering the period April to August 1841, is almost entirely taken up with accounts of activities at Waraputa.

The mission there was never very successful and grew only slowly, although this might have been a deliberate policy because of a lack of planted fields and food. Almost a year after Youd arrived there he was concerned about the smallness of the congregation, and it is clear that both his own house and the church were still not finished. There was, however, a steady drift of Indians from the interior. Alfred, his Macushi interpreter, and his family arrived in May 1841, and in July a larger group migrated from Pirara because of events that had taken place there. According to these Indians, Fr. José had departed for Pará and Leal had retired to Fort São Joaquim, and a brother of Evaristo was in command of the twenty Brazilian soldiers stationed at Pirara. The Indians decided that the purpose of these troops was to carry them off and that they were merely waiting for reinforcements before doing so. Accordingly, the Indians, through subterfuge, escaped to the Rupununi River, where they stole Fr. José's large canoe and fled downstream (CW/O/100: 49).

In one of the few letters that we have written by Doyce he states that at the end of August 1841 there were about a hundred Indians at Waraputa. There had, however, been the usual problems with health and fifteen deaths had occurred in the previous eight months. There had been an epidemic of whooping cough among the Indians and both Youd and Doyce suffered from recurring bouts of fever. In January 1842 the population was put at 100 to 120. The Indians came from a number of different groups, and on several occasions Youd commented that, although Macushi was the lingua franca, the seven different languages in use at the mission were an obstacle to the preaching of the Word (CO111/195: 1086; CW/O/100: 49; CW/O/34: 2).

It was not until the end of November 1840 that the Foreign Office instructed the British chargé d'affaires in Rio de Janeiro, W.G. Ouseley, to inform the Brazilian minister of foreign affairs that Schomburgk had been commissioned to mark out the boundary between British Guiana and Brazil and that the governor of British Guiana had been instructed to resist, in the meantime, any encroachment upon Pirara or upon the territory near the frontier 'which has been hitherto occupied by Independent Indian Tribes' (CO111/174: 2265). Ouseley, in turn, wrote to Palmerston in January 1841 giving report of further encroachments by Brazilians, and of plans to annexe the territory which 'now almost uninhabited and of little value, may hereafter be important', and of the continued enslaving of Indians (CO111/184: 672).[1]

On 11 February, Ouseley acknowledged recent receipt of the despatch of 28 November concerning British plans and the appointment of Robert Schomburgk as boundary commissioner. He had conveyed the contents orally to the Brazilian minister for foreign affairs, who had agreed to act on it urgently and to consider appointing boundary commissioners (CO111/184: 948). It was not until 20 February that Ouseley handed in writing to the Brazilian government the contents of the dispatch and at the same time expressed the hope that steps had already been taken to warn provincial and local authorities of British intentions. Together with this communication he presented to the Brazilian minister a memorandum on the boundary question because, Ouseley states, the minister professed complete ignorance of the locality and circumstances of the matter. Among other things Ouseley dismissed Leal's report of 1838 because his knowledge and information were totally inadequate to carry out the duties assigned to him and the result was that his claim was so 'preposterous that it scarcely deserves notice'. Ouseley also repeated the warning that the governor of British Guiana had orders to prevent further encroachment on the disputed territory and aggression against the Indians. He reminded the minister of the survey in progress and told him that markers were to be set up along the boundary claimed by Britain (CO111/184: 1147, 1388).

As a result of these exchanges the minister of foreign affairs wrote to the president of Pará on 6 March bringing him up to date on these happenings and asking for his advice, on how best to bring the matter to a successful conclusion preserving the dignity of the empire and avoiding such disagreeable occurrences as those that had arisen with France over Amapá. It was important that a decision be reached in a friendly and conciliatory way. On 24 March he let Ouseley know that he had done this and that instructions had been issued to prevent further annoyance to the Indians. He made counterclaims on the line of the frontier and took the opportunity to say that he felt certain that the British government would have no objection if Catholic priests 'equally occupy themselves in the meritorious work of civilization and conversion' among the Indians (AHI/308/4/11; CO111/184: 1389).[2]

The Brazilian government also seems to have been concerned about any reaction from the public, for when the appointment of boundary commissioners was announced it was done, according to Ouseley:

> in a manner which, in so far as it is unlikely to awaken the morbid feelings of national jealousy of the Brazilian Population and Deputies, may be considered judicious. Treated as a matter of secondary Importance and the true features of the case kept in the background, the report seeks only to avoid giving any hold for present discussion (FO13/170: 78).

Ouseley also sent a letter on this matter to Governor Light in which he expressed some further opinions. He was of the view that the imperial government had had little to do with the aggression and was unlikely to support the acts of the president of Pará. Even so, he continued, there was national jealousy concerning the northern boundary, and if local, petty civil and military authorities had acted in order to show zeal and gain popularity it would be difficult for the imperial government to discourage them. Misconceptions, even outright fabrications, would appear in the newspapers, which were already exciting the public against the British. He suggested to Light that publicity should be given to British actions in order to counteract misrepresentations. He also thought that a demonstration, if not the use, of force might be necessary, and that such proof of determination, if properly explained, would not cause difficulties for the Brazilian government (CO111/184: 1389).

Ouseley's mention of newspapers exciting the public against the British was remarkably prophetic, for the day after he wrote to Light, the *Jornal do Commercio* of 11 March 1841 picked up, via the French newspaper *Commerce*, a story that had appeared in the English *Morning Chronicle* of 29 December. The piece announced the departure from London of the Guiana Boundary Commission but went on to pass some gratuitous remarks about the 'grasping' nature of the Brazilian government, which had been barefaced enough to have seized Pirara, 'a village in which English colonists were settled as early as 1811', and to have dispersed the mission there. The newspaper then proceeded to criticise the Brazilians for their 'atrocious system of ... predatory incursions', by which the native population had been reduced to slavery. This account is clearly derived from Robert Schomburgk's description of what he observed on the Rio Branco in 1838, as, one suspects, is the claim that the

Indians look to Great Britain for protection. Not so obvious is the source of the newspaper's claim that the survey was being carried out 'in pursuance of reiterated application of the colonists'.³

Not surprisingly, the story caused considerable anger in Brazil and Robert Schomburgk came in for most of the criticism. The newspaper denied that *descimentos* had taken place, although it admitted that recruitment of labour might be heavy-handed on occasions. It went on that Schomburgk's account, 'forgetting in the end all considerations of honour, truth and justice, mortally wounds our pride, murders our reputation, and presents us to the eyes of the world as a barbarous and uncivilized nation!' Furthermore it was Schomburgk who was responsible for changing the British government's attitude and for exciting its imperial designs on Brazil.⁴

While these various things were going on, events at Pirara had taken another turn. On 22 January 1841 an Indian arrived in Georgetown from the interior, to report that the Brazilians continued to occupy Pirara and that there was a stockade around Youd's former house. In accordance with the Colonial Office's earlier instructions, Light sent a commissioner with a letter to the Brazilian military and civil authorities insisting 'firmly though prudently on the withdrawal from Pirara'. At the same time he warned the Colonial Office that 'it would require five weeks at least to convey the smallest detachment of troops to Pirara from hence, and that subsistence must be furnished from hence'. Despite what Light said, his letter addressed to the commandant at Fort São Joaquim is best described as peremptory, containing as it does such sentences as 'no delay will take place on your part, in according to my demand that Pirara be abandoned by all Brazilian subjects' (CO111/177: 742; WO1/579: 742).

The commissioner sent by Light was William Crichton, Inspector-General of Police. Crichton had been a postholder on the Essequibo and then superintendent of rivers and creeks in the Essequibo before being appointed Inspector General of Police.⁵ He had had a lot of experience of the interior but he was not altogether an uncontroversial character, as later happenings will reveal. Crichton, together with a Lieutenant John Hackett of the 70th Regiment, whose purpose was to make a reconnaissance in case of some future military action, left Georgetown on 4 February and arrived back on 30 March. Both men provided lengthy reports on their expedition.

Hackett's report focused on the problems that any military expedition would encounter. He noted that Pirara was at present unfortified but that there were possibilities for fortifying the place. Although provisions were available locally there would be problems with the water supply during the dry season. The terrain would suit the Brazilians rather than the British, who would find the forest impassable as presently equipped. The Brazilian force consisted in total of two officers, thirty-three regular troops and about fifty militia who could be recruited from the cattle ranches. It would require eighteen days to muster the complete force and it would take two months to bring up reinforcements from Manaus, the closest place where they were available (CO111/178: 1368).

Crichton's account concerned itself mainly with the dealings he had with Fr. José and Leal. He and Hackett arrived at Pirara Landing on 4 March, and the next day dispatched a message to Pirara asking for horses to be sent. In fact the messenger met Fr. José, who had heard shots and had come out to investigate. He was worried because it was rumoured that Schomburgk was on his way to take him prisoner and he thought that 'not an Indian would stand in his support'. On the day after their arrival at Pirara, which consisted of twenty-nine houses, some eighty inhabitants and a garrison of six mounted men, Crichton showed his credentials, and informed Fr. José that the Brazilians had encroached on British soil and must withdraw, that a boundary survey was to be conducted, and that no interference with the Indians living within the disputed zone would be permitted. Fr. José agreed that he would withdraw to Fort São Joaquim at the sign of any force, but Crichton assured him that he was only there to invite the Brazilian's withdrawal, although he referred to 'those measures of force which a perseverance in the occupation of Pirara must eventually call forth'. To this Fr. José responded that:

> he could not persuade himself into a belief that the Brazilian Government would think of contending with such a Power as Great Britain for a few square miles of the Plain of Pirara yet nevertheless he could not evacuate the Place under any other conditions than an act of force without an order from his own Government.

Leal, who had been sent for, arrived from the fort on 13 March and argued more determinedly that the territory belonged to Brazil. The matter of ownership of the cattle also came up and it was thought that this question would be settled by negotiation between the respective governments, although Crichton added that he did not think Brazil could argue that they had right to the territory just because their cattle had strayed on to it. Leal thought that Great Britain would have difficulty in sending troops to Pirara if the Brazilians held firm, to which Crichton replied that a detachment could be there within a month and that an alternative strategy would be for the Royal Navy to blockade Brazilian ports. Leal supported Fr. José's position that there could be no withdrawal, unless force was used, without permission from higher Brazilian authorities. It was finally agreed that Fr. José would take letters to Pará and be in Georgetown with the reply in August. Crichton wrote two letters; from Pirara and Pirara Landing on 15 and 16 March respectively, for transmission to the Brazilian authorities. The contents of both of them are much the same and whereas they order the Brazilians to evacuate the disputed territory and leave it to the independent tribes of Indians, the tone is on the whole more moderate than that employed in Light's letter. Crichton and Hackett then departed for the coast on 16 March carrying letters for Light from Fr. José and Leal (CO111/178: 1368).

Identical letters from Fr. José and Leal to Light merely acknowledge receipt of the letter to the president of Pará. Of greater interest is a joint communication condemning the activities of Schomburgk and Youd. Schomburgk is accused of having taken the opportunity of the *cabanagem* to present himself at Fort São Joaquim and obtain the friendship of the witless commandant and enter into association with the 'rebel' Pedro Ayres. He is also accused of having insulted the Brazilians by saying that they were no better than wild Indians and by flying the British flag over the Brazilian one 'by which he intended to make the ill-educated (*rusticos*) inhabitants of the place believe that he [Schomburgk] was the greatest man in the world'. Youd, in his turn, is accused of having forcibly entered the chapel at São Joaquim, of preaching heresy, and of having thrown out an image of St Antony that was on the altar, saying that the Brazilians were ignorant to worship a wooden doll. Furthermore he had given arms drill to the Macushi at Pirara, and had said that he was the brother of Christ, the legitimate son of Joseph. Leal also wrote on the same day a second letter to Light complaining that Youd was sheltering deserters at Waraputa and that by his 'pernicious preaching' he had persuaded Brazilians to leave their homes and act against their country. Furthermore, because of the recent civil war, some people had taken refuge in British Guiana, and all those without passports should be considered suspect and be sent back to Fort São Joaquim (CO111/178: 1368).

Robert Schomburgk, who had arrived back in Georgetown in January 1841 to start his boundary survey, denied Fr. José's and Leal's charges in a letter to Light of April that year. He pointed out that he had never met either of them, and therefore their accusations must be based on hearsay. He had not taken advantage of the uprising on the Amazon to gain admittance to the fort since the Royal Geographical Society had obtained him a passport from the Brazilian envoy in London, who had recommended him to Pará, who had in turn recommended him to the authorities in the areas through which he would be passing. He had requested permission from the appropriate authority to winter in Fort São Joaquim and had been given it (he enclosed Ambrosio Ayres's invitation of 25 May 1838). Of his friendship with 'the rebel Pedro Ayres', he observed that 'whatever he may be now, was then accredited to the highest district authority'. As for the accusations of hoisting the British flag above that of Brazil, and of treating the Brazilians like wild Indians, they were too ridiculous to deserve notice. He had not entered the country clandestinely, nor had he passed himself off as a 'great man'. He added that in the past Leal had also accused him of killing cattle (CO111/178: 1367).

Light, in forwarding Crichton's and Hackett's reports to the Colonial Office on 27 April, claimed that the Brazilian occupation appears to have been 'an accidental circumstance' related to efforts to secure cattle that had strayed. It is not clear on what grounds he made this claim, but it led him to state that the Brazilians, if Crichton had insisted, would have evacuated Pirara. Both statements seem a distortion of what Crichton had reported. Crichton had also recommended in his report that the interior be secured by a colony of European labourers. They would find no difficulty in working in the climate prevailing there, and would set a good example to the Indians. The country was ideal for a colony and good for trade, although he did admit that the rivers did not afford easy routes into the interior (CO111/178: 1368).

In a further dispatch on the subject, of 21 May, Light repeated his earlier claim that Pirara would be evacuated without resistance and supported the view that a colony there, protected by troops, would be highly advantageous, not only for securing the territory but for civilizing the Indians and developing trade with the interior of Brazil. On the latter point he was even more optimistic in a letter to the British chargé d'affaires in Rio, to whom he wrote that the possession of Pirara was a 'means of promoting a vast commerce'

RETREAT TO WARAPUTA 83

with the interior of Brazil as the route there through Pirara was much quicker than via Pará. He also referred to 'boatloads of dry goods and merchandize' that the Indians sought for trade in exchange for their products and forest produce (CO111/178: 1434; WO1/579: 1434).

The Colonial Office declined to entertain any idea of a colony, but consulted the Foreign Office on 17 July on the question of sending troops to Pirara (CO112/23: 199). The Foreign Office replied on 22 July:

> I am directed by Lord Palmerston to acquaint you in reply for the information of Lord John Russell, that his Lordship is strongly of opinion that it is desirable to adopt the measures recommended by the Governor of British Guiana.

This communication from the Foreign Office was extensively minuted by members of the Colonial Office. Concern was particularly expressed about how such an action would be paid for, but on the military side fewer problems were foreseen. It did not matter if the troops in Georgetown, of which there were 760, were weakened by sending a detachment of them to the interior because:

> it is difficult to know what use they are of there at present. The Country has long been in a state of profound tranquillity, and there is no apparent danger of external aggression.

It was finally concluded that troops should be sent to Pirara, and a letter to Lord Hill, General Commander-in-Chief, informed him that Lieutenant-General John Maister, military commander in the Caribbean, was being instructed to do this and asked him what description of troops would be best suited for the purpose, although it was assumed that they would be part of a Black regiment. The commander-in-chief concurred with this assumption for various reasons, including the presumption that the climate would not be injurious to the health of Black troops (CO111/184: 1558; WO1/579: 1841).

A note from Ouseley in Rio de Janeiro that the Foreign Office passed to the Colonial Office on 26 June must have helped Lord John Russell reach this decision. Ouseley reported that the Brazilians (who would, at the time Ouseley wrote in April, have been ignorant of Crichton's visit) denied the validity of any British claim to the disputed territory. The facts that the British subjects abandoned the territory when asked to do so and that the Colonial government had failed to defend its claim supported this view (CO111/184: 1389).

Thus on 20 August 1841 the Colonial Office informed Light that, in accordance with his recommendation of 21 May, Pirara was to be occupied by troops and Lieutenant-General Maister had been ordered to take the necessary measures. A detachment of the West India Regiment stationed in British Guiana, the size of which was to depend on the advice of Governor Light, who would also be responsible for briefing its commander, was to be employed for the purpose (CO111/178: 1434; NAG/MBD).

In Pará, the president had received the minister of foreign affairs' communication of 6 March in which he was instructed to avoid conflict and misunderstanding with the British. As a result he wrote on 5 May to Leal, passing on these orders but at the same time giving more ambiguous directions. While avoiding all conflict Leal was neither to cede rights to territory nor cease to preach to the Indians who voluntarily preferred to follow the Catholic faith. Furthermore, although Pirara undoubtedly lay in Brazilian territory it might be convenient to evacuate it provisionally to avoid any trouble, but at the same time the British must not be allowed to occupy the contested area (AHI/308/4/1).

Presumably this communication to Leal crossed with those from the Upper Rio Branco, because once Crichton had departed Fr. José set off for Belém, where he arrived in early June with the various communications, including a letter from Leal to the president. Leal in his letter said that Crichton had given them four months to settle the matter or the British would just fix the boundary, and went on to remark that knowing the English, he did not doubt it. He proposed to maintain a force of ten men under a sergeant at Pirara. He was, however, much concerned about the poor state of Fort São Joaquim. There were six pieces of artillery, but because of the condition of their carriages it was not possible to fire three successive shots. There were only two arrobas (about 30 kg) of saltpetre and 172 shot of various calibre. Within six months he had to report that the situation had worsened as the severe floods of the wet season had further damaged the fort (ANB/IG[1]11; CO111/184: 1739).

The letters from Light and Crichton calling for the withdrawal of Brazilians from Pirara caused considerable ill-feeling towards the British. The main problem was the abruptness of the demands and the threats contained in them. They were described as written in the style that the British had employed with the rajahs of India before despoiling them of their estates. At the same time Fr. José and Leal came in for considerable criticism in Pará for their failure not to have protested in stronger terms against the British aggression.[6] The president of Pará reported the 'irregular behaviour' of the governor of British Guiana to the Ministry of Foreign Affairs on 15 June, but the latter, in acknowledging his report on 2 August, merely told him to continue to act as previously ordered, that is in a conciliatory manner, avoiding all conflict (AHI/308/4/11; Araujo e Amazonas 1852: 287; Baena 1841b: 324–5).

The temporary British consul in Belém,[7] Henry Dickenson, interviewed Fr. José with the intention of obtaining accurate information in order to correct any rumours about the incident that might spring up locally. His account of what happened, as obtained from Fr. José, is close to that just recounted but in addition he learnt that Crichton had guaranteed the safety of the mission during Fr. José's absence (CO111/184: 1739).

The British boundary commission had some difficulty in starting its work, but the problems were not of the Brazilians', but of the colony's making. As mentioned, Schomburgk arrived in Georgetown in January 1841, and was still there in March, having been delayed by the unhelpful attitude of the mayor and town council. Schomburgk wanted to build a temporary wooden observatory from which observations might be made in order to provide a base line for his survey. The town council refused to give him permission to do this on town land, stating that the relevant ordinances would have to be changed first. Light noted that there had been no problem about permission in the past 'for other purposes not quite so useful to society, ... amongst others to a strolling equestrian company'. This matter was finally resolved when Lieutenant-Colonel William Bush, in command of the military forces in British Guiana, offered the use of part of the parade ground, but even this was not straightforward because the subaltern of engineers, absent from Georgetown and not consulted, objected and brought work to a halt until overruled. The boundary survey finally got under way when the party left for the Barima River region and the frontier with Venezuela on 18 April (CO111/177: 1095; CO111/178: 1369).

Although this affair of the observatory delayed the progress of the survey, it was not the greatest threat to the boundary commission's work. The Colonial Office had proposed that the cost of the survey should be born equally by the home government and the colonial government. The Combined Court, dominated by the planters, would have none of this and insisted that the colony's boundaries and the cost of fixing them were a matter for the mother country. It is clear that the Colonial Office was quite unable to understand this position and could not think what arguments to advance against the proposed arrangement, given that the survey was entirely to the colony's advantage. The continuing intransigence of the Combined Court finally elicited the comment 'the question will have to be decided whether the expedition should be abandoned or continued'. In fact, the Combined Court never gave in. In order to get the survey under way Light finally found the money from a contingency fund at the governor's disposal, although the Combined Court even objected to this. Even so Light was unable to meet the half-share of the commission members' salaries from this fund, and they received only half-pay until the matter was sorted out after the survey had been completed (CO111/178: 1435; CO111/180: 2564; CO111/181: 238; 2769; CO111/184: 2539; NAG/CPM/41, 42).

Robert Schomburgk returned to Georgetown from his first boundary survey at the end of July, and submitted to Light his plan for surveying the Brazilian boundary. He stated that he would like to make a start at the beginning of September and would make his headquarters at Pirara, from where it would be necessary to set up a supply line to the coast. In a covering letter, he asked for orders concerning the timing of the commission's departure as the question of who was paying for the survey still threatened to halt the project. He had Indians waiting to act as canoemen, and wanted to know whether to leave in September, or to send the Indians home and wait until the funding had been sorted out before departing. He preferred the latter (CO111/180: 2567).

In the same letter Schomburgk commented on the letter that Ouseley, the British chargé d'affaires in Rio, had sent Light. He fully agreed that Pirara must be held, because among other things 'the wish of the National Chieftains who are defacto the rightful possessors of the soil, to cede the Sovereignty to Her Britannic Majesty, is of importance', and suggested that he might ratify a treaty with them. He was in favour of giving the survey every publicity but against sending an armed force, which would be difficult to do, expensive and would not 'improve the morals of the Natives'. He suggested that a police sergeant with two or three men would suffice to hold Pirara. They could also be of service to the survey team, since they could look after the equipment left at Pirara and organise the supply lines. He also recommended sending a naval ship to Pará as a demonstration of 'friendliness' to persuade the president to keep his 'petty local officers' in order (CO111/180: 2567).

Light did not forward Schomburgk's communications to the Colonial Office until October, by which time he had received the instructions to occupy Pirara. His view was that it would be of benefit to the occupying force if it went to Pirara at the same time as the boundary commission, but he did not think that Schomburgk's suggestion of a civil rather than a military occupation of Pirara was a good idea. Although there were difficulties in the latter, not least the distance, he trusted that the occupation would be useful to the commerce and civilizing of the Essequibo, but was concerned that it would raise international questions of increasing 'difficulty and importance' (CO111/180: 2567).

In mid-1841, the Society gave permission to Youd to take leave, but rather begrudgingly because of the state of the Waraputa mission. This note was echoed by Bernau, who stated that the mission had good prospects but that Youd's absence would be detrimental to the project for the Indians were likely to disperse, and that Doyce, of whom he now held so low an opinion as to think that he would be better off dead, would be totally unable to maintain the mission. William Pollard, who had taken over from Strong as secretary and treasurer to the Corresponding Committee, noted that Youd's health seemed to have improved so that perhaps there was no longer the same necessity for Youd to take leave. The Society welcomed this news and in January 1842 wrote: 'We shall be very glad to find that the Rev. T Youd's circumstances have so far changed as to admit of his relinquishing his purpose of visiting England.' By the time they wrote, the situation at Waraputa had become more problematic, for in November 1841, John Doyce's connection with the Society was terminated as a result of a marriage 'with a young woman of doubtful reputation' (CW/O/67: 11, 13; CW/L/3: 110, 126–8; CW/O/18: 23).[8]

The same month Youd, who was in Georgetown, received a communication from the governor, informing him in secret that the British government had decided to occupy Pirara and to assert its rights to the territory. Governor Light's purpose in informing Youd of the forthcoming expedition, which would be ready to leave during the first week of December, was to recruit him to it. In particular he reckoned with confidence on Youd's 'influence being exercised to ensure cordial welcome and cooperation on the part of the Indians'. He hoped that Youd would be able to help with providing paddlers and assured him that the strictest orders would be given to the troops to respect the Indians. Light trusted that with Youd's assistance Pirara would flourish again and become, under Her Majesty's protection, 'a focus of Christian light to the aborigines' (CW/O/67: 13, 14).

The Corresponding Committee gave Youd permission to join the expedition, although, because it was worried about the future of Waraputa, it did so with some reluctance. What seemed to have swayed the decision in favour of the re-occupation of the mission was talk that the Roman Catholics in Georgetown were endeavouring to send a priest to Pirara. The Committee expressed the hope that the Society would be able to provide a third missionary so that both Pirara and Waraputa might be manned (CW/O/1b: 10).

The decision to allow Youd to accompany the military expedition was criticised by Bernau, who naïvely thought that missionaries should keep out of politics, although 'no blame attaches to Mr. Y's leaving Warapoota ... for far as matters had gone the having a Roman Cath. in our rear would have been an evil of fearful consequences'.[9] After the incident was over, he claimed that he learnt from Youd that the Governor had wished to make him 'some kind of political agent between the British and Brazilian Government' and judged such an appointment to be 'irreconcilable with that of being a Missionary' (CW/O/18: 25, 27).

During the autumn preparations for the military expedition went ahead. On 30 October Light instructed Lt.-Col. Bush, commanding officer of the military in British Guiana, that the military expedition was to consist of two subalterns, thirty men, an assistant surgeon, and an assistant commissary-general. Black troops had been selected because they could 'be relied on as much as the White Troops'. It was necessary to have ten special canoes built, which would be ready by the end of November. Their construction was under the supervision of Crichton who, together with McLintock, the postholder from Pomeroon, was responsible for recruiting the hundred paddlers required. A local merchant proposed to send up a 'commercial venture' with the expedition and Light had 'no doubt but that a lucrative opening into the interior will speedily follow' (CO111/181: 2768; NAG/MBD).

Youd thought that the force was too small and that it should be increased to fifty men. Light argued that all in all there were nearly

RETREAT TO WARAPUTA

fifty 'fighting men' and given that the visit by Crichton and Hackett had been magnified into an accompanying force of 2,000 men, no doubt similar exaggeration would operate on this occasion. Furthermore the British would have the support of the Indians, 'always hostile to the Brazilians' (CO111/181: 239).

There were the inevitable delays and the boundary commission, which left first, did not do so until just before Christmas Day. In part the delay was the result of further doubts over the funding of the survey, and finally Light took it upon himself once again to find the money out of the contingency fund at his disposal, as it would cost as much to keep the expedition in Georgetown while the Combined Court made up its mind whether or not to contribute as it would to carry out the survey (CO111/181: 238).

It was not only with reference to the boundary commission that there were questions of funding. Even before the military expedition had left Georgetown, some worries about the expense of the whole undertaking were being aired. General Maister, on receiving instructions to occupy Pirara, had addressed Robert Schomburgk with certain questions about communications and means of supply. He was not encouraged by the answers he received, and wrote to the Colonial Office on 9 November indicating the enormous difficulty and expense that would be incurred by maintaining the troops at Pirara (WO1/579: 2362). In mid-January 1842, the Colonial Office transmitted these concerns to the Foreign Office:

> the Detachment of the Force, small as it is, will be a matter of very heavy expense; and that an early settlement of our differences with the Brazilian Govt. ... as a means of enabling us to dispense with these outposts appears to be an object deserving of the most serious attention (WO1/579: 2768).

Any delays on the British side were more than matched by those on the Brazilian, where the Ministry of Foreign Affairs even recommended a dilatory approach in order to give time for the collection of more accurate information on which to continue negotiations (Ponte Ribeiro 1842: 30). In fact the slowness of communications achieved this effect, for it made any rapid response almost impossible.

In September 1841, Colonel João Henriques de Mattos was appointed boundary commissioner. Born at Barcelos on the Rio Negro in 1784, de Mattos had played a part in many of the political events of Pará during the early decades of the nineteenth century, including the *cabanagem*, when he fought on the Loyalist side.[10] Doubt was almost immediately thrown on his competence to undertake the necessary survey, it even being claimed that he was lacking in the first principles of ordinary arithmetic. Preparations took their time and it had not been possible to obtain the survey instruments required, even if de Mattos knew how to use them (which was in doubt), when he finally set out from Belém on 14 February 1842. In fact the instructions issued to him by the president of Pará were of a fairly general nature; he was to report on the geography of the region, its economic potential, and on the numbers, condition and allegiance of the Indians. He may enter into preliminary discussion with the British commissioners, without compromising the Brazilian position, in order to discover what they were proposing. The Ministry of Foreign Affairs, in writing to approve the appointment, reiterated that prudence was to be used to avoid any conflict and that conciliatory means were to be adopted (AHI/308/4/2; AHI/308/4/11; Baena 1841a; Barata 1973: 114–15; Ponte Ribeiro 1842).

Meanwhile the diplomatic exchanges were proceeding unevenly, mainly because the slowness of communications resulted in a misunderstanding of what incident was being talked about. In November 1841, the Brazilian minister in London, Marques Lisboa, complained to the Foreign Office about the British demand for the evacuation of Pirara by the Brazilians and expressed astonishment at such behaviour. This was the reaction to Crichton's visit and when the Foreign Office replied a month later it was to inform the minister that he was out of date, since instructions for the military occupation of Pirara had already been sent out and the Brazilian authorities had been informed of this in August. It was further suggested that discussion on the topic would be premature until the boundary commission had completed its work, which, it was trusted, would lead to a satisfactory and amicable settlement (CO111/184: 2506, 2788).

In fact, it was not until 10 December 1841 that the Brazilian minister of foreign affairs was informed by the British minister in Rio, Hamilton Hamilton, of the British decision to occupy Pirara (CO111/197: 854).[11]

Notes

1. It is not clear where the British chargé d'affaires obtained this information and to what period it applied.

2. Manchester, in his book on *British preëminence in Brazil*, states: 'On March 24, 1841, the Rio court stated its position in an able dispatch written by Aureliano de Souza e Oliveira Coutinho, and by refusing to treat as long as military occupation continued, forced England to order the withdrawal of the expedition' (1933: 307–8). It is not clear how Manchester concocted this account of events. In March 1841, except for Crichton's brief stay (described later in this chapter) of which the news reached Rio much later, there was no British military expedition at Pirara and Coutinho's letter contains no demands of this sort.

3. I have not seen the version of this piece as it appeared in *Commerce* and therefore as it was received in Brazil. Accordingly I do not know what further embellishments the story may have received between its publication in the *Morning Chronicle* and *Jornal do Commercio*.

4. The article gave rise to an exchange of letters between the British chargé d'affaires and the Brazilian minister of foreign affairs. The former asked that an official denial be made and the latter retorted that the Brazilian press was free and not subject to government direction (see FO128/36: 12–26).

5. For an account of the duties of postholders and superintendents of rivers and creeks, see Menezes 1977a.

6. There were those who considered such criticism as unjustified. Baena wrote that for him the idea that protests preserve honour was nothing less than metaphysical and that protests were evidence of weakness (1841b: 324–5).

7. Cowper had been transferred to Pernambuco earlier that year (FO13/173).

8. We hear little more of Doyce. In October 1848, Bernau, in one of the last letters he was to write from Bartica Grove, mentions that Doyce had died in a miserable state, unhappy in his marriage and in total neglect (CW/O/18: 37).

9. It is not clear whether Bernau was referring to the Brazilian priest or to the one that the Georgetown Roman Catholics were rumoured to be sending. Presumably Bernau would have regarded them as equally pernicious.

10. As a result he had, not surprisingly, made enemies. For example, Francisco José de Souza Soares de Andréa, president of Pará, wrote in June 1838 with reference to a list of potential vice-presidents on which de Mattos's name appeared that he did not judge him worthy of being on the list even in last place, accusing him of treachery and military incompetence (ANB/IJJ⁹110).

11. Hamilton Hamilton was British minister in Rio de Janeiro from May 1836 to August 1846, but was on leave of absence from December 1837 until July 1841, during which period W.G. Ouseley served as chargé d'affaires. There is no obvious reason why there was quite such a long delay in informing the Brazilians of the British intention to occupy Pirara.

CHAPTER 6

THE OCCUPATION OF PIRARA: 1842

The boundary commission, under the command of Robert Schomburgk, left Georgetown on 23 December 1841. As well as Schomburgk the expedition included two new members who replaced those who had resigned from the first part of the survey. William John Fryer, who, before migrating to British Guiana, had served in Spain first as a doctor and then as an officer in Colonel Sir George de Lacy Evans's volunteer corps in the Spanish Carlist wars, was taken on as Schomburgk's secretary and assistant and was also expected to provide some medical care. A young man, Edward A. Goodall, was recruited at the last moment in London to be the artist.[1] If we were to accept Goodall's account of his relationship with Schomburgk we would see the latter as a martinet who reprimanded and punished the young artist for his high spirits. On their first meeting Goodall noted:

> he seems a very nice little man but rather petulant, however. It is too soon for me to think of giving an opinion at present, as he is very agreeable and kind. That may perhaps wear off when we get into the bush (1962a: 39).

This proved an accurate prediction and Goodall's diary contains many examples of Schomburgk's temper. On the journey upstream Goodall was punished for setting fire to a tall hollow Mora tree by being made to do some sketches after a long day's travel. Then at Pirara there was an exchange between them over Goodall's leaving the camp without permission and 'the little man', as Goodall often refers to Schomburgk, 'as usual, worked himself into a towering passion and tried to drown what I said'. On another occasion Goodall writes: 'The little man looks as sour as vinegar this morning and had already vented his spleen on Mr. Fryer' (1962b: 54–5, 57). However, things cannot have been as bad as Goodall implies since he and Schomburgk travelled a long way together, often under conditions of extreme hardship, and appeared to have remained on good terms. For his part Schomburgk, even if he did not show it, respected Goodall's competence. Of their first meeting he wrote that 'I am not only pleased with his specimens of skill, but likewise with his manners. ... I have every hope, that he will be all that can be desired'. Nor does he fail when writing to Light to mention Goodall's industriousness and 'amiable conduct'(CO111/204: 493; RGS/RHS/Corr: 19/8/41).

Schomburgk's younger brother Richard accompanied the expedition at the request of the Prussian government in order to make collections for the Royal Prussian Museum and the Botanical Garden in Berlin. There were nine other permanent expedition hands, consisting of four Germans, three coloured men, a black cook, and the Macushi interpreter, Sororeng, whom Schomburgk had taken to England in 1839.[2] Numerous other Indians were required to handle the five boats and and provisions for these included rice, salt fish, pickled meat, biscuit, two glasses of rum and a ration of tobacco daily.

The Treasury, irritated by the colony's continued refusal to contribute to the survey, declined to pay Fryer's salary and Schomburgk had to find it out of his own pocket until the expedition was over; the Treasury then relented and reimbursed him. For the same reason both Schomburgk and Goodall received only half their salary and it was not until they were back in London that the Treasury agreed to make good the deficit. Just before departure Schomburgk wrote to Light regretting that the lack of funds did not permit a surgeon to be attached to the commission and that they would have 'to trust to Providence for our health and lives', to which the government secretary, Young, replied that there would be a medical officer with the troops (CO111/181: 238; 204: 493; 206: 670).

The officers of the boundary commission were required to sign articles covering disciplinary matters. The first of these reads:

> Any guilty of profane oaths, cursing, drunkenness, uncleanness or other scandalous actions in derogation of God's honour shall receive such punishment (other than flogging) as he deserves.

The other articles, of similar tone, covered such matters as quarrelling with or threatening a superior officer, complaining about provisions, desertion, insulting or molesting Indians, sleeping on duty, and publishing without permission. Soon after the expedition got under way what were presumably the same articles were read out to all the men, for Goodall records that 'we were ordered to put on our uniform the bugle was sounded for the men's fall-in to have the articles of war read to them' (CO111/181: 238; CO111/178: 1369; Goodall 1962b: 47).[3]

Thomas Youd joined the boundary commission near Bartica Grove for the journey up to his mission station at Waraputa. There he awaited the military expedition under whose protection he was to re-establish his mission at Pirara. Richard Schomburgk and Goodall had diverging views on the missionary. The former described the sermon preached on 2 January as 'excellent ... exactly suited to the occasion' (RS, I: 239); whereas the latter complained that 'we had a long-winded sermon, so long that none but a missionary would have had breath to have held out for this length of time' (Goodall 1962b: 47).[4]

The journey, although without major incident, was made at a leisurely pace. The only problem was the lack of reliable information on what was happening at Pirara. At a mixed settlement of Macushi and Carib on the Rupununi River the news was that the Brazilians were still in possession of Pirara and that all the Macushi had been enslaved. At the larger village of Haiowa further upstream the story was that the Indians had not been enslaved but had withdrawn to the Kanuku Mountains, that Fr. José was near Fort São Joaquim supervising the construction of a new residence, and that the only Brazilians at Pirara were a few cattle minders. Even so, as the expedition approached Pirara Landing due precautions were taken and members of the party were armed. Pirara Landing was reached on Wednesday, 9 February and on the following days four miles of the Awarikuru Creek were cleared of fallen trees in order to allow the canoes to approach closer to Pirara (CO111/195: 1086; RS, I: 274, 299).

On the day after the expedition's arrival at Pirara Landing, Fryer accompanied by two of the Germans and others set off for Pirara in order to deliver the dispatches for the Brazilian authorities that Light had entrusted to Schomburgk just before his departure. They returned the next day to say that only three Brazilians (and four families of Indians) remained at Pirara and that they were not to be found immediately, 'having strolled off to a neighbouring drinking-party'. Fryer had sought them out and sent one of them to Fort São Joaquim with Governor Light's letter for the commandant. This letter informed the commandant that the British government had directed the military occupation of Pirara and that the arrival of troops was imminent. This information had been transmitted to the Brazilian minister in London and, no doubt, his government would have already apprised him of it. Accordingly Light felt certain that the Brazilians would immediately withdraw while negotiations between the two governments were going on. 'Withdrawal, although permitted with all the honour and courtesy due to a Friendly Power, must on no account whatever be delayed or postponed.' Light looked forward to hearing that there had been no violence and trusted that the British settlement at Pirara 'may be a means of extending ... amicable intercourse and commercial relations' (CO111/181: 238, 239; CO111/195: 1086; RS, 1922 I: 295, 298–9).

The following day, 12 February, just as the boundary commission party was about to leave for Pirara, gunfire heralding the approach of the military detachment was heard (Goodall 1962b: 51; RS, 1922, I: 299).

On 23 December Light is able to report that the military expedition would leave next week. The detachment, drawn from the 1st West India Regiment of Foot, which had white officers and black men, turned out on embarkation to be slightly larger than originally proposed. It was under the command of Lieutenant Edmund Hayter Bingham, and the second subaltern was Lieutenant John Andrew Wieburg. Lieutenant Seddon William Settor Bush, son of Lt.-Col. Bush and regimental adjutant, was to accompany the expedition as far as Pirara and then return with the boats. The assistant surgeon was Richard Robert Dowse and the assistant commissariat general was Mr Lowe, who had as an assistant a commissariat issuer, Mr Curtis. The troops consisted of two sergeants, a drummer and thirty-six rank-and-file. The expedition took three months' provisions consisting of a daily ration per man of a half-pound of salt meat with rice, biscuit, rum and sugar. To transport everything there was a fleet of ten canoes and eighty Indian paddlers under the command of Crichton and the postholder McClintock, both of whom spoke an Indian language (RS, I: 221; CO111/181: 239; WO1/580: 565).[5]

Governor Light gave Lt. Bush strict instructions, under 17 headings, on how he was to proceed. Many of these were concerned with the Indians. The main object of the expedition was to take Pirara and protect the Indians, assert British rights to the territory and afford facilities for settlement by British subjects. The commanding officer should insist on discipline among his men and prevent clashes between them and both the Indians and Brazilians.

If he maintained friendly relations with the Indians he would be able to resist any force the Brazilians mounted against him, and to this end he should acquire the friendship and confidence of the Indians. His good relationships with the Indians would help with provisioning the expedition and reduce the number of deserters, although Indians who pursued deserters should be instructed not to injure them. It should be remembered that Indians never forget a wrong and would revenge it in due course. Finally, since rum sent Indians mad, the troops should be prevented from bartering their ration with them (CO111/181: 239).

Then there were other instructions relating to the organization of the expedition. On arrival at Pirara the Brazilians should be 'quietly and civilly' required to withdraw, with every respect being shown to them, although it should be made clear that no resistance would be countenanced. Because the ownership of the wild cattle was in doubt a careful account should be kept of all those slaughtered. The soldiers were to cultivate their own crops, yams, sweet potatoes and cassava, and although these took a long time to grow in the event of a prolonged stay the expedition could become independent of the Indians. Pits, 12–14 ft deep, were to be dug for water during the dry season. The troops were to be located in a fortified site outside the village and should be prevented from entering Indian houses. The officer was to assess commercial opportunities and keep a journal of civilian occurrences involving either Indians or Brazilians and submit it periodically together with a military journal.

The instructions close with some general observations, some repeating those mentioned above but also adding that good relationships with Youd were important for the successful outcome of the expedition, particularly his help with regard to the Indians, and that the greatest respect was to be shown to him personally (CO111/181: 239).

The military force did not leave Georgetown until 11 January, and although it made a rather faster journey than the boundary commission, it was not without incident, mainly involving clashes of personality. The very detailed journal (CO111/195: 1091) kept by Crichton is our main source of information concerning what happened, although it has to be treated with caution since he was one of the chief protagonists. Crichton and McClintock between them had been responsible for arranging the construction of the boats and mustering the mainly Amerindian paddlers. The fleet of

THE OCCUPATION OF PIRARA

ten canoes was first assembled and loaded a little upstream from Bartica Grove, where the troops arrived by steamer from Georgetown on 11 January. Because there were more people than allowed for, the canoes had to be repacked and it was not until after midday on the 12th that a departure was made from Bartica Grove. By the evening of the first day Crichton had noted the officers' desire for exclusiveness when he wrote in his journal that he had 'mentioned to the officers on the way from the Grove that I had some excellent fresh Fish for Dinner but as they took no notice of it I concluded they intended to mess by themselves.' The whole of the next day was spent rearranging the stowage of the canoes as the officers wanted a boat to themselves and their baggage stored separately from that of the men. Lieutenant Bingham even objected to the presence of the civilians and Crichton told him that as far as he was concerned he, Crichton, and all the other non-military personnel could leave, but that the Indian paddlers would leave with them. Other members of the military staff also presented difficulties. Commissar-General Lowe ordered that no rations were to be drawn for McClintock, and the assistant surgeon instructed that the Indians were not to be provided with medicine. Crichton countermanded both these orders by threatening to return downstream to collect the necessary stores and medicine and thus hold up the whole expeditionary force.

Crichton reported that even by the second day the 'officers seem already to be heartily sick of the expedition and are wishing themselves in Georgetown'. He also noted that the officers stayed up very late that evening singing and drinking. This was a pattern of behaviour which he records on many occasions, adding on one day that the songs were not 'very choice' and on another that he had had to break up a drunken quarrel.

However, the dangers of the journey appear to have brought home to the officers their inexperience and helplessness, and they became more communicative. By 18 January, six days after leaving Bartica Grove, the officers admitted to the unpleasant conditions under which they were living, having no coffee and having to cook for themselves because the men they had selected as servants did not know how. It was then agreed that the two messes should merge, which was what happened for a few days until a further dispute separated them again.

On 20 January, the force arrived at Waraputa where Youd was waiting to accompany them. He entertained them well, being very liberal with 'his old Port'. On the next day Youd mentioned that Schomburgk had told him that he, Schomburgk, had authority to try to procure the evacuation of Pirara before the troops arrived. This was presumably a reference to the letter that Light had given Schomburgk for transmission to the Brazilian authorities announcing the imminent arrival of British troops in the hope that it would cause the immediate evacuation of Pirara. This news greatly angered the officers, who 'seemed to consider that the interference of Mr Schomburgk would rob them of all honor attached to the Expedition'. They therefore decided to try and press on as fast as possible and overtake Schomburgk.

On 24 January, Crichton had a big row with Bingham and also with Bush who, Crichton complains, had from the start behaved as though he were the commanding officer. The row had to do with the behaviour of a soldier whom Crichton reprimanded and to whose defence the officers sprang. It is a rather confusing incident and it is not worth trying to unravel it, but the result, which is perhaps indicative of the existing tensions, was that once again there was a separation into two messes. After this, except for some petty skirmishing carried on through an exchange of letters, an angry silence settled on the two parties that lasted for the rest of the journey. However, this falling out also characterised the relationship among the officers; Crichton recorded an argument between Bush and the surgeon on 3 February and commented that this was not the first they had had and that Bush had quarrelled with every officer except Bingham.

Despite these internal dissensions the expedition made good time and was at the Carib village at the mouth of the Rupununi on 2 February. They found there that Schomburgk's party was only five days ahead of them. There was also a message left for them in a bottle by the members of the boundary commission, who had drunk the military force's health with its contents. Even this managed to cause offence to the officers because the members of the survey team had referred to themselves as 'officers'.[6]

Twice on the journey, despite the express orders of Governor Light, the troops were allowed to occupy Amerindian villages. On the second occasion, an Indian woman on the way to her field was assaulted by a soldier. Youd complained to Crichton on her behalf, but Bingham was reluctant to believe the accusation. However, when the woman described her assailant as having the marks of ritual scarification on his face, it was decided to hold an identity parade,

THE OCCUPATION OF PIRARA

which proved fruitless when it was discovered that all the men were so adorned. Crichton told Bingham that it was a mistake to have allowed the troops into the village since first impressions were all-important and news of what had happened would rapidly spread among the Macushi.

This incident occurred on 8 February, and the next day Bingham decided to push on with the troops to catch up with Schomburgk, leaving the heavy baggage to come at its own speed. The arrival of the troops in the Awarikuru Creek on 12 February is described by Richard Schomburgk as follows:

> [T]he big boat came into view round a bend of the river: it was chock full of a motley-dressed crowd of black figures whose full-voiced throats broke out into a thundering hurrah. Soon after, a landing was made by the officers with Lieutenants Bingham and Bush in the lead, all cursing and swearing at the uncustomary exertion: they greeted us with a hearty handshake. What must the rapids have been to upset their military bearing, what must the undergrowth of 'pimplers' have been like to tear in tatters the tunics adapted for parade! A dirty coloured shirt, ten times dirtier linen, half-torn trousers which had long forgotten their original colour, and a broad straw hat constituted the uniform of the commandant, as well as that of the rank and file. When the officers ... learnt of the peaceful state of affairs, they seemed anything but displeased, while the full-toned 'God save the Queen' on the bugles rang triumphantly in thousands of echoes through the forest which otherwise was so noiseless (I: 300).

and by Edward Goodall thus:

> I was sketching ... when I heard the officer commanding the detachment shouting out 'God damn your eyes, jump out, jump out and be damned to you'. Soon after they all landed I overheard the conversation between the officers and Mr. Schomburgk, the officer saying 'I never had such a job in all my life, damned if I ever did! What an outlandish place this is: it must be the last place God Almighty made' (1962b: 51).

Once landed, Lieutenant Bingham paraded his troops and warned them that although the Brazilians had temporarily left Pirara they might well return in increased numbers. Then it would be their courage that would prevent their being led off into captivity to the 'mines in the province of Minas where prisoners never lived to enjoy the bright blue sky or breathe the fresh air of heaven again' (RS, I: 301). At supper that evening less inspiring comments on the whole venture were passed:

[F]or without being a military genius, the impracticability of this monstrously costly and, if matters really came to a crisis, unsuccessful expedition was patent to everybody. Had the Brazilians wanted to remain owners of Pirara they could have easily crushed the small force to death before relief could have been even thought of. The presence at the mouth of the Amazon of a single frigate, of which many were lying idle in Barbados, would have produced the same effect at barely a sixth of the cost (RS, I: 301).

The next day Robert Schomburgk set off for Pirara to recruit Indians to carry the baggage. He was surprised to find still in the village, as well as the Brazilian soldiers, Evaristo. Richard Schomburgk confirms that whereas he had proved a considerable nuisance to Youd at Pirara, on the latter's withdrawal he had rendered indispensable services to Fr. José, who had obtained a pardon for him and appointed him mission assistant. Despite the fact that Governor Light had issued an expulsion order against him, he managed, through 'his cringing friendliness and complaisance' towards the army officers, to avoid this happening. Crichton also recorded that on his arrival at Pirara on 18 February Evaristo was instrumental in finding him lodgings. Goodall wrote of him: 'He plays very beautifully on the guitar, is a capital shoemaker, hammock manufacturer and amongst his other accomplishments can hurt a bull and cut a fellow's throat as well as any man.' Richard Schomburgk, while also recognising these skills, had no doubt that he had been left behind as a spy. According to Evaristo, the Brazilians had expected the arrival of Schomburgk and had no intention of impeding his survey. However, they had had no warning of the approach of any military expedition (CO111/195: 1086, 1091; Goodall 1962b: 51; RS, I: 306–7).

Crichton, with the main supply boats, arrived at Pirara Landing on 12 February and on the following day the supplies for Pirara were shipped up to Awarikuru Creek. The surgeon, who had now been ill since 15 January, remained at Pirara Landing waiting for a horse to take him to Pirara. Youd told Crichton that the officers planned to make the paddlers carry the stores and equipment to Pirara so Crichton and McClintock went up to Awarikuru to see what was happening. They were asked to stay to dinner by Richard Schomburgk; an invitation they felt bound to accept although the presence of the officers at the table made for a chilly atmosphere. Crichton recorded that 'no compliments passed between us'. The question of the paddlers acting as porters was raised by Bingham during the meal, and Crichton expressed his doubts about their willingness to do so. They were exhausted and had no sandals for crossing the savannah. Furthermore the local Indians were well accustomed to doing such work. The problem was resolved next day when thirty to forty Indians sent by Schomburgk to collect his stores agreed to return for the military supplies (CO111/195: 1091).

The main body of both expeditions, military and boundary, advanced to Pirara on 14 February, leaving Lieutenant Wieburg and Mr Fryer behind with a small party to protect the supplies. The soldiers donned their 'redcoats' for this exercise so that Richard Schomburgk is able to describe their advance as that of a 'thin red line'. Pirara was occupied with due ceremony; the troops, drawn up in close formation, presented arms while Lieutenant Bingham declared the Queen to be the rightful owner of the place and the Union Jack was hoisted. The two remaining Brazilian soldiers surrendered their ammunition, amounting to several hundred rusty cartridges (RS, I: 301–2, 304–5).

Since Youd had last seen Pirara a number of changes had taken place. The Indian settlement was much decayed and the population had dwindled to a handful. Youd's own house, which had been occupied by Fr. José, still stood, but the church had been pulled down and replaced by a much larger building in front of which had been erected an immense cross. An equally large house had been built for Leal, and this was taken over as temporary accommodation for the troops. This building was fortified with sandbags and two cannons, which were fired each morning and evening, were set up to defend it. The accommodation of the military and boundary expeditions were at some distance from one another, but the two parties were on good terms and dined together regularly (CO111/195: 1085, 1086; RS, I: 304–5, 309–11).

After dark on the evening of 15 February, the day after the arrival at Pirara, two Brazilian horsemen approached the village and were detained by the guard at bayonet point. They had come from São Joaquim and were bearing a letter from Leal, dated 16 January, to the governor in Georgetown. Bingham, thinking it was a response to Light's recent letter, opened it to find that it was a reply to Light's letter to Leal of 1 February of the previous year, the communication that had been delivered by Crichton. In it Leal stressed that Youd had left voluntarily, admitting that he did not know where the frontier lay. Leal also claimed that Youd had been sent by a missionary society with the British government's permission (CO111/195: 1085).

According to Richard Schomburgk (I: 311), the horsemen were sent back to the fort next day with a further message, which asked Captain Leal to come and fetch the soldiers and equipment left at Pirara. In fact this letter from Bingham to Leal, dated 17 February, simply informed the latter that the former's orders were to make a peaceful occupation of Pirara but that any interference from the Brazilians was to be met with the 'most determined resistance'. He added that the matter was one to be settled by the respective governments.

Crichton arrived at Pirara on 18 February to find that the officers had complained to Schomburgk about his behaviour, so that after church service on the 20th they barely spoke to one another. Crichton describes Robert Schomburgk on this occasion, presumably making him sound ludicrous on purpose given that his journal was to be submitted to Governor Light, as dressed 'in Full Regimentals with a sword as long as himself nearly – a chapeau Bras with a Plume above it a yard in length at least' (CO111/195: 1091).[7]

When, on 23 February, there was still no reply from the Brazilians, Bingham sent Lieutenant Bush with a dispatch pointing out that there had been no reply to Governor Light's letter or to his, and that he now required an early indication of the Brazilian's intentions (CO111/195: 1085). Bush, however, missed both Leal and Fr. José. The latter sent a message from Pirara Mouth on 25 February saying that he would be in the village the next day. On his arrival he was greeted by Youd in 'full canonicals', the military in full dress uniform and a nine-shot salute from the mortars.[8] Richard Schomburgk describes his approach thus:

> [T]he Friar in black vestments and bare-headed, by his side a black Brazilian soldier protecting him from the scorching heat with a large sunshade, following him several soldiers without weapons, and bringing up the rear his horse (I: 311).

Fr. José apologised for the delay in his arrival and explained that when the messengers arrived Leal had been near the Kanuku Mountains rounding up wild cattle and he himself had been at his new residence some two days from the fort. Accordingly it had been difficult to coordinate their movements, and it was important to do so as they were to act conjointly. However, Leal should be at Pirara the next day, and a Brazilian boundary commissioner was due shortly at the fort. Leal arrived on the following day 'at a whizzing gallop' with some forty mounted men and a young woman.[9] Only four of the horsemen were described as soldiers and according to Richard Schomburgk they 'could have been taken at first sight for a troupe of wandering minstrels rather than for the military escort of a high officer'. The young woman, Senhora Liberadiña, was the wife of the rancher Ignácio Lopes de Magalhães, who founded in the 1840s the ranch of Bôa Vista which was, in due course, to grow into the state capital of Roraima. If we accept Richard Schomburgk's word, she had formed a romantic attachment with Leal (I: 311-12).

The official meeting was set for the next day, 28 February, at 1 p.m. Crichton, who had returned to Pirara Landing for two nights, arrived back early that morning, 'before Mr Youde's coffee was ready'. He went to pay a formal visit on Leal and Fr. José, by whom he was warmly received. Their conversation seems to have been a friendly dress rehearsal for the later serious negotiations, and certainly most of the relevant topics appear to have been covered (CO111/195: 1091).

At the formal meeting Leal and Fr. José produced their orders from the president of Pará, and stated that they did not dare, at the cost of their lives, evacuate Pirara voluntarily. They 'expressed a determination of not evacuating Pirara unless forced at the Point of the Bayonet, but that they would rather be made Prisoners and sent to Georgetown'. Leal proposed that, if he gave his word that he would in no way interfere with the British occupation, he be allowed to remain at Pirara with two or three soldiers, all unarmed, until he received orders to withdraw. Bingham replied that he was unable to accept this since his orders were explicit that no Brazilians were to remain at Pirara. He therefore insisted that they retire, and said that he would if necessary use force. Since the British force was so much stronger, Leal and Fr. José admitted that they had no choice, but they would do so only under protest and regard it as an insult to their country. Bingham put his demands in writing, declaring that all soldiers and people under Brazilian command must leave and hoping that this would be achieved without violence (CO111/195: 1085, 1086).

In response a formal letter of protest was written by Leal and Fr. José in which they accused Bingham with the:

> manifest transgression of law and politics with which he surpassed the limits prescribed by honour, moderation and prudence, for the violence with which by force of bayonets, he made the Brazilians evacuate

the village of Pirara, and if it had not been for the prudence with which we behaved, certainly some collision would have occurred.
... We appeal to God as our witness of our loyal and just persuasion that Brazil & the entire world will not cease to note the behaviour of the English Govt. and to the end that it may reach the knowledge of all, we send this present protest (CO111/195: 1579).

Given these circumstances Schomburgk wanted to know whether he would be allowed to continue unhindered with the survey of the Takutu and Mahu. He was assured that there was no problem about that, but that no markers he set up would be recognised as delimiting the frontier; they would merely be treated as being for scientific purposes. In his turn Fr. José reported (wrongly) that a former president of Pará, Bernando de Souza Franco, had been appointed as boundary commissioner and would shortly be arriving at Fort São Joaquim. Schomburgk was uncertain as to how to deal with such a commissioner since his instructions made no allowance for his entering into any form of negotiations concerning the frontier. He addressed this question to Governor Light and, in due course, the Colonial Office answered in a letter of 1 July to Light, reaffirming that Schomburgk's task was to carry out the survey and that the negotiations would be conducted at governmental level on the basis of his maps (CO111/195: 1086).

It is difficult to know just how resistant the Brazilians were to the British demands for withdrawal and how much force Bingham had to exert. At the same time there is no doubt about the fact that the opportunity was taken for a considerable trade in horses, cattle and other goods between the two sides. For example, Goodall gave his pistols to Leal in exchange for 20 dollars' worth of Indian 'curiosities' and a hammock worth ten dollars. Fr. José sold six of his cows to Youd and Leal three horses to Youd and one to the officers (Goodall 1962b: 53; RS, I: 315–16).

Schomburgk mentions that he showed Fr. José and Leal every civility and attention during their stay at Pirara and, according to Richard Schomburgk's description, their visit was characterised by considerable conviviality:

> As the Commandant and the Friar were our guests during their stay, the officers like ourselves supplied the table with all the delicacies in their possession so as to make the first meal as sumptuous as possible which we absolutely succeeded in doing. The Friar became especially lively after the emptying of only a few bottles of champagne, which, as he asserted, he had not tasted for 30 years. Stiff ceremony relaxed

more and more with every bottle of wine until at last the guitar was sent for and Aberisto [Evaristo] came forward with several vaqueiros to play and sing: striking some simple chords on his instrument for half an hour at a time he accompanied the jubilant Friar and Captain Leal as they relieved one another by turns with their songs of folk and freedom, and improvised sentimental ditties respectively. Any stranger who might have noticed us would have had difficulty in imagining two hostile parties at this free and easy dinner party. Even our Mr Youd was cheerier and brighter than ever and although but speaking broken Portuguese he entered into friendly conversation with the Friar (I: 312).

Even so Richard Schomburgk recognised tensions beneath the surface, especially so far as Leal was concerned, of whom he wrote 'only Captain Leal in the middle of his sentimental songs now and again cast over the assembled company the most penetrating glances that distinctly enough betrayed the hostile instincts raging within his breast'(I: 312). According to the same witness, Leal's parting words were that 'he desired nothing else than that he might have to appear at the head of an army before Pirara, so as to repay hospitality in a way which at the present moment was impossible' (I: 315).

The Brazilians evacuated Pirara in early March.[10] They rounded up and took with them a quantity of cattle belonging both to the Brazilian government and to Fr. José. They also took with them the vesper bell from the chapel, hung from a beam and carried by a number of Indians (RS, I: 315–16).

On 2 March the supply boats set off on their return journey to Georgetown. With them went Lieutenant Bush, Crichton and McClintock as planned, and Dr Dowse, whose worsening health forced him to retire. Crichton's feud with the military had not been patched up. Although Crichton kept his journal every day until they arrived in Georgetown on 12 March, there is not a single reference during the journey to any of these officers. Indeed, it would seem that he was on better terms with the Brazilians than those of his own side. He noted in his journal on 20 February that he had not received any of the meat from a bullock that had been slaughtered at Bingham's command, whereas on 1 March he recorded breakfasting off a good steak that Fr. José had given him and also that he had received a turtle from the same hand that day. In return he sent Fr. José '6 bottles of wine, 1 flask of gin, 1 bottle mustard & box of gun caps' and to Leal he gave his 'day & night spy glass'. (CO111/195: 1091).

Not surprisingly the return of Crichton and Bush to Georgetown introduced their dispute to a wider audience. Bingham had sent letters to Light and Lt.-Col. Bush complaining about Crichton's lack of cooperation, his domineering behaviour, and his coarseness and vulgarity. Of Crichton's refusal to help with Indian porters at Pirara Landing, he 'deemed was done in purpose to annoy'. A series of letters passed between Governor Light and Lt.-Col. Bush, but the former, who sided with Crichton, dismissed the accusations as vague and unimportant and proposed that the matter be dropped as Crichton was back in Georgetown and there was thus no further opportunity for friction (CO111/195: 1091).

Light, when forwarding Bingham's complaint to the Colonial Office on 18 March, pointed out that Crichton was over 50 years old and had had much experience of the interior, whereas of the military contingent he noted that:

> Lt Bingham is a young man of about twenty two years of age, his second officer not so old – the medical man and Commissary equally inexperienced and nearly of the same age. The Soldiers, Black Troops – the color not much in favor with the Indians.

Much of the trouble, he imagined, arose from 'the ill humour of a young man' and 'fatigue in a first introduction to the hardships of a soldiers life' (CO111/195: 1085).

At that time Light had not seen Crichton's journal as the latter was ill on his return to Georgetown. However, when he forwarded the journal to the Colonial Office on 31 March, his support for Crichton had not diminished and he added to the accusation of inexperience on the part of the officers that of snobbery:

> On first setting out, the officers attached to the detachment, effected in common with many other young military gentlemen, to consider themselves of a higher grade in society than Civilians and avoided all social intercourse for some days with Mr. Crichton's party.

A Colonial Office minute to this letter reads:

> Nothing could well be more unlucky or worse managed than this Military Expedition to Perara. It seems to me that the sooner such Soldiers and such Commanders, return to Head Quarters and find themselves under the authority of some experienced Officers, the better.

The minute goes on to suggest that the blame really lay with the senior officers who selected the men, and another minute simply

THE OCCUPATION OF PIRARA 107

states 'I think this whole expedition has been a mistake' (CO111/195:1091).

However, whilst Bingham was busy with making complaints about Crichton, charges against Bingham, which were taken much more seriously, were also being made. As we have seen, the instructions given to Bingham by Light before his departure from Georgetown were very explicit so far as the treatment of Indians was concerned. He had also been instructed to station his troops at a point not close enough to the village for them to enter it but near enough to protect it. Bingham failed to follow these orders. It has already been noted that on two occasions during the journey upriver troops had been allowed to occupy Indian houses and that in one village there was a case of assault on an Indian woman. Light remarked that this was 'disobedience of which I shall take notice'. In fact, Light wrote to Bingham on 16 April admonishing him for not submitting a journal as instructed, for entering Indian villages, and for residing in Pirara. He warned him to obey his orders but approved the measures taken to repossess Pirara (CO111/195: 1091, 1348).

At Pirara, the troops had been allowed to occupy a large house in the village on the grounds that it was necessary for them and their supplies to be under cover. The convenience of the large building in the village meant that there was some delay in carrying out the governor's instructions. However, even if the initial billeting of the troops in the village was justified, their continued presence there was not. In what appears to be Youd's last letter to the Society, of 23 February, he complained that the troops were stationed in the village contrary to orders and that his own instructions were to defer founding a permanent mission until the troops were outside the village. Youd mentions that he intended to apply for a land grant for the Society but could not do so if the fort was to be built there. Bingham, aware of these complaints, replied angrily that he did not intend to build the fort in the Indian village and asked whether Youd expected them to live under canvas in the meantime. Youd told him that it was quite usual for soldiers to do so, especially in wartime. Youd expressed concern that Bingham was hostile to the mission (CW/O/100: 26).

Relations between Youd and Bingham seem to have been generally strained. The former complained to Crichton on two occasions that Bingham had ordered seats to be removed from the Catholic chapel when the instructions had been that this building and Fr. José's house were to be left alone (CO111/195: 1091). On

5 March there was also a row between them over the large cross that had been erected in front of the chapel. Youd wanted to take it down and put it inside the chapel, on the grounds that it was:

> altogether inconsistent to have the well known sign of a Roman Catholick Mission standing so conspicuous and useless in the midst of a Protestant Mission when neither antiquity, magnificence or value can be brought forward as a reason why it should remain (CO111/195:1579).

Bingham, however, gave orders that it was to remain standing until permission for its removal had been gained from the governor. He argued that its removal was an unnecessarily provocative act and one that was:

> likely to cause ill-feeling between ourselves and the Portuguese, more especially as I had heard a report that such conduct on his [Youd's] part had been the cause of the misunderstanding before (CO111/195:1579).[11]

Goodall (1962b: 54) also refers to this incident and remarks that it was unfortunate that some Brazilians were present in the village at the time. This action of Bingham in preventing Youd from taking down the cross seems inconsistent with his own earlier decision to pull down the Brazilian flagstaff, an action that had annoyed Fr. José as 'without attending to those courtesies which are observed between friendly powers'. Light, however, sided with Bingham on this occasion and the cross remained standing (CO111/195: 1091, 1579).

But it was the continued presence of the troops in Pirara that was the main bone of contention. Crichton recorded an argument that Bingham and Youd had over this. The latter stated that if the troops were to remain in the village, he would have to leave as the Indians would not stay. Bingham got in a rage and said that he could not move unless the Indians prepared the quarters for the military force outside the village. Youd responded to this that the soldiers should prepare their own quarters, that the Indians could not be compelled to do it, and that the use of force would drive them away. Robert Schomburgk supported Youd in this matter. Even so little was done immediately, and on the day of his departure downstream, Crichton received a letter from Youd enclosing a copy of a letter he had sent to Bingham. In the former Youd reiterated that unless the troops were moved out of the village there would be no possibility of a mission and that he wanted Governor Light's

THE OCCUPATION OF PIRARA 109

instructions obeyed. In the latter, he pointed out that there had been an incident in which a soldier had molested a young Macushi woman at Pirara Creek. He thus proposed that there should be set hours for the troops to visit the waterside and that the Indians should be warned to stay away at those times (CO111/195: 1091).

When exactly the troops moved out of Pirara is uncertain. According to Bingham's journal the troops left the village on 5 March and were occupied until the 20th of that month with the construction of their new quarters and intermittently until 18 April on its fortification (CO111/195: 1579). However, Goodall provides a rather different timetable. According to him, by 6 March only a suitable location for the troops' quarters had been found, and that it was between 9 March, on which day there was 'a regular row between Mr. Youd and the commandant, the former wishing to get the soldiers out of the village', and the 12th, when Goodall visited the new quarters, that the military force moved out of Pirara Village (Goodall 1962b: 54).

The removal of the troops from Pirara did not entirely prevent the molestation of the Indians. Robert Schomburgk, in his role as justice of the peace, heard a complaint in June about a soldier who had, on more than one occasion, entered an Indian house and, having made its owner drunk, attempted to molest his wife. Visiting Brazilians were accused of similar behaviour and Schomburgk wrote to Bingham saying that it was his duty to see that the Indians were not wronged nor provided with drink (NAG/MDB).

The new military quarters, Fort New Guinea as the building was called, were on a slight hill, three-quarters of a mile from the village to the east of the Pirara Creek. The fort was described by Richard Schomburgk (I: 361) as follows:

> The fortification was encircled by a ditch several feet wide and deep as well as by a five-foot high wall. Of what such use a fort would really prove if it came to a question of serious fighting with the Brazilians I could not rightly appreciate, even with my naturally slight tactical knowledge. The military had to fetch their water from a tolerable distance and, owing to the tropical heat, the Brazilians could have very easily forced the garrison to capitulate by cutting off the supply, even if they had not wanted to drive them out of their stronghold by setting fire to the magazine and barracks with fire arrows, in the shooting of which they are unusually proficient.

When Bingham received Light's reprimand for failing to carry out his orders properly, he responded with some vigour. He defended his decision to move into Pirara village on the grounds that it was 'the most efficient and effective way possible' to carry out his orders to take military possession of the place since the position he had taken up 'was alone adapted' for its protection. Furthermore Fr. José had never objected to the occupation of his house, which was the only building available suitable for the protection of stores and the health of his men. He was sure that if the governor had been present he would have approved his actions (CO111/195: 1579).

He continued that he had now moved out of the village but had not occupied the site identified by the governor. The reason for this was that the site proposed was unsuitable, being commanded on three sides and close to an unhealthy swamp. The place he had chosen, 1,200 yards from the village to the east of the Pirara Creek, was better but far from perfect as it was overlooked by the village which, if occupied by a hostile force, would be difficult to retake.

As for the complaint that a soldier had 'approached' an Indian women, he claimed that he did what he could to apprehend the guilty man, but in the end had dismissed the incident as being of 'a most trivial nature'. He also took the opportunity to cover his back by writing to General Maister in order that he

> may be assured that in my taking Military possession of Pirara I have exercised my judgement to carry out the military part of it entrusted to me in the most efficient manner and at the same time with due regard to the health and advantage of Her Majesty's Troops employed' (CO111/195: 1579).

The military detachment then settled in for what proved to be almost six months' stay. This was a period of boredom, hunger and discomfort punctuated by rumours and alarms. Days were divided up by fatigues at 6 and 10 a.m. and a parade at 4 p.m. Otherwise there was not much to do, and with the onset of the rainy season at the end of May conditions deteriorated considerably. Bingham recorded that they woke one morning to find 2 inches of water on the floor of their quarters, and the fort, being located on relatively dry land, was plagued by snakes. All the officers were reported at one time or another as being down with ague, and if there were few mentions of soldiers so suffering this may simply reflect Bingham's concerns (CO111/195: 2522).

Shortage of food was a continual problem. The way in which Light had visualised the expedition feeding itself had always been hopelessly optimistic. Bingham quickly found this out and reported it to Light early in their stay. His journal contains many references to the problems they had in obtaining bread from the Indians, and to the difficult journeys that had to be made during the wet season to procure it. At one point he complained that there had been no fresh food for five days and that everyone was living on salt pork. However, the situation would have been worse had not on 20 March four Brazilian deserters arrived who, being proficient cowhands, were employed to round up cattle; they managed to provide a fairly regular supply of meat (COIII/195: 1579, 2522).[12]

Boredom seems to have been the main problem for most people, and this was offset in various ways. Goodall comments that 'Pirara is so uninteresting, that reading is the only pleasure' but he also played backgammon, draughts and cards. The initial lack of any playing cards among both parties was rectified by Goodall himself, who made two packs, the faces of which portrayed members of the expeditions and local Indians. Youd's sermons did not provide Goodall with any entertainment and he regularly comments on their undue length and variously describes them as 'intolerable' and 'tiresome' (Goodall 1962b: 51, 54, 64; RS, II: 95).[13]

There was a fair amount of heavy drinking. On Sunday, 13 March, Goodall records that: 'In the course of the morning two officers called, one of whom stopped the whole day and returned half overseas with Mr Fryer to his quarters at New Guinea.' On the next day: 'Mr Low called on us early for a dose of salts with Mr Fryer who also felt very seedy.' Again on the morning of Monday, 6 June, after a heavy day of carousing on the Sunday with a visiting Brazilian: 'Bingham and Low returned to the fort this morning and remained in their hammocks the whole day having their heads bathed with vinegar' (1962b: 55, 64).[14] There were also extempore amusements, such as seeing how many vultures one could kill with a single shot by loading a cannon with musket balls and firing it at a flock of the birds surrounding the carcass of a dead cow (RS, I: 361).

There were also visitors from Brazil. Leal came at least twice; on 22 April he called, accompanied by Evaristo, who had now rejoined the Brazilian side, in search of the deserters, claiming that they were soldiers. Bingham, however, declined to hand them over, saying that he had no authority to arrest them. On 9 August Leal came to raise the question of who was to accept responsibility for the British killing of Brazilian cattle. He may have visited more often than that, since Richard Schomburgk states that during his absence on the journey to the source of the Takutu, Leal 'had expressed his friendly intentions on the occasion of many a visit, and duly continued to carry on undisturbed his profitable trade in cattle, provisions, and ethnological specimens' and that 'Friar José ... not only continued the alluring trade with the enemy in his own person, but carried it on even more actively through his amanuensis Aberisto [Evaristo]' (II: 85). Who, says Richard Schomburgk, could blame them? Leal complained that he had received no pay for four years, his garrison at the fort for three years, and Fr. José claimed that he had had nothing for ten years. Nor were these the only Brazilians who came either to trade or simply out of curiosity (CO111/195: 1579, 2522).

It would appear that only once, on 19 May, did a supply boat arrive from Georgetown, and Bingham laconically records in his diary 'Arrival of men'. Richard Schomburgk informs us that a replacement assistant surgeon, John George Bowlby, arrived with this boat, which left again for Georgetown around 30 May (CO111/195: 1579; RS, II: 85–6).

A feature of the military expedition's stay was the almost total lack of intelligence about Brazilian intentions; a lack readily filled by rumour. On 20 April there was a report that 100 Portuguese troops had arrived from Pernambuco (CO111/195: 1579). At the end of May, Richard Schomburgk wrote on his return from the Takutu expedition that the officers were in possession of the information that 'The militia on the Rio Negro and Rio Branco were already called up, two regiments of regular troops were on the march from Para, and the garrison of Fort Sao Joaquim was by this time strengthened by the forces from the nearest fortress on the Rio Negro' (II: 85). On 1 June, considerable alarm was caused by what was thought to be the sound of a heavy cannon from the direction of Fort São Joaquim, but two Indians sent out to reconnoitre found nothing. A few days later, a Brazilian visitor was able to inform Bingham that there were just three soldiers at the fort, that no reinforcements had arrived, and that the authorities in Pará had said that they must await permission from Rio before acting. On 25 July, some Brazilian soldiers, including a drunken sergeant, visited and let it be known that 350 soldiers were approaching, but Bingham declined to believe them. On 9 August, Leal made one of his visits and announced that there were thirty soldiers at São Joaquim and that a further sixty were due with the Brazilian boundary commissioners in sixteen days' time (CO111/195: 2522).

THE OCCUPATION OF PIRARA 113

While the military expedition was experiencing a period of boredom and inactivity, the boundary survey was proceeding. The expedition to survey the Takutu River to its headwaters set out on 26 March. The first boundary markers were erected at the confluence of the Takutu and Mahu, and Schomburgk took the opportunity to declare 'in the Name of Her Majesty Victoria ... the right bank of the River Takutu to form the South Western boundary of Her Majesty's Colony of Guiana'. A number of other markers were set up at various points along the full course of the river, and Schomburgk noted, when in the vicinity of the settlement that had been the object of the Brazilian slave raid in 1838, that these markers would help protect the Indians by identifying them as Her Majesty's subjects. After an arduous journey the expedition arrived back in Pirara on 22 May, in time to celebrate Her Majesty's birthday (CO111/195: 1710).

It will be remembered that Leal and Fr. José had, at the time of their withdrawal from Pirara, given consent to Schomburgk's proceeding with the survey but had warned that only its scientific status could be recognised. The appearance of boundary markers with the initials VR on them near the mouth of the Mahu gave rise to an almost immediate protest from Leal and Fr. José in which they reiterated that they did not recognise these markers as having any validity as boundary markers, but regarded them as solely for exploratory and scientific purposes (AHI/308/4/2).

Schomburgk's comment to Light on this protest is revealing:

> This protest is worded in a tone which augurs the best results for the ultimate ends of my mission. It was naturally to expect a Protest from the Brazilians Authorities near the Frontier against my having established certain markers along the River Takutu, and from what I knew of the violent temper of Captain Leal I was prepared to receive a Protest expressed in the strongest terms, in lieu of which the subterfuge is used to consider these markers merely as made during an exploratory and scientific journey.

Furthermore, he had heard that among the inhabitants of the Rio Negro and Rio Branco opinion was in favour of Pirara remaining in British possession. The reason for this was that the Upper Amazon and Rio Negro were likely soon to be separated from Pará and that when this happened the new state would look to British Guiana for trade. He continues:

> I know even from good authority that Fray Jozé is favourable to the

project of transferring the trade to Demerara, and leaving Pirara in undisputed possession of the British but whether it agrees with his opinion to push the British Frontier as far as the Takutu I have not been able to ascertain as yet. It is certain however, that there exists no good understanding between the Commandant at Fort S. Joaquim and the Missionary of the Rio Branco; and the latter does not espouse the hatred of the former towards the English (CO111/195: 1836).

Schomburgk presumably knew about Fr. José's involvement in the Amazonas independence movement and the uprising of 1832, but what he is unlikely to have known about was the priest's more general dissatisfaction. On 24 April Fr. José had written to his vicar-general, and, having rehearsed the physical and spiritual hardships he had had to endure and the lack of support he had experienced, he raised the possibility that despite his love for his country he may have to go and spend the rest of his life among foreigners in British Guiana (AHI/308/4/2). It is difficult to judge how sincere he was being in making this threat. It may have been a new tactic in his efforts to win material support, but if so it was a potentially risky move and he must have considered the possibility of having to flee to British Guiana if his scheme backfired. In fact, as we will see, it produced little response.

On Sunday, 29 May, soon after the boundary expedition had returned from the headwaters of the Takutu, Goodall notes that Youd was expected to leave for England soon, and accordingly 'we had the last sermon that we shall probably hear from him for some time' (1962b: 63). Youd left Pirara on 3 June. During the few months he had been there the mission reverted to its previous thriving condition, with many Indians returning to live there and others travelling up to 20 miles in order to attend church service on Sundays. Following his departure, however, the Indians immediately began to abandon Pirara so that only a month later Bingham noted in his journal that there was hardly an Indian left there (CO111/195: 1579, 2522; RS, II: 99).

According to Richard Schomburgk (II: 98) Youd left because he was instructed by 'the President of the Missionary Society in London' to withdraw to Waraputa until the question of in whose territory Pirara lay was decided.

> On Mr. Youd informing his faithful Macusis of the orders received, they were deeply upset, and very bitterly grieved, because they well knew that neither the military nor we would remain in Pirara for

The boats of the Boundary Commission at Yupukarri Inlet or Pirara Landing, the Rupununi end of the Pirara portage.

A temporary camp of the Boundary Commission. It is not possible to identify the individuals depicted but it is worth noting the uniforms, flags and mortars.

Tuesday 15th Feb. 1842. 'In the evening after dinner we heard a slight noise among the soldiers and, on going out to see what was the matter, found that the guard had stopped two mounted Brazilians with the points of their bayonets, much to the horror of the two men. When I arrived on the spot the scene before me would, if I could have managed it, have made a very good sketch. The two horsemen had brought a letter from the commander of the Brazilian fort, which the officers were reading by the dim light of a firestick, the guards still with their bayonets close to the noses of the horses, while their soldiers, some in their shirts, eagerly listened to the letter being read' (Goodall 1962b: 51).

Wednesday 2nd March 1842. 'At two o'clock the Brazilians were ready to start. . . . Captain Leal, on a beautiful little horse was cavorting about showing his horsemanship. . . . The only woman of the party was also mounted and dressed something like a Norman peasant, with the exception of wearing trousers and sitting cross-legged on her horse. The old Friar then made his appearance' (Goodall 1962b: 53). Captain Leal, Senhora Libradiña and Fr. José are readily identifiable at the head of the column.

Pirara after the British occupation in 1842.

The quarters of the Boundary Commission at Pirara. Note the large cross erected by Fr. José and the cause of a dispute between Youd and Bingham.

Fort New Guinea, the quarters of the detachment of the 1st West Indies Regiment outside Pirara. 'A small entrenchment guarded by barracks built of palm-fronds, to which the officers' quarters as well as the magazine, also covered with palm-leaves, were attached. The fortification was encircled by a ditch several feet wide and deep as well as by a five-foot high wall' (Richard Schomburgk, I: 361).

Monday 4th April 1842. 'Began and all but finished one [a sketch] of the junction of the rivers Mahoo and Takutu'. Tuesday 5th April 1842. 'The greater part of our men were engaged in branding tins with the Queen's broad arrow and carving V.Rs. In the afternoon they were all dressed in uniform and ranged before the Commander, together with the Indians when Schomburgk, drawing his sword, claimed on behalf of Her Majesty, the right banks of the Takutu and Mahoo' (Goodall 1962b: 58). The boundary marker can be seen on the tree.

ever. They had all along attached themselves to him with absolute devotion, and now charged him with the most pathetic entreaties not to leave them again to the mercy of the Brazilians. His sacrificing love could not withstand such appeals: he soon made up his mind, and within a few days was off to Georgetown to hurry from there to London and personally press the prayers of the wards committed to his charge before the President of the Missionary Society (RS, II: 98).

There is a problem of timing here, because whilst the Church Missionary Society did indeed write ordering Youd to withdraw to Waraputa, the letter containing this order is dated 1 July 1842 (CW/L/3: 151–2). In fact, the sequence of events was as follows: the Society, as has already been noted, was in a poor financial condition, and at the beginning of 1842 it wrote to the Corresponding Committee informing it of its decision to reduce its activities in British Guiana with the exception of the missions to the Indians (CW/L/3: 126–8). On 31 March, the Society wrote again, in response to the Committee's communication of 17 December in which it had requested that a further missionary be made available, stating that whereas it would like to see Bartica, Waraputa and Pirara 'occupied on behalf of the Indians', it could not afford to maintain three mission stations. Instead the Society was going to approach Lord Stanley at the Colonial Office with a request for financial support, especially for Pirara and in particular for Youd's salary. The Society thought it had a strong claim given that Light had requested Youd to accompany the military expedition to Pirara and to remain as missionary there (CW/L/3: 135–7; CO111/197: 1240). On 15 June, the Society repeated its wish to retain both Waraputa and Pirara, but this would depend on the reply from the Colonial Office which had not yet been received (CW/L/3: 147–8). This was sent on 21 June and was not exactly helpful, since the Colonial Office observed:

> that as Mr Youd's expulsion from Pirara had been made a subject of complaint it might naturally be supposed that his re-establishment there was desired, but of course it will be for the Society to judge where their Missionary may be most usefully stationed (CO112/23: 346).

There is another problem here, because as we will see in the next chapter, an agreement had already been reached with Brazil and the order to withdraw the troops had been sent to Light a week before Lord Stanley replied to the Society. Although the agreement declared the disputed territory to be neutral until the boundary question was settled, it explicitly allowed for the continuation at Pirara of representatives from the Roman Catholic and Protestant churches. It might have been thought that the British government would wish to keep a toehold in Pirara by sponsoring the presence of a Protestant missionary there, but this was not the case. Nor did the Church Missionary Society advance this argument, which was rather stronger than those it employed in support of its request for government funding.[15]

On 1 July the letter was sent instructing Youd to retire to Waraputa because the Colonial Office had turned down the application for financial support and because of the unsatisfactory state of affairs at Pirara as described in the Corresponding Committee's letter of 14 May. However, it is just possible that it was the Committee that took it upon itself to order Youd to retire to Waraputa, because in that letter of 14 May, it was mentioned that thought was being given to such a move, particularly if the soldiers were not better restrained by their young and inexperienced officers (CW/L/3: 151-2; CW/O/67: 14; CO111/197: 1240).

In other words, when Youd left Pirara at the beginning of June, the Society was still hoping to retain Pirara as a mission. Therefore, if Richard Schomburgk is right that Youd did receive instructions to retire to Waraputa, the Committee must have put its thoughts into action. This seems to be the most likely course of events, although what the Committee may not have banked on was Youd's returning to England rather than staying at Waraputa. Youd already had permission to return to England on leave and Pollard, in his letter to the Society of 29 July, complained that Youd was determined to go to England as he wished to see his father. Pollard stated that, in Youd's view, Waraputa was not healthy and 'that Pirara is the place he wishes to be is evident'. Even so, he continued, it was equally clear that the Society could not afford to maintain the mission there, but he erroneously concluded that, even if it could, it could not because under the agreement the zone was neutral until the question of the boundary was settled; thus ignoring the fact which we have just noted that missionaries were permitted to remain there (CW/O/67: 15).

Youd must have known about the withdrawal of troops from Pirara before he left Georgetown for England, because we learn from a postscript of 31 July to Pollard's letter of the 29th that Youd was to leave next day on the ship *Demerara*, under the command of a Captain Miller. What Youd's response to this news might have been we do not know, as he died at sea a few days after leaving

Georgetown. He was buried, according to Richard Schomburgk, on Barbados (II: 100), and to Bernau, at sea (1847: 134).

Schomburgk put Youd's death down to yellow fever (II: 100), whereas Bernau was far more fanciful about it. He claims that Youd had offended an Indian by persuading his sons not to attend a dance. The story continues, according to Bernau's published version of 1847 (127–8), thus:

> The father, believing the Missionary had influenced them [his sons], swore that he should pay for it with his life. On the next day he sent a leg of deer, which, there is too much reason to fear, he had poisoned; for Mr. and Mrs. Youd, having partaken of it, were soon afterwards taken ill. Mrs. Y. being near her confinement, refused to have recourse to an emetic, and died in the course of the same night; whilst himself, having taken one, by that means saved his life.

A few days later a second attempt was made on Youd's life.

> [I]t would appear that he [the Indian] must have administered a second dose through a second hand to avoid suspicion. Mr. Youd saved himself by means of another emetic ... After his return from Pinara [sic], however, the same person made his appearance also at the latter place [Waraputa], and must, somehow or other, have administered a third dose, in which he fully succeeded. Mr. Youd having fallen asleep at his meal for the space of an hour on his awakening, occasioned by acute pain, he had recourse to an emetic again; but it was too late, and the poison took its full effects. He then tried other remedies which lengthened his life, but so weakened him, that, after a fortnight's time, he died on his passage home.

One might imagine from the detail that Bernau provides that Youd gave him all the information on his last trip downstream to Georgetown. This was not so, because it was not until January 1844 that Bernau first reported this version of the Youds' deaths, having been told it by some Indians. Indeed, it only emerged as a result of the extraordinary death of the Indian involved. The latter, when he heard of Youd's death, discharged his gun in celebration and when he was repeating the exercise the gun blew up and killed him. Initially Bernau was inclined to question the truth of this story but the suddenness of Mrs Youd's death and the strange behaviour of the murderer left doubts in his mind which, he admitted, would be difficult to clear up (CW/O/18: 29). Nearly a year later he obtained the additional details that form the basis of the account as it appears in his work *Missionary Labours in British Guiana*, and these seemed to convince him of the truth of the matter (CW/O/18: 33).[16] In fact, there is absolutely no evidence to suggest that either of the Youds was poisoned, and Mr Youd makes no mention of it in either his journal or his extant letters. Even so it has given rise to a version of Youd's death that still carries some credence.[17] On the other hand, that the story came in the first place from Indians should occasion no surprise because their explanation of the two deaths fits well with Amerindian understanding of the causes of misfortune and death, which depends on anthropomorphic agency and the *post facto* attribution of cause that best suits the circumstances of the deceased's personal relationships and acts.

Of Youd, Bernau wrote in his journal:

> It must be said of him that he served the Lord in the Missionary work with a devoted heart; and that in his lonesome travels in these wilds he has borne with submission the many deprivations and trials incident to a Missionary's life (CW/O/18: 26).

He later added:

> His [Youd's] plans were somewhat deficient, limited and undigested, while his sanguine expectations prepared for him in many instances cruel disappointments (CW/O/18: 29).

Richard Schomburgk was more fulsome in his praise and described Youd as 'the noblest and most thorough-going of missionaries' and correctly predicted that it would be difficult to replace him with another who would show to the Indians the same 'devotion and sacrificing love' (II: 100).

Notes

1. For an account of Goodall and his recruitment to the boundary commission, see Menezes 1977b.
2. Not all of them lasted the whole survey. The cook and one of the Germans were dismissed for theft, another of the Germans was seriously wounded in a shooting accident and had to return to Georgetown, and a third gave up because he had enough of the hardships the expedition entailed.
3. I have not found a copy of these articles but they are described as being similar, with the addition of two extra articles, to those signed by the members of the expedition before departure to Barima in April 1841. There is a copy of those articles in CO111/178: 1369.
4. The following Sunday at Waraputa Richard Schomburgk and Goodall were both equally amused by the Indians who escaped through the church window during Youd's lengthy sermon (RS, I: 247–8; Goodall 1962b: 48).

THE OCCUPATION OF PIRARA 119

5. It is not clear why the force was increased in size at the last moment. On 23 December, Light was still referring to the expedition as being composed of two subalterns, an assistant surgeon, an assistant commissariat general and thirty men. Bernau (1847: 124–5) said that the detachment consisted of upwards of sixty men. However, the embarkation return, at least, as far as the officers are concerned, coincides with what is known from other sources. Richard Schomburgk gives a different figure for the number of canoes and paddlers, nine and 120 respectively. He also says that they took four months' provisions.

6. Goodall's diary for 27 January (1962b: 49) reads: 'We passed without any accident the rapids of Rappu, the last of the falls when Mr. Schomburgk, and I came too, landed on a small rock in the centre of the river. A salute was fired and we drank to the health of the officers of the Pirara detachment, to which Mr. Youd, the missionary parson, loyally replied, in champayne.'

Richard Schomburgk in describing the same incident makes it clear that this is the occasion on which the message was left (I: 264–5): 'we ourselves opening a bottle of champagne to celebrate the successful passage of the dreaded cataracts. This being done, a 50ft. long bambu was fetched and the empty champagne bottle tied to it: we had previously enclosed in it a sheet of paper conveying greetings to the officers of the military expedition with the wish that fortune might prove just as kind to them in crossing the falls as she had been to us.'

However, the curiosity is the presence of Youd (who was accompanying the troops) reported by Goodall. Richard Schomburgk does not mention him, and his reference to Mr Youd's corial on p. 264 presumably refers to the canoe borrowed from Mr Youd (see p. 254). An Indian paddler of the military expedition had died on the night of 25 January, and Crichton complained that Youd had left early on the morning of the 26th without offering to take the funeral service. He also records that Youd was back with the military expedition on Sunday, 30 January when he preached (CO111/195: 1091). It is just possible that Youd travelling light caught up with Schomburgk and returned again. The reason why he should have done so is more obscure but it may have had something to do with Schomburgk's authority to demand the evacuation of the Pirara before the troops arrived. Youd brought the matter up again with Crichton on 31 January, the day after his return.

7. It was clearly an occasion for obligatory dressing up, as Goodall was able to avoid church because his only pair of white trousers had a 'slight rent'. Schomburgk seems to have been a stickler for correct dress and on another occasion, while on the expedition to the source of the Takutu, Goodall was reprimanded for wearing a blazer rather than his uniform jacket (1962b: 52, 58).

8. Richard Schomburgk's description differs from that of Crichton. The latter pointedly makes no mention of the military, stating that Robert Schomburgk and Youd received Fr José and saying that even the salute was fired on two small howitzers belonging to the boundary commission (CO111/195: 1091).

9. Goodall (1962: 53) puts the figure at 'a dozen to fifteen horsemen'.
10. On 2 March, according to Goodall (1962b: 53), and on 3 and 4 March according to Bingham (CO111/195: 1579).
11. Presumably Bingham was referring to the occasion at Fort São Joaquim in July 1838 when Youd preached in the chapel there. This incident, as we have seen, was later exaggerated into his having desecrated the place.
12. Richard Schomburgk met three Brazilian deserters on their way to Pirara at the Macushi village of Nappi during his expedition to the Kanuku Mountains (I: 327). He gives no dates for this journey, although we know he must have left on or after 2 March since he claims to have observed the Brazilians evacuate Pirara. Schomburgk met the deserters on the third day after his depature from the Pirara, and Goodall records (1962b: 53–4) the arrival of three Brazilians on horseback at Pirara on 5 March. It is just possible that these were the same men, but Schomburgk would have had to have left on 2 March, the same day as the Brazilians, for this to be so. But by Schomburgk's own chronology this did not happen because he places both the visit of a group of Maionkong Indians and the departure of the boat crews between the Brazilians' evacuation and his journey to the Kanuku Mountains.

Goodall gives 21 March as the date of Schomburgk's return (1962b: 56). Between then and 26 March when the expedition to the source of the Takutu River set out Schomburgk made his first visit to the newly erected Fort New Guinea where he saw the three deserters he had met at Nappi. Certainly by this time there were two Brazilians vaqueiros bringing in cattle to feed the force for we have mention of them in Goodall's diary entry for 21 March.

13. Goodall's reaction to Youd seems to have been a personal one rather than one caused by anti-religious feelings. Richard Schomburgk says the Macushis' nickname for Goodall was 'Domini', because he 'often read the prayers at service' (II: 257).
14. The stores of both expeditions obviously contained a good supply of drink of various sorts. The military officers were not keen on trying the local Amerindian drink made from cassava, in which the fermentation was achieved by the chewing and spitting of bits of the root. They said 'they would as soon drink the contents of a spitoon'. Schomburgk remarked that if they had spent as long in the interior as he had, they would 'be damned glad to get it' after a day's march across the savannah (Goodall 1962b: 52).
15. It is unlikely that the Society would have been unaware of the agreement with Brazil as Lord Glenelg, Secretary of State for the Colonial Department from 1835 to 1839, and James Stephen, a permanent secretary at the Colonial Office, were both officials of the Society.
16. A note appended to this letter by the secretary to the Corresponding Committee, Pollard, reads: 'I feared that poor Bernau had had a dose also – just before the illness which obliged him to leave for Barbadoes – the paralysis of his limbs appeared a very extraordinary symptom.'
17. See, for example, Brett 1868: 222 (but not 1851); Veness 1875: 115–20; Stevenson 1908: 159–60; and Menezes 1977a: 219. It is interesting that

THE OCCUPATION OF PIRARA

Veness cites Youd's own description of his wife's death, which makes no mention of poisoning, but then falls back on Bernau's account which he quotes virtually verbatim but without acknowledgement.

Lloyd (1895: 232), while accepting the basic story, provides a different account of the fate of the poisoner: 'Mr. Youd died at sea on his way to England, from poisoning, and the Indians assert that the man (a Macoushi) who poisoned him was subsequently struck dead by lightning while in the church one Sunday imitating a parson preaching.'

CHAPTER 7

THE WITHDRAWAL FROM PIRARA: 1842

While the military force was in the field events were taking place on two other fronts, but because of the slowness of communications there was considerable delay between what was happening in Pirara and reaction to it elsewhere. First were the diplomatic exchanges between London and Rio de Janeiro, and second the reaction in Pará to the occupation of Pirara.

Even before the military expedition left Georgetown there had been an advance on the diplomatic front. As we have noted, the British minister in Rio, Hamilton, informed the Brazilians on 10 December of the British intention to send troops to occupy Pirara. On 8 January, the Brazilian minister for foreign affairs replied, accusing the British of not having given the Brazilians time to act. He pointed out that Ouseley had presented Palmerston's letter of November 1840 concerning the proposed survey only on 20 February 1841. The Brazilian government had sent out a directive on 6 March, ordering that no actions were to be taken against Indians that might give grounds for complaint and that harmony was to be maintained with the British. Even so Crichton had been at Pirara within a month of the receipt of Ouseley's note, whereas the Brazilian government's instructions had not reached Pará until 6 May. Accordingly it was not surprising that Brazilian intentions were unknown on the distant frontier of Pirara by the time Crichton got there. There was then a slightly absurd exchange of notes about timing between the two sides. The British minister claimed that if the Brazilians had acted when first told about the proposed action there would have been no problem, since it resulted from delay on their part rather than any precipitate action on the part of the British. The Brazilians responded that on questions of such seriousness it was to be expected that the information would be conveyed in writing, and although Ouseley had twice been advised of this, the note and memorandum had not been received until 20 February 1841 (CO111/197: 854, 1116).

Despite this rather futile exchange, in which both sides showed that they had no idea how long it took to travel from Belém to the Upper Rio Branco, the Brazilian minister's letter of 8 January did contain a positive proposal. The minister had picked up from Crichton's report the suggestion of declaring the region around Pirara a neutral zone until such time as the survey and negotiations had settled the matter. Accordingly the Brazilian minister proposed that:

> Reserving then all its Titles, in order to make them available at the fitting time, the Brazilian Govt agrees to order the retirement of its authorities and of any Military detachment from Pirará, and to recognise provisionally the neutrality of that Place under the condition stated by Gt Britain, that the Tribes of Indians should remain independent, and in exclusive Possession of the Territory until the definitive decision of the contested limits; and likewise that consequently no English force should remain at the same Post, but only Ecclesiastes of the two Religions, Catholick and Protestant, employed in the Civilization of the aborigines; and the Subjects, without Military Character of both Nations, who may happen to be required for the Preservation of private Property, or purposes of jurisdiction and superintendence or such relations as may originate from the provisional state of things which it is in view to establish, and on which point the two Govts may come to an understanding through their Plenipotentiaries (CO111/197: 854).

The British minister forwarded news of the proposed agreement to the Foreign Office in London on 22 February, but it was not until 4 May that the correspondence was transmitted by the Foreign Office to the Colonial Office for comment. By that time some report of the occupation of Pirara had reached the ears of the Brazilian minister in London, Marques Lisboa. During March and April there were some discussions between him and Lord Aberdeen in which the latter apparently gave assurances about an amicable outcome to the affair. The Brazilian minister appears to have transmitted this news to Rio de Janeiro without delay and some weeks before the British had reached a definite decision about their next step (CO111/197: 2021).[1]

The arrival at the Colonial Office of a proposed agreement was very opportune, as it had recently received from General Maister the information that, as predicted, the cost of the expedition was going to be very high. One minute to Maister's letter expressed the view that 'the object is not worth the expense' and that the troops should be withdrawn, and another that the 'only object in sending a force there has been to enforce that which is now conceded; the evacuation of the place by the Brazilian troops & non-interference with the Indians, the missionaries or other peaceable inhabitants'. The colonial secretary wrote to the Foreign Office: 'With his [Earl of Aberdeen's] concurrence I propose to give immediate directions for the withdrawal of the force now maintained at Pirara at an expense apparently utterly disproportionate to the object, and now happily rendered unnecessary' (CO111/197: 854; WO1/580: 1105).

A further letter from the Foreign Office to the Colonial Office on 31 May agreed with latter's proposal to withdraw troops from Pirara but wondered whether before the determination to do this was made known to the Brazilians, there should not be a more formal agreement. This was not the only worry expressed about the withdrawal, and a minute of 30 May to a despatch from Light of 18 March reads: 'It seems unfortunate that this place was ever occupied as the abandonment of it will appear like an abandonment of our claims to the Territory.'

Nothing came of these concerns, and a communication was finally despatched to Governor Light on 15 June with instructions to withdraw the troops. However, it was not until 4 July that the Foreign Office directed the British minister in Rio de Janeiro to inform the Brazilian government that the troops were to be withdrawn from Pirara on the understanding that the proposed conditions were abided by (CO111/195: 1085; CO111/197: 1126; CO112/24: 94; FO128/37: 152).

On 14 July Light confirmed that he had received the instructions to withdraw the troops from Pirara and had ordered Lt.-Col. Henry Capadose, the new commanding officer of the troops in British Guiana, to make the necessary arrangements. The latter replied that it would take until the end of July or the beginning of August to put the order into effect.

The authorities in Pará were, in the meantime, mainly in the dark about what was going on. The vice-president, Sousa Franco, in a communication to the Ministry of Foreign Affairs, dated 14 February (the very day that Pirara had been occupied), noted that there was no recent news from that part of the province. He had received from the ministry the information that the British were threatening to send troops to Pirara and commented that 'this is a case of premeditated aggression which ... ought to be repelled with all the means at our disposal' (AHI/308/4/2).

The news of the occupation of Pirara reached the vice-president in April in the form of a letter from Fr. José, written on 8 March to the administrator of the Treasury in Manaus and forwarded by the latter. He gave an account of the occupation of Pirara that in most respects does not differ from that recorded in the British documents although, as is to be expected, there is that much more emphasis on the strength of their protestations and the threats of violence that forced them to retreat. He confirmed that they had told Robert Schomburgk that the markers he put up would only be recognised as being of scientific value. Fr. José took the usual opportunity to deplore his condition and added that in this distant and unprotected place, without knowing what to do, there was neither day nor night that his eyes were not exhausted by tears at the thought that Brazil was going to lose the valuable Rio Branco savannahs.

The vice-president's reaction to this news was to write to the military commander of the Lower and Upper Amazon, Lt.-Col. Manoel Muniz Tavares, on 25 April, asking whether the order of 6 November 1841 to reinforce the garrison of Fort São Joaquim with 30 men had been executed[2] and to inform him of the instructions that were being given to the military commander of the Upper Amazon, Major Raimundo Correa de Faria. These were to send 100 troops to Fort São Joaquim, place them there in a state of defence and await further orders. The force must be disciplined, be ready to enter into action, and if attacked must defend Brazilian soil until the last. On 27 April, he reported the matter to the minister of foreign affairs and continued that if the authorization were given it would be easy to expel the invaders but that the imperial government may wish to give its highest consideration to the consequences of such an act (AHI/308/4/2).

It is not clear when the news of the occupation reached Rio, but the Brazilian minister of foreign affairs protested about it to Hamilton on 17 June. Hamilton replied on the 28th of that month saying that he too had only recently heard of the event as a result of the British consul at Pará having forwarded a copy of the provincial president's protest (CO111/197: 2021).

At this point Sousa Franco's involvement in the affair ended as a new president of Pará, Rodrigo de Souza da Silva Pontes, was installed. Silva Pontes arrived from Rio at the end of April and had been well briefed at the Ministry of Foreign Affairs. In particular, he must have been aware of the draft proposal for neutralizing the disputed territory. One of his first tasks was to write to Governor Light protesting at the occupation of Pirara, sending one copy of it via the British consul and another via Lieutenant Bingham at Pirara. He also wrote to de Mattos concerning his commission to survey the boundary.

There had been much discussion in Rio about the composition of the boundary commission. In particular the question had been raised whether de Mattos should have been allowed to proceed alone without instruments, maps and proper qualifications for the job, and it was decided to revise his instructions. Thus the president's letter ordered de Mattos, if he was not yet up the Rio Branco, to await the arrival of the other commissioners with the necessary instruments, and, if it was too late for this, to restrict himself to those parts of his commission which did not require the use of instruments – in other words to conduct a general rather than a scientific survey. He was to verify the scale of the English occupation, to protest if the English tried to curtail his movements, but on no account to do anything to cause trouble between the two countries (AHI/308/4/2; AHI/294/1/3).

On 6 May, the president forwarded to Rio de Janeiro a batch of letters and reports relating to the occupation of Pirara.[3] Most of them have already been taken note of, as they are copies of the letters that passed between Governor Light, Captain Leal, Fr. José and Lieutenant Bingham. The exception is a covering letter from the military commander of the Upper Amazon, who, in transmitting these to the president on 28 March, admitted that he was perplexed since the territory occupied was that whose ownership was to be agreed by commissioners from the two countries. It seemed to him that the English were seeking free access to the Amazon and only awaited a cause to take it. He did not know what to do and would await orders. On the same day the commander wrote to his superior officer, the military commander of the Lower and Upper Amazon, explaining that Pirara was a long way from Fort São Joaquim but that even if they were closer there was no force there sufficient to oppose the English, who 'as always have shown their proud character; they do what they want and nevertheless call themselves a friendly nation.' In turn the military commander of the Lower and Upper Amazon informed the president by a dispatch of 11 April that while awaiting orders he had recommended to the commander of the

Upper Amazon the strict observance of the order of 6 November 1841 to send thirty troops to Fort São Joaquim. The president, in his covering letter to these documents, feared that the British planned to stay at Pirara and found colonies there (AHI/308/4/2).

On the same day, 6 May, Silva Pontes also addressed a further protest to the British government about the actions of Governor Light. The new British consul, Richard Ryan, who had arrived in Belém on 2 April, acknowledged this on the 9th, saying that while he would convey the communication without loss of time he was certain that the British government would be able to justify the governor's actions (AHI/308/4/2).

On 10 May, President Silva Pontes sent a further letter to Rio in which he echoed the view of the military commander of the Upper Amazon that the British occupation of Pirara was merely the first step towards the banks of the Amazon. Soon, he argued, they would find a reason, some disagreeable happening, to take Fort São Joaquim. For the sake of national honour, the fort must be defended but it needed improvements. He requested help, money, engineers, some small warships and above all a steamboat, because without one communications were so slow that it was impossible to make a speedy response to any hostile initiative. The letter also contained doubts about what action he should take. Since he had been ordered to avoid any break with the British, he wondered whether improvements to the fort should proceed in case even this was grounds for dispute (AHI/308/4/2).

The following month attempts by the British Guianese government to attract Brazilian immigrants were immediately seen by the president as suspicious. He was certain that these immigrants, because they were the most accustomed to rural life and work in the tropical climate, would be used to found the colonies at Pirara, where they would facilitate the British access to the banks of the Amazon (AHI/308/4/2).

The next news to arrive from the Upper Rio Branco was a dispatch from Fr. José, dated 9 April, which appears to have reached Belém in early June. He reported that the British troops had retired a quarter of a league (approximately one mile) towards the Rupununi, that Youd was still in Pirara village, that Schomburgk was at Pirara Mouth, measuring and demarcating without waiting for the Brazilian commissioners, and that the British were helping themselves to cattle, saying that due compensation would be paid. He also reported that an Indian arriving from Venezuela had told him that

Pedro Ayres was in that country, preparing to attack Fort São Joaquim. He could not confirm this news but would make a reconnaissance in that direction to see if he could ascertain anything.

The president's reaction was to order an appropriate armed force to the frontier. He was worried, it would appear, as much by the news of Pedro Ayres's activities as by the threat represented by the British, although he suspected that these might be connected. On 8 June he wrote to the military commander of Pará, Brigadier Francisco Sergio d'Oliveira, another veteran of the *cabanagem*, summarising the situation. First, the English were not satisfied with occupying Brazilian territory but were killing cattle, claiming that they had been authorised to do so by their government, which would pay for the animals slaughtered. Second, it was rumoured that Pedro Ayres was preparing to attack the fort from the headwaters of the Rio Branco, and the president feared that this was a plot to provide a pretext for further invasions by the English. Third, the president referred to a recent newspaper and pasquinade campaign that called for revenge on the English. His interpretation of this campaign was that it was not born of a sincere spirit to avenge the wrongs done, nor yet an expression of true patriotism. In fact he suspected that the English themselves had started it in the hope that it would provide a justification for further action. While such machinations could be handled in the capital, they were more difficult to control in the interior, where seeds of anarchy and disorder still existed.

For all these reasons, an expedition should be mounted immediately, with the brigadier in charge or, if he was unable to go, an officer should be chosen in whom there was complete confidence. The size of the detachment was up to his discretion, but every care should be taken not to provide the English with an excuse for further intrusion. He should check to see what progress had been made on repairing Fort São Joaquim and whether the garrison had been reinforced, as ordered by his predecessor. A report should be made on the activities of the English with particular reference to the slaughter of cattle, to the movements of the boundary commission and as to why the military force had withdrawn towards the Rupununi, leaving the missionary in Pirara. The aim of the expedition was not to make war but to make the frontier safe from any attempt on the part of Pedro Ayres, to make others respect that which belonged to Brazil and to ensure that the interior and frontier of the province were free from disturbances. Further, should he find

THE WITHDRAWAL FROM PIRARA

any persons who showed anger towards the English he must calm them. He should proceed with whatever sized force he felt necessary to complete his mission, leaving enough troops in the city of Belém for routine duties. Three boats were available to transport his men (AHI/SP: L293, M4, P7).

The president, however, cancelled this order according to a letter he sent to the Ministry of Foreign Affairs on 26 July. He was then of the opinion, given that the story about Pedro Ayres came from an unreliable source, that it may be a ruse on the part of the British whereby Brazilian action would give them a pretext for more extensive occupation of Brazilian territory. He felt supported in this interpretation by the violent anti-British campaign in the local press and by the distribution of pasquinades, calling for a war to the death against the 'robbers of Demerara'. Furthermore the political situation was delicate because of the forthcoming election, and he considered it inadvisable to reduce the military force in the provincial capital. He hoped that the force already sent to Fort São Joaquim by his predecessor would be sufficient to repel an attack by Pedro Ayres. He also drew attention to a report that contraband English goods were for sale 'at very reasonable prices' on the Rio Negro (AHI/308/4/2).

The British consul in Pará, Richard Ryan, kept the Foreign Office informed of these military movements. On 19 May he reported that a detachment, probably not exceeding 200 men, was to be sent to drive the British out of Pirara. A month later he wrote that 400 troops had been ordered to embark immediately, and then some three weeks later, at the beginning of July, that this order had been cancelled as the force might be needed locally. The reason was 'the dissolution of the legislative chambers at Rio de Janeiro, as the President fears disturbances may occur in the Province during the approaching elections' (CO111/197: 1441, 1714, 1805).

Ryan's communication of 19 May, containing the protest from the president of Pará of 2 May at the 'palpable and grave infraction' of Brazilian rights by the forcible deprivation of territory, reached Light, via New York, in July, just after he had received the orders for the withdrawal of the British troops. He was alarmed at the consul's news that the Brazilians planned to reoccupy Pirara with 200 regular troops augmented by militia, although in the absence of a steamboat it would take three months to transport them to Pirara. Nor were Light's worries assuaged by the consul's opinion that:

as in all probability the Commander appointed to take the Troops on the Demerara Frontier, will be of the general cast of officers here, full of pride, and consumately ignorant, it is to be feared, if he finds the British Force weak in numbers that he will without hesitation endeavour to drive them from their Post, and sacrifice them if he can (CO111/195: 1813).

What concerned Light was the timing of the withdrawal, since it would appear as though the British had fled at the first intimation of a threat from the Brazilians. The result would be that the Indians, owners of the land, would lose confidence in the British and once again fall under Brazilian oppression. Furthermore the Brazilians would become increasingly confident in their territorial claims, perhaps even allying themselves with Venezuela over the matter of the boundaries.

> A retreat caused by their [Brazilian troops'] appearance would have a fatal effect on the minds of the Indians, would be magnified by the presumption of the Brazilians into a great victory over Her Britannic Majesty's troops, and would have a bad effect throughout the whole of the Northern States of S. America whose pretensions would not fail to increase, by the idea that Great Britain had yielded on the first show of resistance.[4]

He hoped that a clash could be avoided, but had no fear if there was an attack on the British detachment as it was well entrenched. It could not, however, hold out against a blockade and it would have to surrender before help could arrive from Georgetown. He trusted that the president of Pará was acting without the authority of orders from Rio de Janeiro and suggested that he 'should be made to feel the displeasure of the power against whom he has dared to move' (CO111/195: 1815).

Light was also concerned about one aspect of the agreement, which was that Pirara was to be left jointly to the Roman Catholic and Protestant missions. While Fr. José was there there would be no problems since he was well disposed towards the British, with whom he carried on trade, and he was not over-occupied with his flock. However, the situation might be very different with the arrival of a more zealous priest. Light accepted that at present the disputed territory was of no value to either side, but he argued that since British Guiana was likely to develop faster than Brazil it would become important, so nothing should be yielded now. He proposed that there should be occasional inspections of the situation by a competent person to report on the state of affairs and the progress of civilization, and to receive complaints about any violations of the neutrality. Such visits would furnish Britain with evidence that it had not abandoned its claim to the territory and its watchfulness over the Indians' interests. This suggestion was approved by the Colonial Office on 5 October (CO111/195: 1813).

Because there would be a delay in assembling the boats to collect the troops, Light sent a message to Bingham telling him to prepare to withdraw and warning him of the 'hostile disposition' of the president of Pará. He was told to keep secret from the others at Pirara the news of the approaching Brazilian force, but should it arrive he must make every effort to avoid hostilities. Light also sent a copy of the agreement to be communicated to the commandant at Fort São Joaquim, and Bingham was to advise him of his intention to withdraw as soon as possible. Finally he noted that 'it will be sufficiently evident from your communication of the Agreement that the withdrawal of the detachment is occasioned by the Agreement ... and not by the expected or actual presence of Troops from Para' (CO111/195: 1817).

Inspector Crichton was entrusted with delivering to Pirara the order for the military expedition to withdraw, although it is doubtful that he went in person.[5] The message reached Pirara on 22 August and it was very welcome. Bingham recorded that: 'The joyful intelligence was hailed with three hearty cheers. There is not an officer here who would not have volunteered for Sierra Leone in preference to remaining on this desolate waste.' Richard Schomburgk described similar scenes of delight, and added that the present peaceful withdrawal was welcomed because everyone was still convinced that a Brazilian force 'quite eight times the stronger' was assembled on the Rio Branco and was ready to attack when the dry season arrived. Nor was this rumour restricted to the members of the expeditionary forces, for Robert Schomburgk reported that similar news had been circulating among the Indians who, as a result, had been flocking to Pirara for protection (CO111/195: 1817, 2514, 2522; RS, II: 108–9).

Two days later Lieutenant Wieburg set off for São Joaquim to deliver the letters to the commandant; he returned a week later with the information that there were only fourteen soldiers at the fort. During his absence the large boats sent to collect the troops had arrived, having had a slow and difficult journey against the wet season flood. They were loaded with all haste, and on 1 September, after setting fire to Fort New Guinea, the military expedition departed. After a trouble-free and quick journey the troops reached Georgetown on 14 September (CO111/195: 2522; NAG/MBD: 14; RS, II: 110–12).

Robert Schomburgk, writing to the government secretary, expressed his pleasure at the withdrawal of the detachment since, in his view 'it has done more harm than good'. Ruminating on what he described as an 'ill-conceived project', Richard Schomburgk claimed that it had cost not less than '24,000 dollars' and repeated the view that 'with this sum they [the British government] could have carried out their intended purpose far more securely, even more cheaply in fact, if they had simply blocked the mouth of the Amazon' (NAG/MBD: 14; RS, II: 109).

Pollard, Secretary of the Corresponding Committee, on hearing that the troops were to be withdrawn, stated that he was 'heartily glad of it for the sake of the poor Indians'. Bernau joined in the criticism of the expedition and referred to the Indians as suffering from the 'contamination of the soldiery' and the 'resentment of the Portuguese'. However, he went further than this and questioned whether it had been wise to have founded the mission at all since 'there is little ground to believe that any material good will result from it to the poor Indians'. He rightly recalled that no express permission was ever given for its founding, and less correctly that what had been approved was a reconnaissance with the aim of attracting the Indians to a downriver site (CW/O/67: 15; CW/O/18: 25).

In human terms, the cost, except for the discomfort, sickness and deprivation, was low, at least during the military expedition. There were no deaths and no injuries, at least as a result of hostilities. Not a shot was fired in anger. However, there were casualties. Both Lieutenant Bush and Dr Bowlby died shortly after, the former on a boat for England and the latter from yellow fever on St Lucia (RS, II: 112).[6]

As has been noted, Leal and Fr. José had jointly protested to Schomburgk in early May about the setting up of boundary markers and had repeated their earlier condition that only the exploratory and scientific purposes of such markers would be recognised. They also stated that the survey should await the arrival of the Brazilian commissioner, but, Fr. José noted, in a cover letter to the copy of their protests sent to the Pará authorities, Schomburgk 'waits for nothing'. The report of Schomburgk's activities reached Pará by the end of July, and the lack of progress on the part of the Brazilian commissioners was a continuing source of worry to the president. No commissioners had arrived from Rio, and Colonel de Mattos, whose journey from Belém to Manaus had taken ninety-two days and who had not yet received the president's orders of 2 May revising his instructions, reported on 4 June that he was unable to proceed further for lack of supplies and canoes, caused by the departure of a detachment of troops for Fort São Joaquim shortly before his arrival. He went on to complain that the commandant of Fort São Joaquim, Captain Leal, in being a policeman and lacking military experience invited affronts from the English, and suggested that he should be replaced by a properly qualified military officer and that the fort should be fully garrisoned. In fact the former had been done almost as soon as the authorities at Pará had news of the occupation of Pirara, for on 25 April Major of Artillery Hygino José Coelho, another officer with experience of fighting the rebels during the *cabanagem*, had been appointed military commander of the frontier although Captain Leal had been left as administrator of the state ranches. Coelho, like de Mattos, seems to have had some difficulty in arranging his journey up the Rio Branco. He was still in Manaus in early June and had not reached Fort São Joaquim by mid-September (AHI/308/4/2; Hurley 1936: 36).

Colonel de Mattos occupied his time while waiting in collecting depositions on matters relating to the frontier and the activities of Schomburgk and the Ayres brothers in 1838. Much of the information collected repeats what has already been noted, but it was now stated explicitly that the declared scientific nature of Schomburgk's expeditions was merely a cover for its real purpose, the preparation for the usurpation of Brazilian territory behind which Schomburgk himself was the 'soul and spirit'. His witnesses further confirmed the dangerous relationship that existed between Schomburgk and the traitor Pedro Ayres, who then held an important and threatening position on the frontier at Marabitanas as director of the Canton of San Fernando in Venezuela (AHI/308/4/2).[7]

By early August, the president of Pará was becoming increasingly concerned by reports of Schomburgk setting up boundary markers as he pleased. He feared that this was further evidence of the British intention to march to the left bank of the Amazon. He resurrected the order to Brigadier d'Oliveira to make a reconnaissance of the Upper Rio Branco and made a formal protest to the British about Schomburgk's activities. Ryan duly transmitted the protest to the

British authorities and informed them that 500 men were being sent to retake Pirara and that the brigadier in charge had left on 11 August (AHI/308/4/2; CO111/197: 2178).

The failure of the Brazilian boundary commission to get under way was not helping the situation, for when the president protested on 1 August to the British consul that Schomburgk had acted alone and had not waited for the Brazilian commissioners, Ryan replied that he did not think the Brazilians intended to go ahead with the survey as they had not even named their commissioners. This placed Silva Pontes in some difficulty and his first inclination was not to respond to the consul's assertion, since it was so far from the truth. He then decided that if it were not denied this would be taken as a confession of the truth. However, by a stroke of luck de Mattos, who, while still in Manaus, had finally received the instructions of 2 May not to proceed further but to remain in Manaus if he had not already entered the Rio Branco, chose to ignore these orders for some reason that remains unrevealed. Silva Pontes's first thought had been to summon de Mattos back to Belém and dismiss him from the commission. He decided, however, to allow him to continue because in that way he could counter the British consul's claim by pointing out that a named commissioner had already reached the Rio Branco (AHI/308/4/2; CO111/197: 2178; CO111/206: 145).

In reporting all this to the minister of foreign affairs, Silva Pontes stated that he would do everything in his power to reinforce the frontier but that he had not got the proper means to do it. Worst of all, he argued once again, was the slowness of communications within the province, which meant it was impossible to react quickly to any incident and difficult to implement any orders without a steamboat. A week later he repeated his plea for action on the fortification of the frontier and the increasingly pressing need for the other members of the boundary commission to leave Rio and get to work before it was too late (AHI/308/4/2).

During the same period, early August, the president wrote to the minister of foreign affairs on the achievements and woes of Fr. José, according to himself. His name, stated the president, would not be unknown to the minister as a result of the Pirara affair. He had been the most reliable reporter of events, and despite his age and sickness, his religious feelings and patriotism made him forever vigilant in the defence of his country and zealous in the conversion of the Indians. His energy, however, was beginning to fail him and he needed an assistant, but the laws of the province prevented the president's use of money for such a purpose. It would be a very serious matter if for lack of help Fr. José was no longer able to continue in post. The president requested the Ministry of Foreign Affairs for help with the large sum it would cost (AHI/308/4/2).[8]

The president got some timely support for his request in the form of a letter from the vicar-general of the Upper Amazon, who wrote saying what difficulties Fr. José was facing as the generosity of the English was attracting Indians to their side. The president informed the minister of foreign affairs of this as some expenditure might be required in order to counteract the English practice (AHI/308/4/2).

Unbeknownst to the president until near the end of the year, Fr. José had also been tempted by this generosity. As has already been mentioned he had written in April to his vicar-general raising the possibility that despite his love for his country he might have to go and spend the rest of his life among foreigners in British Guiana. It is difficult to judge how sincere he was in making this threat, but the impression it gives is that it was a new tactic in his efforts to win material support. This interpretation is strengthened by the fact that the vicar-general took so long to react. He did not reply until 1 November, and when he did it was with a letter full of exhortation. The vicar-general understood all Fr. José's trials and tribulations and his lack of the wherewithal to do his work, but in the end the reward was in doing God's work. He finished his letter by saying that he was sending Fr. José for his comfort two dozen small cups, one dozen large cups, two dozen plates, two arrobas of sugar (about 65 lbs), an alqueire of rice (about 13 litres), and a barrel of wafers for celebrating mass (AHI/308/4/2).

During October Silva Pontes received news of the agreement reached about the disputed territory from the Ministry of Foreign Affairs. He was worried that this territory would include that area contained within the boundary markers set up by Schomburgk and proposed that neutrality should be confined to the region of Pirara. Since there was no doubt that Fort São Joaquim was on Brazilian soil improvements to it could and should be carried out, but nothing could be done for lack of resources – money, manpower and transport. Finally, clearly mixing up the agreement and earlier information, he informed the Ministry of Foreign Affairs that the British troops had withdrawn only as far as the Rupununi, which he interpreted as further evidence of the bad faith of the agents of the British government (AHI/308/4/2).

About the same time the Brazilian Ministry of War came to life and wrote to Silva Pontes on 30 October approving various actions he had taken to resist the British invasion, but pointing out that before the cost of the major repairs of Fort São Joaquim could be agreed the law required the submission of a plan and estimate. The letter ends with the sentiment:

> It is an act of great foresight to have reinforced the garrisons on the frontiers; and although we may not be in a state to make war with England, if the forces of that country attempted to commit acts of violent usurpation on any part of Brazilian territory, with the military, even in the case, which is to be feared, that our forces were to yield to others more numerous, for it is not so bad to be conquered than to permit a slur to be cast on national honour and dignity without, at least, offering any resistance to protect them (Braz M2, Ann 2: 120–1).

Fr. José and Leal do not appear to have forwarded until 20 September the letter delivered by Wieburg on 26 August concerning the agreed neutrality of Pirara and the departure of the British troops. Nine days later Fr. José wrote to the vicar-general for advice on what to do in the light of these events. He asked whether, with the troops gone and Youd recalled to England by his government, he should go and catechise the Indians at Pirara, since under the terms of the agreement he had the right to do so (AHI/308/4/2). No answer to this proposed move seems ever to have been sent and Fr. José made no attempt to act on his own initiative. It remains a mystery that Brazil as much as Britain failed to take advantage of this clause in the agreement. It is of course possible, even likely, that neither country's heart was much in the affair.

Notes

1. I have not found any documentary evidence for these talks and the only reference I have seen to them is that mentioned here.
2. This order of 6 November 1841 has not been found but it apparently instructed the military commander of the Lower and Upper Amazon to send fifty men to Manaus, thirty of whom were to proceed to Fort São Joaquim. It is not obvious what incident gave rise to this order unless it was a delayed response to Crichton's mission in February of that year. It would appear from the vice-president's letter that it had never been confirmed that his order had been carried out, as indeed it had not been.
3. These included a letter of 1 March from Fr. José to the president reporting the invasion of and succeeding events at Pirara. It is almost identical

in contents to the letter of 8 March to the administrator of the treasury at Manaus already noted, except that the emotional ending is missing.

4. The view that the British fled on the approach of a Brazilian force did gain some credence. The missionary Bernau, writing only five years after the event, states that the troops were suddenly recalled and the fort blown up on the report of the approach of 3,000 Brazilians (1847: 125–6). There also seems to have been some criticism of the withdrawal in the Georgetown press, but unfortunately I have been unable to track this down. The newspapers in the Guyanese National Archives are not available for consultation because of their condition and I have been unable to locate them elsewhere.

It was not only contemporaries who got things wrong, as this garbled version of the event by Michael Swan demonstrates:

> The Governor of British Guiana sent twenty-nine coloured troops of the First West Indian Regiment under two lieutenants to dislodge the Brazilians. The British encamped some miles from Pirara and sent word that they expected the Brazilians to remove themselves to the other side of the Ireng [Mahu]. The Brazilians decided they were stronger and refused to budge. Poor Lieutenant Bingham was without orders for such an emergency and he dispatched a messenger back to the Coast to ask whether he should attack or not. Time went by and the British stores were exhausted; Lieutenant Bingham was reduced to the humiliation of asking his potential enemies for food, which was refused. The second detachment of soldiers arrived to find their compatriots half starved. The Brazilians, sizing up the new situation, departed for their homeland, allowing their half-breed troops the pleasure of a small night foray. An outpost of Empire had been successfully held (1958: 130).

5. The British Case in the boundary dispute certainly assumed that Crichton was the bearer of the dispatches (Brit C: 83). Light's orders, however, were that Crichton should proceed to the Mazaruni 'where he will hire Indian paddlers to convey the messenger to Pirara' (CO111/195: 1817). The messenger was presumably a policeman, as Bingham records in his journal on 22 August that he had 'heard that the Police Boat had come to take me to Demerara, cannot conceive for what cause' (CO111/195: 2522).

After this Crichton played no further part in the affair, and in February of the following year Light was forced to dismiss him from the post of inspector-general of police because he had opened and copied official communications with which he had been entrusted (CO111/199: 658).

6. When Richard Schomburgk wrote that in the short course of nine months four of the Europeans who had foregathered in Pirara so late as March had gone to their last rest, he was presumably referring to Youd as well as to Bush and Bowlby (even if the last did not arrive at Pirara until May). The fourth person is the German expedition hand, Nicolas Reiter,

who died while returning with the military expedition after having been dismissed for stealing drink (II: 110, 112).

7. This is presumably San Fernando de Atabapo at the junction of the Rivers Orinoco and Guaviare. One would not have thought that Pedro Ayres would have represented much of a threat from there, but the Brazilians constantly worried about their distant frontiers as they still do today.

8. The only response to this seems to have been a letter of 7 June 1843, in which the president is asked to convey the emperor's appreciation for all the good work that Fr. José has rendered the church and state, and the emperor's hope that he will continue to do so with equal zeal (AHI/308/4/11).

CHAPTER 8

THE CLOSING SCENES
1842-43

Leal's protests about the activities of the British boundary commission were proving ineffectual, given the continuing failure of the Brazilian commissioners to put in an appearance. In July 1842 Leal wrote to Schomburgk informing him that the commissioners were due any day and, accordingly, asking that Schomburgk refrain from any further aggression until they arrived. In reply Schomburgk stated that he had no instructions to treat with the Brazilian commissioners. On 9 August, while on a visit to Pirara, Leal predicted the commissioner's arrival in sixteen days and Schomburgk wrote a letter to de Mattos, welcoming him and trusting that an amicable solution to the boundary question would be reached. On this occasion Leal's information was accurate, for de Mattos did start up the Rio Branco at about this time. However, he was taken seriously ill on the journey, and for lack of medical aid he retired to Manaus, getting back there on 6 September. Two days later he wrote to the president of Pará, assuring him that he would complete his duty once he was fit again (CO111/195: 2514; AHI/308/4/2).

Leal's visit to Pirara had not been simply to give news about the approach of the boundary commissioner, for a more important matter had arisen. On 3 May, the administrator of revenues had written to him expressing surprise at his failure to inform the administrator about the cattle that the British military expedition had killed, and holding him responsible for any loss that the nation might have so incurred. Leal came to ask Bingham to help him out of this mess and wrote to him:

> it becomes necessary that in reference to the above, you should declare to me in writing, the order by which you were authorised to take possession of the cattle of His Imperial Majesty, in order that by such a document I may be relieved from the responsibility in which I am placed.

Bingham obliged and informed Leal that:

> it is not in my power to give you a definite answer, but I have no doubt if application be made to the proper quarter (namely his Excellency the Governor of British Guiana by whose authority I have acted) that the cattle in question will duly paid for.

Bingham further told Leal that an account had been kept of every head killed for the detachment (CO111/195: 2522).

During the wet season the British boundary survey team had been unable to progress, not simply because of the weather but also through lack of supplies and money. At the beginning of June Schomburgk sent, in the same canoe as that in which Youd travelled, Nicolas Reiter, one of the German hands, to Georgetown to make the necessary arrangements. This action caused some offence to Light, who thought that an official member of the expedition rather than a 'menial fellow' should have come to Georgetown to deal with such an important matter (CO111/195: 1710). Schomburgk received a rebuke for this to which he responded with some heat, giving a variety of reasons why it had not been expedient for him or another official member of the expedition to visit Georgetown. Among other reasons, it was because:

> There was another circumstance which rendered my stay in Pirara almost peremptory – the mind of the Indians in and about Pirara, became unsettled from the moment they understood that Mr. Youd was leaving these regions. A sojourn among them for several years had procured me their confidence, and whenever they felt themselves aggrieved they resorted to me, and I found it easy to smooth all matters of discontent; I did not consult therefore my comfort but considered it my bounden duty to remain at Pirara (CO111/195: 2516).

He concluded his letter with the classic complaint that those in the field have against those sitting at home:

> I am grieved that His Excellency has found it necessary to censure my conduct where according to my humble opinion I have acted according to the strictest dictates of my duty. The cheerfulness with which I have encountered hitherto the numerous obstacles, and the increasing labour which my duty impose upon me, the fatigues and deprivations of my situation, have been therefore in vain to elicit even an approving remark (CO111/195: 2516).

To this government secretary Young replied on behalf of the governor that the governor had always been very supportive of

THE CLOSING SCENES

Schomburgk, commended his reports to the Colonial Office, and provided money without which the expedition could never have gone ahead. He wrote:

> These comments on your letter are not made for mere purpose of rebuke but in order to convince you that His Excellency has not been sparing of support and assistance to continue and extend those useful public services which have attracted the attention of Scientific Societies, the confidence and patronage of Her Majesty's Government, and have been honourably distinguished by the Sovereign of your native Country (CO111/195: 2516).

The supplies for the boundary commission arrived at the same time as the message ordering the troops to withdraw. These ensured that the next step in the survey, the ascent of the Mahu River, the journey to Mount Roraima, and the descent of the Cuyuni River to join up with the earlier survey, could go ahead. Schomburgk sent Light at the end of August the outline of his plans for this part of the expedition, but also raised some queries about what should happen after its completion. He asked whether he should proceed with the survey of the boundary with Dutch Guiana, over which there was little disagreement, or concentrate on preparing the maps of the territory that was in dispute. He would expect an answer to this when he got back to Georgetown. Light forwarded this letter to the Colonial Office on 3 October, asking for a decision to be made on this matter and reminding London that he was having to find half the cost of the survey out of the contingency fund as the Combined Court continued to block any payment. The Colonial Office did not receive this dispatch until mid-December and various minutes generally supported the view of suspending the survey, although one minute reads:

> The only questions which seem to make the determination of the boundary a matter of *present* importance, are those connected with the protection of the Indians. But these questions seem to suggest strong motives for an early adjustment. ... If the territories in question be British, it seems to concern British honour & humanity that these barbarities ... sh[d] not be practiced within them.

The question was passed to the treasury (CO111/195: 2514).

After the departure of the troops, the British commission set out on 11 September to survey the western frontier to Mount Roraima. They made camp on the Takutu, below Fr. José's fazenda,[1] while Robert Schomburgk went to make an astronomical fix of the junction of the Rio Branco and Takutu. He called at Fort São Joaquim on 17 September in order to pay his respects to the Brazilian commissioner and to show that the British wished to settle the matter of the boundaries 'in the most amicable fashion'. There he learnt that de Mattos had been taken ill and had retired downstream again (CO111/204: 493).

Leal referred to Schomburgk's visit in a despatch of 20 September and reports that Schomburgk was continuing his boundary demarcation towards Mount Roraima. What he did not mention was Schomburgk's invitation to the 'élite' of the fort to luncheon at the commission's camp at the mouth of the Mahu River (AHI/308/4/2).

Once again, the British party thought its honour was at stake and every attempt was made to provide as lavish a meal as possible. It is worth quoting Richard Schomburgk's account of this event at some length (11: 126–8):

> [T]he menu ... consisted of mutton soup, pickled salmon, green peas and carrots with bacon and turtle steaks, as well as small English pickles: madeira, port, champagne and Rhine wine. ...
>
> Like pretty butterflies, with Captain Leal and Senhora Liberadiña in the lead, they [the guests] came into view through the green bushes, jumped nimbly off their steeds, and were brought over to us under the 'thunder of the guns,' while several of the vaqueiros took the little horses under their care.
>
> A creole Negro who belonged to the élite of the Fort rendered himself conspicuous with the foppishness of his clothes, but the real beauty of the whole show was a Senhor Simony whose dark coloured skin showed up exquisitely against his snow-white trousers, gold-spangled fire-red waistcoat and scarlet blouse. Such silly simian fondness for finery must be born in the African's blood. Some of the young women could have run Senhora Liberadiña, who was already known to us, very closely in a beauty competition, for it would be very doubtful to whom preference should be given for charmingly slim proportions, delicate hands and feet, brilliant eyes, classic noses, or pretty mouths with regularly set teeth: the only pity was that they had disfigured these by filing the incisors to a point. Their dress was just as tasty for, as I subsequently had an opportunity of observing at Fort Sao Joaquim, the favourite colour was blue, and all of them wore clothes of this nature while a very pretty material, much like our figured lace, and which every Brazilian girl crochets herself, covered the bosom. The long black hair was held up in plaits with a tortoise-shell comb, while around the bare neck hung several sweet little coral-seed necklaces, to which were attached a rosary and various relics. Senhora Liberadiña for instance wore amongst other things a

piece of the true Cross which Friar José had probably cut from the first tree suitable.

The greeting over, we sat down to table where we really had to restrain ourselves from bursting into loud laughter because, with the exception of the commandant, forks were just as little known to all our guests as were the victuals placed before them, and, under the circumstances, it was hard to give advice although all were to learn. They saw how Captain Leal and we were putting them to use, and though quite anxious to follow our example, were unable to keep pace with us, and it was only very rarely that they got each bit into their mouth at the first attempt. The many fruitless manoeuvres and evident clumsiness of his friends seemed to put Captain Leal in a dilemma. The embarrassment of the ladies was also increasing, and to put them at their ease, my brother took it upon himself to propose that they should eat according to the custom of the country, i.e., use their fingers instead of forks. Everything now went on swimmingly. It was on this same day that I learnt many a little habit which in Europe would be regarded as a grave breach of good manners: for instance, spitting a good deal while eating, and the frequent rinsing of the mouth, which would then be skilfully emptied in a long stream shot out to a considerable distance without rising from the seat. After dinner, both ladies and gentlemen puffed their cigarettes, and the enjoyable day was brought to a close with singing and dancing to the accompaniment of a guitar.

The Brazilians departed next day but not before Leal had negotiated the exchange of twelve baskets of manioc flour, which he would deliver on the expedition's return from Roraima for a double-barrelled shotgun which he took with him.

The expedition set out again on 24 September, but two days later was delayed by the news that Fr. José was coming up river to 'pay respects'. Robert Schomburgk, in consideration for his 'age and weak constitution', decided to wait for him. Because he had missed the 'sumptuous banquet', what remained of the delicacies was provided for him in exchange for which he offered some baskets of manioc flour, two turtles, feather ornaments and two hammocks. His real purpose, however, was to ask Robert Schomburgk to bring him on his return from Georgetown some black material for an altar-cloth and glass shades for the lamps which he tried to keep burning in his chapels but which the wind tended to blow out. He had also brought with him a musical box which played tunes suitable for Mass and which was no longer working; inspection quickly showed it to be past repair, which news almost brought tears to Fr. José's eyes. However, a couple of bottles of wine as a parting present cheered him up again. Fr. José also had some comments to make on the boundary question and he:

> breathed the wish, as on a former occasion, that every thing might be settled amicably. He showed me several letters, which he had received from his Superior, the Vicar-General of the province, which lauded his amicable conduct towards 'the English', and desired him to continue the same, and to prevent every possible rupture ... Fray José is considered to have political influence, and I know from experience that he is generally esteemed in the province of Rio Negro.

This view of him was shared by the president of Pará (CO111/204: 493; RS, II: 132–3).

As a result of the assurances given by Lord Aberdeen to Marques Lisboa in April, to which reference has been made, the Brazilian government seemed to have assumed that a settlement had already been reached. Thus it was that on 18 June the minister for foreign affairs wrote to the president of Pará informing him that the British had agreed that the status quo should be maintained and that the demarcation of the frontier should cease. The president of Pará wrote in these terms to Light on 1 August (AHI/308/4/2).

In fact the British decision to withdraw the troops and to agree to the proposals put forward in January did not reach Hamilton in Rio de Janeiro until August, and he conveyed them to the Brazilian authorities on the 29th of that month. In early September the Brazilian government accepted the terms, confirmed that instructions would be sent to the president of Pará ordering their rigorous observance, but expressed concern about what steps would be taken to safeguard Brazilian property, particularly cattle, in the disputed territory. At about the same time dispatches were received in Rio from the president of Pará containing the information transmitted by Fr. José in his letter of 9 April. This gave the out-of-date news that the British troops had retired to a fortified position outside Pirara, that Youd was still in the village, that Schomburgk was putting up boundary markers, that cattle were being killed and that Pedro Ayres was preparing to attack Fort São Joaquim (CO111/197: 2409).

In October, there was an exchange of letters on these matters between Hamilton and the Brazilian minister of foreign affairs; a correspondence characterised by a failure to appreciate the long lapses in time between the events and the news of them reaching Rio. The Brazilian minister reported that the latest news from the president of Pará, apparently referring to the state of affairs in April, was that Schomburgk was still erecting boundary markers, Youd was still alienating Macushi Indians 'from their ties to the Empire' and the British force was still there. These things, he protested, were in direct contravention of the promises made by Lord Aberdeen in April. Hamilton responded by pointing out that it would have been impossible for news of the agreement to have been transmitted to Pirara by the end of April (CO111/206: 145)

The most serious complaint related to the boundary markers set up by the British commission, and in October and November this matter was taken up between the Foreign Office and the Brazilian minister in London. The latter requested that the markers be removed, but the Foreign Office proposed that since the markers had been put up purely for scientific purposes they should remain where they were. In its reply the Foreign Office took the opportunity to comment on the failure of the Brazilians to get their boundary commissioners into the area earlier. The Brazilian minister, however, insisted on the removal of the markers and the Foreign Office agreed to this, although in an attempt to have the last word it referred to the recently received information that the president of Pará had ordered 500 men to reoccupy Pirara. This, it argued, was clearly against the agreement on the basis of which the British troops were withdrawn and it was hoped that it was not true. The Brazilian minister strongly denied that there would be any contravention of the agreement (CO111/197: 2203, 2214, 2241).

The decision to remove the boundary markers was conveyed immediately to Light, who replied that, for the moment, there was little he could do about it as Schomburgk was uncontactable. Further, he argued, perhaps a little disingenuously, that:

> the authorities of Para and Pirara must be perfectly aware, that these marks are presumptive, not those of assumption – they have been thoroughly made cognisant of this.

He continued that Brazil must not be allowed to make a spurious claim to territory on the basis of wandering cattle. The territory, he reiterated, belonged to the Indians who:

> glad of British protection would yield to its power – Hereafter the district claimed, according to Mr. Schomburgk, may be useful to Great Britain – and on that principle should be insisted upon (CO111/ 195: 44).

We have already seen that the president of Pará, in early June, had ordered Brigadier d'Oliveira, military commander of the province, to proceed to the Rio Branco frontier, then cancelled the order because of the possibilities of civil disorder associated with the elections, and finally reinstated it by an order of 4 August. No evidence has emerged as to the size of this expedition, but we can be fairly certain that it did not approach anywhere near 500 men. It made fairly good time and having left Belém on 11 August, it arrived at Fort São Joaquim on 12 December. During the three months since Robert Schomburgk had been there, Major Hygino José Coelho had arrived to take over command of the frontier, with Captain José da Costa Pereira in charge of the troops. Captain Leal had been removed from all military duties but remained as the administrator of the national ranches.

Brigadier d'Oliveira found São Joaquim to be a fort only in name, and described it as being more a rural settlement than a military establishment. It was in a state of ruin, the seven cannons were without carriages, there was none of the necessary equipment to fire them and there were only two pounds of bad saltpetre. He recommended changes in the layout of the fort and noted that the cost of repairs, which were under way, would be reduced because of Fr. José's patriotic offer to supply wood and tiles. The expedition moved on to the national ranch, São Bento, and then to Fr. José's mission on 20 December. The commander was much impressed by the work of the missionary, and recommended that the president provide gifts for the Indians to combat the presents from the English and send people to teach the Indians technical skills. With these many of the Indians would in a short time be converted to Catholicism and become a useful labour force (AHI/308/3/2).

With reference to the British occupation of Pirara, the Brigadier thought that Leal might have to answer to the Conselho de Guerra for his retreat from Pirara. On the other hand the instructions that Leal had received from former Vice-President Bernardo de Souza Franco had contained such contradictions that they left him not knowing what to do. For example, in a dispatch of 5 May 1841 he had been ordered to avoid all conflict with the British but not to cede any rights to terrain. At the same time he was advised to evacuate Pirara provisionally, despite the fact that it undoubtedly lay in Brazilian territory. Accordingly Leal had done nothing while awaiting definite orders (AHI/308/4/2).

The expedition ascended the Takutu, observed the boundary

markers placed by Schomburgk at various places but did not go to Pirara itself out of respect for its neutrality. Information about happenings at Pirara was obtained from a Wapishiana chief and it was learnt that the British flag still flew there and that British guns were still there, in contravention of the agreement. The roof of Fr. José's church had fallen in, and it was suggested that this damage was not simply the result of time and weather. The brigadier commented that the land the British wanted to take was good for cattle and it was important that ranches were founded there (AHI/308/4/2).

There is also more information about Pedro Ayres who, as we have noted earlier, was now reputedly director of the Venezuelan canton of San Fernando. His relations with Robert Schomburgk had originally been friendly, but they had broken down as a result of uncompleted commercial transactions. Pedro Ayres was not to be trusted and should be watched closely. The brigadier suggested that some action should be taken to improve the defences of the boundary in the direction of San Fernando and proposed to Fr. José that he move his mission upstream to Sta Rosa, where he could keep an eye on things (AHI/308/4/2).[2]

It is not certain when this military expedition left the region, but it was probably around mid-January. It was still at Fort São Joaquim on 8 January, and the brigadier was back in Belém by mid-February when he made the above report to the president. The latter, in forwarding the dispatches to Rio de Janeiro the following month, urged the government to implement the various recommendations made in the report, for reasons of both internal and external defence. The president was concerned about the Indians and regarded it as essential to show that the British claim that the Indians were seeking their protection was false. The English were creating this notion while trying to attract the Indians by every 'seductive means'. He particularly supported the recommendations that skilled teachers be introduced into the villages and that help be provided for Fr. José in the work of the mission (AHI/308/4/2).

At the same time as the Brazilian military expedition was in the region, so was part of the British boundary commission. Robert Schomburgk had decided to split the expedition; while he completed the survey of the northwest frontier with a small party, the other members would return to Pirara and wait for him there. Richard Schomburgk and Fryer visited the fort on their return journey in order to collect the manioc flour they had bought from Leal and spent the night of 21 December there. By this date the Brazilian force was at Fr. José's mission on the Uraricoera, but the British party was told that the Brazilians, guided by Leal, were visiting Macushi villages and that they wished to visit Pirara (CO111/204: 494; RS, II: 234–7).

Schomburgk and Fryer found considerable work proceeding on the reconstruction of the fort. Fryer reported that a force of fifty men was stationed there and that Coelho claimed that there were 100 labourers engaged in its renovation, including the remounting of the guns on new carriages. Fryer believed that the purpose of Brigadier d'Oliveira's visit to Macushi villages was to recruit labour, without which little progress would be made on the repairs. This information was interpreted by Light for the Colonial Office in these terms:

> The intention of employing Indians to strengthen the fortifications of San Joachim, is tantamount to saying they will be coerced – the Brazilians have no money to pay even their garrison – luckily the Indians, with the exception of the few who know they are under the protection of the British Government, have abandoned the neighbourhood of Pirara (CO111/204: 494).

Richard Schomburgk provides a full description of the fort and of the conditions of the soldiers stationed there (II: 235–6):

> Its walls are built of a red fine-grained sandstone. ... The fourteen embrasures were supplied with eight nine-pounders. The gun-carriages were nearly rotten in general, the majority of the guns on the bare ground, and peaceful pasture sprouting at their sides. The eastern face of the fort formed a bomb-proof casemate which the commandant occupied: under it were the sleeping-quarters of the soldiers. Sixty men of the Provincial Militia in white cotton pantaloons and jackets with black facings, a few sergeants of the active service and Major Coelho formed the garrison. ... In a straight line with the Fort, along the banks, stood the real dwelling of the commandant, and of the Friar, the church, and the small huts of the vaqueiros. ... The daily rations ... consisted of 1lb. beef and a quantity of farinha, for which one bullock was killed daily. The poor soldiers had not received pay for three years: they bothered us almost to death to buy the tobacco, which they seemed to possess in large quantities, in the form of 5 to 6ft. long rolls of varying thickness.[3]

Schomburgk and Fryer were disappointed not to meet Captain Leal, who owed them a quantity of manioc flour. Leal, as we have seen, was absent but they learned that he was now the administrator of the national ranches, where he received 'a quarter of the profits'.[4] They were told that he had been impeached in Pará 'for having carried on relations of too friendly a nature with the nation's enemy [and] relieved of his post as commandant'. No other evidence has been found to confirm this claim, although there may well have been grounds on which to charge him. We have already noted that the administrator of revenues was attempting to hold him responsible for the cattle killed by the British, and Brigadier d'Oliveira had considered whether he should be made to answer for surrendering Pirara to the British. As we shall see, Colonel de Mattos was to make charges of corruption and embezzlement against him. In fact Leal's replacement as commandant of the fort seems simply to have been a reaction to the threats from the British and Pedro Ayres by the appointment of a more experienced soldier (RS, II: 234–5).

Despite the reputed fate of Leal, Major Coelho was 'full of friendship and courtesy'. Even so, the British party stayed only briefly and then set out for Pirara. They reached Fr. José's fazenda on the Takutu on Christmas Eve and it was there that they learnt of the death of Youd, 'one of the bravest and noblest of men'. By late December they were back in Pirara, whose population was now reduced to an old Indian woman and the German, Tiedge, who had been left behind to look after stores and equipment. The village was in a poor state; part of the Roman Catholic chapel had already fallen in and a number of other houses had suffered likewise. The party settled down to await the return of Robert Schomburgk, who was not expected until April (RS, II: 234–40).

Early in the New Year 1843, Coelho and Leal came to Pirara carrying letters for Light from Brigadier d'Oliveira. One of these was the protest from the president of Pará, dated 1 August, at the continued demarcation of the boundary without the cooperation of Brazilian commissioners; he requested that the boundary markers be removed. The others were from Brigadier d'Oliveira himself. The first, dated the day after his arrival at Fort São Joaquim, was formally to announce his visit and to stress its temporary nature. He also reported that Coelho was the new commandant and had been ordered to maintain harmony and good relations with the British. The second, of 28 December, was a complaint that British subjects were still exploring in the region in defiance of the agreement. He also sent Light, presumably in response to the information that British goods were circulating on the Rio Negro, a copy of the Brazilian government's ordinances relating to trade with neighbouring countries, and he trusted that in future these would not be ignored (AHI/308/4/2; CO111/204: 494, 659).

Coelho and Leal told the British that four Brazilian commissioners were expected shortly and that they planned to set up boundary markers from the Pacaraima Mountains through the village of Annai to the Siparuni Mouth. Light's comment on this was that if they proposed to do that they were not in a position to complain about Schomburgk's activities (CO111/204: 494).

Not long after the visit by the Brazilians, four deserters from São Joaquim arrived at Pirara, seeking to reach Waraputa. They were helped on their way by the Macusi chief, Basiko, in return for a gun one of them had stolen from the fort. A few days later Coelho and Leal accompanied by soldiers returned to Pirara in pursuit of them, and when Basiko was discovered with the gun he avoided hanging only on the protestations of the British. On this occasion, the Brazilians reported that de Mattos was expected daily at São Joaquim (RS, II: 241–2).

While this was going on Robert Schomburgk had arrived back at Georgetown in late January 1843 to find that there was still no decision on whether the survey of the eastern boundary, along the Courantyne River, was to be carried out. Light wrote to the Colonial Office on 30 January in rather exasperated tones, pointing out that without his support the survey would not have taken place, but that: 'Fortunately I have had both courage and inclination to assist Mr Schomburgk.' There was very little left to be done, and Light writes: 'I shall consider ... [myself] justified in making such advances as may be necessary' to finish the job and trusts that the Colonial Office would 'support me determinedly' because the settling of the frontier question will be of great benefit to the colonists 'in spite of themselves' (CO111/204: 493).

Schomburgk also wrote in support of completing the boundary survey. He pointed out that since he had to return to Pirara to arrange for the erasure of the boundary marks and to escort the other members of the boundary expedition to the coast because they lacked the 'necessary experience to pass the numerous and dangerous falls of the Essequibo with every chance of success', it would not add greatly to the cost if he returned to the coast by the Courantyne and thus completed the survey (CO111/204: 493).

The Colonial Office had not been treating the matter of the boundary survey with any sense of urgency. The Treasury had written to the Colonial Office on 30 September 1842 recommending that the survey be totally discontinued if the colony remained unwilling to contribute its half share. The Colonial Office did not respond until 5 January 1843, when it agreed that the survey of the Dutch boundary should not be undertaken, but argued that the survey was not solely in the colony's interest for it was also a military matter. Unless the boundaries were defined, a once and for all exercise, there may be need for repeated expensive military operations. The Colonial Office thought that Her Majesty's Government should pay for the completion of the calculations and the maps and for conducting negotiations with Brazil and Venezuela. The Treasury replied on 28 January, stating that whereas they would accept the expenses of the Brazilian and Venezuelan frontier survey they would not do so for the Courantyne expedition unless the colony paid its share. The Colonial Office wrote back to say that Light had recently confirmed that the colony still refused to contribute (CO111/197: 2020; CO111/206: 216; CO112/25: 48, 60).

The arrival of Light's dispatch of 30 January on 6 March put some urgency into the matter and set off a flurry of minutes. The Colonial Office was undecided about what should be done, but it finally had its mind made up for it by a further dispatch from Light dated 15 February, stating that he had given Schomburgk permission to proceed with the survey of the Courantyne and that Schomburgk had departed the previous day. A minute to this letter states: 'You will see that the Governor has superseded any further question as to the prosecution of Mr Schomburgk's researches.' The Treasury wrote on 21 March reiterating its position as laid out in its letter of 28 January, but was informed on the same day that the survey had gone ahead. As a result the Treasury agreed, on 3 April, to pay up (CO111/204: 493, 579; CO111/206: 592, 670; CO112/25: 71).

Robert Schomburgk arrived back in Pirara on 24 March. He had received the instructions to remove the boundary markers, although Light had written rather cynically to the Colonial Office:

> the trees will remain on which these marks have been cut, ... and the presumption of title to the territory be still in existence. Let the Brazilian Government show a counter title if it can (CO111/204/493).

Schomburgk found the other members of his party in good health. The Roman Catholic church was in ruins, and there were few

Indians left but these had been troubled by two Brazilian woodcutters who had visited the village and had attempted to molest the women. There was still no news of the Brazilian commissioner's arrival; Fr. José was expected at Pirara for a visit any day, and there was a rumour that the Brazilian government had ordered a young missionary priest to take up residence at Pirara in order to instruct the Indians in the Catholic faith. Smallpox, which had arrived with the boats that came to collect the troops, had ravaged the Macushi and had now spread to the Wapishiana. One of the first things Schomburgk did was to send Fryer with letters (Light's responses to the president of Pará and Brigadier d'Oliveira) to Fort São Joaquim and with orders to efface the boundary markers on the Mahu and Takutu; this was duly done (CO111/204: 1034, 1577).

Coelho, who had already paid a call in early March thinking that Schomburgk was back, and Leal visited Pirara to pay their respects on 16 April. The former reported, in a dispatch to the president of Pará of 22 April, that the boundary markers had been removed; that on their arrival at Pirara the British flag was flying and on the following day before they left the Brazilian flag had been hoisted and saluted by a salvo from the mortars. This letter somehow came to be published in the Paraense newspaper *Treze de Maio* on 8 July and gave rise to diplomatic complaints, as both Ryan in Pará and Hamilton in Rio interpreted it to mean that the Brazilian flag had replaced the British one. There is, however, no suggestion of that in the wording and it seems far more likely that they were flown together (AHI/308/4/2; CO111/204: 1577; CO111/206: 2195).[5]

Schomburgk learned from Leal that there was manioc flour available at São Joaquim, and sent Fryer to buy ten baskets (whether this was the manioc flour owed since the previous September or a new lot is not certain). On his return Fryer reported that de Mattos had finally arrived the previous week; he brought a letter from him in which de Mattos regretted that he was unable to visit Pirara because of the low level of the water in the Takutu. He and Robert Schomburgk never met, as the latter left on 30 April for the survey of the Courantyne Rivier and never returned to Pirara (AHI/308/4/2/; CO111/204: 1577; de Mattos 1844; RS, II: 270).

By the time Colonel de Mattos arrived at Fort São Joaquim, some fourteen months after his departure from Pará, he had been dismissed from the Brazilian boundary commission, although he was unaware of it. We have already noted that the president of Pará had earlier been on the verge of dismissing him but had not done so in order that he could inform the British consul that a member of the boundary commission was already on the Rio Branco. However, some rather odd and not fully explained information about de Mattos came to the notice of the president of Pará in December 1842. He received from the Brazilian minister in London, Marques Lisboa, a report, dated 22 August, throwing doubt on de Mattos's loyalty. It would appear that de Mattos was related by marriage to the British and that a letter from him containing inexact information which would damage the Brazilian cause was in the hands of the British (AHI/308/4/2).

This letter is almost certainly the one that Colonel de Mattos had written to his wife from Manaus on 28 March 1842 and which she had allowed the British consul, Ryan, to copy. It contains a mildly garbled description of the occupation of Pirara, probably taken from Fr. José's account. In itself it seems fairly innocuous, but it leaves unanswered the question of why de Mattos's wife had passed the letter to the British consul. The other surprising thing is that Ryan himself regarded the letter as confirming the assertion, made in the president's formal protests of 2 and 6 May, that Pirara had been occupied. This suggests that Ryan himself was as much in the dark as to what was going on as the authorities at Pará (COIII/ 197: 714).

The president worried that this was somehow part of a wider British plot to destabilise the situation and provide justification for further advances into Brazilian territory, which linked not only de Mattos and Ryan, but also Fr. José whom, he had only just learnt, had contemplated going over to the British. Silva Pontes's reaction was to try and get rid of them all. In December he wrote both to London and Rio de Janeiro complaining about Ryan and saying that the latter's report that Brazilian troops were on the way to expel the British from Pirara was the type of information that would justify further encroachments by the British. Ryan, he said, should be replaced (AHI/308/4/2).

Silva Pontes did not, however, think that de Mattos's relations by marriage were in themselves sufficient cause to relieve him of his duties, but he now lacked confidence in the colonel's ability to carry them out. Accordingly, using de Mattos's illness as a pretext, he dismissed him from the boundary commission with effect from 16 December. In a further example of the way in which information became quickly distorted Ryan reported to the Foreign Office some fifteen weeks before de Mattos even arrived at Fort São Joaquim that the Brazilian had reached his destination in such bad health that he had been forced to resign and return to Pará (AHI/308/4/2; COIII/206: 605).

Whereas it had proved relatively easy to get rid of de Mattos, Silva Pontes regarded Fr. José as a different matter; there was no one to replace him with as he had a poor opinion of the priests in Pará. What the province seriously needed was the help of some missionaries worthy of the name. Furthermore, care had to be taken, for even if Fr. José no longer possessed the popular influence he once had he must be respected as a daring and enterprising person. There ought to be means by which the life of those whom England had an interest in corrupting may be made more comfortable (AHI/308/4/2).

The Brazilian minister in London also became involved at this time, although it is not clear how, with the problem of Pedro Ayres. He wrote on 12 October to the Venezuelan Legation in London warning them that Pedro Ayres, who was now in their country and had a very bad reputation in Pará, had entered into questionable relations with 'individuals who are our enemies – yours and ours'. He had planned an attack on Fort São Joaquim, and the precautions that the Brazilians had taken against such an event had given offence to the British, who might take advantage of the situation in order to adjourn the evacuation of Pirara. The minister was sure that his Venezuelan colleagues would understand that Ayres's foolish conduct might lead to serious complications, if it had not already done so. A copy of this letter was sent to Silva Pontes, who replied at the end of March 1843 thanking Lisboa for his efforts to enhance the security and tranquillity of the empire (AHI/308/4/2).[6]

On his arrival in the Upper Rio Branco Colonel de Mattos first proceeded up the Uraricoera to visit Fr. José's mission at Serra do Bancó, where he was subjected to the priest's usual list of complaints about his sad condition, chronic illnesses, advanced age and lack of assistance. Fr. José was once again persuasive enough about the mission's potential if only help was forthcoming for de Mattos to accept his claims and report to the president of Pará a list of his woes and necessities (de Mattos 1979: 150–2).

After returning to the fort de Mattos visited Pirara, where he met the members of the boundary expedition who had accompanied Robert Schomburgk only part of the way to the Courantyne. De Mattos, whom Richard Schomburgk describes as white-haired and too advanced in years to carry out his assigned duty (he was 59),

THE CLOSING SCENES

appears to have spent a fair amount of time at Pirara. Relationships were friendly, and Richard Schomburgk refers to the many cheerful hours they had together (II: 314–15). On their final evening at Pirara, the British made a special effort:

> From out of the remnants of our larder we were able to give Colonel de Matoz a splendid farewell dinner, which on account of a few bottles of wine, assumed a cheerful character because his disappointment over the ill-success of his efforts was soon washed away, and with the assurance of his never-to-be-forgotten friendship we helped him, late at night, on to one of our friend Youd's horses. ... Sad to relate, as we heard before we left next morning, the Colonel had not been able to stick on his saddle but had fallen off and sprained his arm' (II: 316).

The 'ill-success' referred to in this passage probably relates to two things. Fryer and Richard Schomburgk had quickly learnt that de Mattos, as we know, had failed to bring any surveying instruments with him and tried to obtain, first by deception and then openly, the British observations. Indeed, he wrote to Fryer: 'you will be pleased to inform me, which are the said points determined upon and where marks have been fixed, in order that I may with greater facility and with more certainty find them.' Fryer reported that he had refused to give him any information, whereas Richard Schomburgk claimed that the Brazilian was provided with false information (CO111/204:1577; RS, II: 314–15).

The other failure was de Mattos's attempts to persuade the Macushi chief, Basiko, to swear allegiance to Brazil, offering as an inducement a 'beautiful gold and silver spangled uniform and polished sword'. Basiko, according to Richard Schomburgk, remembering the way the Brazilians had oppressed his people and the recent threat of Coelho and Leal to 'hang him like a dog' preferred to accompany the British to Georgetown, there to receive, on the recommendation of Robert Schomburgk, from the hands of the governor 'a beautifully ornamented chieftain's staff, and a large printed patent of office'. Richard Schomburgk admitted to being perplexed by Brazilian–Amerindian relations, since he noted that de Mattos brought no trade goods with him with which to pay the Indians for their assistance, but that rather they were expected to offer their services without recompense (CO111/204: 1577; RS, II: 315).

While de Mattos reported that he spent some time in the neighbourhood of Pirara, he made only the briefest reference to meeting members of the British boundary commission and certainly did not mention the fraternisation recorded by Richard Schomburgk. In fact de Mattos merely stated that he had to return to the fort for supplies after 'constant work and privations'. It was when he did so that the order dismissing him from the commission finally caught up with him. As instructed he returned to Belém, arriving there on 3 October, and the following year presented his lengthy report (1979: 152, 158).

The report on the Upper Rio Branco that de Mattos submitted is in a number of ways at variance with that provided by Brigadier d'Oliveira, who had been there only a few months earlier. According to de Mattos repairs to the fort had begun on 17 December 1842 with two stonemasons, two carpenters and two blacksmiths. However, the stonemasons had deserted and had been replaced by two soldiers of the detachment. The soldiers' pay was thirty-seven months in arrears and desertions were not uncommon.[7] By the time he came to leave there were only two carpenters and a stonemason at work, and the rebuilding had almost ground to a halt through lack of building material. Major Coelho had asked to be relieved of his post and Captain Costa Pereira, commander of the detachment, had been recalled. These two officers were to be replaced by a more junior officer, Lieutenant Felisberto Antonio Corrêa de Araujo (1979: 156–7).[8]

In his report, as its title might suggest, de Mattos considered at some length the economic and military decay into which the Upper Amazon had fallen. In particular he noted the sharp decline in the number of cattle and horses belonging to the state, from 3,000 of the former and 2,000 of the latter in 1838 to 500 or 600 and 150 respectively in 1843.[9] This he attributed partly to poor management but also to corruption and 'scandalous behaviour' on the part of the administrators, in particular Leal. He accused the latter of selling cattle for personal gain, of appropriating cattle to set up a ranch in the name of his daughter and of selling to the English manioc flour and dried beef that should have provisioned the fort. Leal was also accused of selling manioc beer, made on the ranch of his mistress, to the Brazilian soldiers, which had given rise to disorderly behaviour and violence among them.[10] Leal was not the only person mentioned as so implicated and Richard Schomburgk's reference (II: 122) to the penniless Fr. José having 'a considerable number of cattle' on his ranch on the Takutu after thirty months in the area suggests that the practice of 'borrowing' from the state might have been widespread.

THE CLOSING SCENES 157

Nor may this have been their only illicit activity, as both Fr. José and Leal appear to have carried on trade with Georgetown, something forbidden under Brazilian law.[11] Although we do not know what became of Leal, no evidence has been found to suggest that as a result of de Mattos's report any action was taken against him (1979: 158-63).

Despite the concerns about his loyalty that led to de Mattos being dismissed from the boundary commission, this did not have a serious effect on his later career. Before he died in August 1857 he was to be military commander of the Upper Amazon in 1847-48 and a vice-president of Amazonas on the Province's inauguration in 1852 (Barata 1973: 114; Reis 1931: 174; Souza 1873: 11).

The dinner with de Mattos on the final evening of the British team's stay at Pirara was the last direct meeting between the two sides in the incident. The relationship between the Brazilians and the British had on the whole been one characterised by courtesy and often cordiality. Robert Schomburgk was able to write:

> I have been on the best understanding with the authorities at Sao Joaquim – even with Leal whose shrewdness and cunning must be fully acknowledged – politeness is a cheap kind and I pay him in compliments which he returns in flowery speeches and sentiments (NAG/MBD).

There were moments when feelings ran high and the British often adopted a patronising and supercilious air that caused deep resentment, if not among those directly involved, then more widely in Brazil. The British were much better provided for in every way than the Brazilians, and they made every effort to be hospitable. This relative affluence was clearly attractive to the Brazilians and as well as tempting Fr. José to desert it provided a source of obtaining goods through trade. Paradoxically enough it was these commercial relationships that produced the greatest tensions. The British complained about the failure of the Brazilians to fulfil their side of trading bargains and it was an incident of this sort that was said to have produced a rift between Robert Schomburgk and Pedro Ayres.[12] On the Brazilian side the main ground for complaint was the British refusal to hand back deserters, and their apparent disregard for Brazilian property in the form of the cattle they killed.

The abandonment of Pirara by the Amerindians that began with Youd's departure had been furthered by the military withdrawal. As has been noted, by the end of 1842 the only person, other than one member of the expedition, living there was an old woman and some of the houses were beginning to fall down. Then, during May 1843, an accidental fire, caused by a child, destroyed part of the village including the former Roman Catholic chapel, the late Youd's house and various other dwellings. When Richard Schomburgk came to leave the place for the last time in June 1843, he wrote of:

> the village rapidly hurrying, dreary and desolate, to absolute decay. Deserted by all its residents, a large proportion of the houses already tumbled down, and those still upstanding surrounded with a wanton increase of weed and bush, and the wide streets once more surrendered to the absolute sway of rank vegetable growth, the last vestage of Life bade farewell with us to the spot that once had been so full of it, that but a year ago had still raised in everybody such glorious hopes, that was doomed to utter ruin by the death of the one man whose energies had called its prosperity into being.

Ironically, however, the large cross, set up by Fr. José, which Youd had tried to have taken down, was still standing and Richard Schomburgk saw in it 'a symbol of the hope that perhaps there soon would dawn another day that might prove more favourable for the Indian tribes' (II: 316).

This part of the boundary expedition reached Georgetown in late June,[13] but Robert Schomburgk and Edward Goodall did not get back until 13 October after the most difficult journey of the whole boundary survey. The members of the expedition remained there, completing the calculations and the maps, until 19 May 1844, on which date they took the mailboat for England where they had arrived by 25 June (CO111/204: 2202; CO111/210: 1214; CO111/218: 1233; RHS 1845).[14]

It was the time for congratulations. Light congratulated their lordships at the Colonial Office for the successful termination of the survey, referred to the 'danger and fatigue' of those involved and of his own part wrote 'but for the fortunate command I had, of funds independent of the colonists, must have been long delayed, or perhaps have totally failed'. Robert Schomburgk recommended Goodall for the 'zeal and diligence' in the performance of his duties and Fryer for his 'exemplary conduct'. The Colonial Office conveyed its thanks to Light, Schomburgk and the other members of the boundary commission 'for the exertions which have been made by you & them in carrying forward the objects of it [the survey] under circumstances of difficulty'. It was, however, Schomburgk himself who rightly received the most praise. A Colonial Office minute

THE CLOSING SCENES 159

reads; 'I believe that no man has undertaken more in the Public Services from the pure love of science and with a moderate pecuniary recompense.' Lord Stanley, seeking public honour for Schomburgk, recommended him for a knighthood, to which Queen Victoria gave her assent in December 1844 (CO111/210: 1214, 1215, 1240; CO111/218: 1233: CO112/24: 218; CO112/25: 291, 334).

Notes

1. Fr. José appeared to have had three residences in the area: a house at Fort São Joaquim, his mission of Porto Alegre near the Serra do Bancó, and his fazenda on the Takutu.
2. As previously noted, Pedro Ayres was presumably at San Fernando de Atabapo on the Orinoco. It would be even more difficult to mount an attack on Brazil from there via the Uraricoera than via Marabitanas.
3. Except for the fact the beef is more often dried than fresh, the basic diet in the region was exactly the same in 1968 as it was in 1842. The tobacco also came in the same form.
4. One suspects that Schomburgk meant one quarter of the calves. For a description of this method of payment, traditional to the interior of Brazil, as it was practised on the Rio Branco savannahs in 1968, see Rivière 1972: 87–9.
5. The Portuguese reads: 'no dia deseseis quando cheguei a Pirarára, estara a Bandeira Inglesa a insada, e em desesete as seis horas da manha insau a Bandeira Imperial com dois tiros de morteiro.' By the time the news reached Light, having travelled from Hamilton to the Foreign Office and then via the Colonial Office, it is claimed that 'on the day after the British flag was removed from Pirara, he [Coelho] had caused the Brazilian flag to be hoisted there' (CO111/26: 308).
6. Whether the Venezuelan authorities acted on the Brazilian minister's warning I have not ascertained. Nor have I discovered what finally became of Pedro Ayres. This is the final reference I have to him.
7. This figure accords with the three years mentioned by Richard Schomburgk (1922, II: 236), but not with the report by the military commander of Pará that the troops had been paid up until the end of December 1842 (AHI/308/4/2).
8. His name according to de Mattos was Correia, but he signed himself Corrêa de Araujo (AHI/308/4/2).
9. We have already noted that Schomburgk regarded the figures of 3,000 tame cattle and 500 horses which he was given in 1838 to have been an exaggeration.
10. de Mattos (1979: 163) describes, quite erroneously, manioc beer as being as strong as cane spirit. In fact, its alcoholic content is very low.
11. It is not clear with what frequency this trade was conducted but there is evidence for its existence. On 31 August 1841, Youd at Waraputa refers in

his journal to the Roman Catholic missionary's man of business on his way to Georgetown on a bartering expedition (CW/O/100: 49). In June 1843, Richard Schomburgk mentions buying a large canoe from Leal that had recently returned from a business trip to Georgetown (II: 317).

12. The practice of which the British complained may have been normal, and certainly was not only directed at the members of the military expedition and the boundary commission. Richard Schomburgk recounts the fate of a coloured man, Levingston or Livingstone, who arrived at Pirara in March 1843 to trade with the Amerindians and Brazilians (II: 269–70):

> Though Captain Leal and Friar José already appeared at Pirara some days later as buyers, our warnings had nevertheless made Levingston so suspicious that without further guarantee he declined the proposal of both gentlemen. ... He escaped this trap however only to fall into another, because soon after our departure he got into the clutches of Matoz [de Mattos], the Boundary Commissioner, who bought everything he possessed and promised, as soon as he got back to Para, to send him a draft on the Colonial Bank in Georgetown. This order, however, had not arrived up to the time of my departure for Europe, just like the seven baskets of farinha for which Captain Leal was still indebted to us.

For the further misfortunes of this trader, including the death of the dogs he bought from a pulmonary infection, see RS, II: 313–14.

13. Richard Schomburgk's dates at this point are particularly unreliable. He states that the captains of the canoes arrived at Pirara on 7 June and that the baggage had been transported to the landing stage by the 18th. He gives the date of his final departure from Pirara as 11 June and his arrival in Georgetown as 19 June, but refers to it having taken thirteen days from Pirara to Bartica Grove (II: 315, 316, 323, 326).

14. Richard Schomburgk, because of the size of his collections, had to sail separately on a merchant ship, which he did on 4 June. Although it is of trivial importance, the exact date on which the expedition left Georgetown varies according to the source. Richard Schomburgk gives 18 May; Robert Schomburgk and Secretary Young, the 19th; and Light the 20th (RS, II: 407–8; CO111/210: 1214).

CHAPTER 9

THE AFTERMATH

The departure of the British survey team from the scene did not signal the complete end to the affair. The main action moved to the negotiating table, but there were still some loose ends to be tied up in the field. In particular there was the matter of the Brazilian boundary commission.

The two commissioners who had been appointed, Lt.-Col. Adolfo Antonio Frederico de Seweloh and Lieutenant Innocencio Veloso Pederneiras, arrived in Belém in November 1842, but the following May Ryan reported that they were still there, awaiting 'definitive orders' from Rio. He doubted that the Brazilian government had 'any real intention of allowing them to proceed'. The president of Pará stated in April that they were delaying their departure in order not to reach the Rio Branco when the weather was bad. But there were also other problems. Once again doubts were raised about the competence with surveying instruments of one of the commissioners, Pederneiras, and various criticisms were directed at the other. The newspaper *O Paraense* (17 June 1843) asked why a German had been chosen rather than a Brazilian, reminded its readers that Schomburgk was also a German and wondered why Seweloh frequented the house of the British consul; an accusation supported by Ryan's comment that the information he had about their progress was 'as reported by themselves'. Nor do the two commissioners appear to have been on the best of terms with one another. Pederneiras complained more than once of the way he was treated by Seweloh, and on one occasion informed the president of Pará that Seweloh had been condemned to death for murder in his own country. Even so they set out on 21 May, but hardly had they done so than the president received from the Ministry of War orders to recall Seweloh as he had been dismissed. The reason for his dismissal was that he had written an official complaint about his poor pay 'in such a style that he ought not to continue in such an important commission'. The president carried out this order and instructed

161

Pederneiras to wait in Santarém for the two new commissioners who had been named. They were Frederico Carneiro de Campos, who was to be in charge of the commission, and Pedro Taulois. These two commissioners arrived at Belém in the steamboat Guapiassú on 11 July and left on the same vessel for Manaus on the 28th (AHI/308/4/2; AHI/SP/294/1/3, 296/3/15; CO111/204: 1459; CO111/206: 147, 605, 1617).[1]

The report of the Brazilian boundary commission, dated Rio de Janiero, 26 July 1844, is rather thin and lacking in details about the journey. According to Baron do Rio Branco the commission visited Pirara in July 1843[2] and found there a chapel and fourteen Indian houses, all in a state of ruin (1897: 43). It does not, however, seem to have spent long in the area and it was later said that all it did was to correct the maps of the eighteenth-century surveys (Ribeiro 1876: 7).

Perhaps the final act in the whole event was a murder that took place in the disputed territory in October 1843. The accounts of this incident by the time they reached the coast had, as usual, become fairly garbled. A sworn statement, made on 31 October by a colonist, Nicholas Fallon Huggins, who had been visiting the Upper Essequibo, is the main source of information. It reads:

> That on Friday the 13th October 1843 a man named Simon acting Captain of the Macusi Tribe, came to the Waraputa Mission to Report to the Minister Mr Pollitt, that the Portuguese had killed an Indian named Charles, formerly a servant to the Rev[d] Mr Youde and also inflicted three severe wounds on an Indian woman (name unknown) and pursued others from their dwellings, and for what Purpose the Reporter never enquired but supposes that it must be their design to capture and bring them into slavery. The Reporter states also that he was informed that the said Portuguese has been waiting from time to time for the Minister Mr Pollitt, hearing that it was his intention to visit that Post, and they said, that if he came there, he should never return (CO111/204: 2306).

On the basis of this, Pollard, secretary to the Corresponding Committee, reported in November that the Brazilians had made a further incursion and carried off some Indians, of whom one had been killed and another wounded. The Indian killed was Youd's former servant, called Charles. The Macusi chief, Simão, came to Waraputa seeking the new missionary's help but the latter had already left. Bernau's report to the Bishop of Guiana later the same month differs from this. There is no mention of the Brazilians having carried off Indians and in the version which he had heard it was Evaristo, known 'on account of his treacherous conduct in the late expedition', who had cut the throat of a Macushi man and wounded two Macushi women. Bernau reported that it was not clear whether Evaristo had been obeying orders from superiors but says that he was reputed to have declared that 'we seek occasion to fight with the English'. A month later he elaborated on this and stated that the relations of the wounded man had shot Evaristo in revenge (CW/O/18: 29, 53; CW/O/67: 23).

Governor Light suggested that this was a matter that should be handled by Her Majesty's Government and that protests should be made at the highest level if the molestation of Indians in the neutral zone were to cease. He also proposed to the Bishop of Guiana that someone be stationed at Waraputa, as the presence of a missionary there would help prevent further oppression and dispersion of the Indians. The bishop asked Bernau to send one of his assistants (Mr Christian), to which Bernau replied that whereas he had no objection to such a move it would involve some expense. He proposed that: 'under such extraordinary circumstances, however, his Excellency the Governor may, perhaps, have it in his power to supply the means in order that his wish may be accomplished.' No missionary went to Waraputa and no more was heard of the matter (Brit C, Ann 2: 80–1; CO111/204: 2306).[3]

The version contained in the British protest, delivered to the Brazilian authorities on 20 March 1844, is that a British subject, a Macushi who had been Youd's servant, had been murdered by Evaristo, the Brazilian deserter and son-in-law of the principal Macushi chief. Furthermore Evaristo had threatened violence towards a British missionary (Brit C, Ann 2: 79–83).

The Ministry for Foreign Affairs ordered the matter to be investigated and in due course, May 1845, the president of Pará responded. Reports on the incident had been received from both Lieutenant Corrêa de Araujo, the new commandant of Fort São Joaquim, and Fr. José. The former visited Pirara where he met Charles, the Indian who had reputedly been murdered. Chief Basiko said that he had had no news of such a murder and if such a thing had happened it must have been at Waraputa or elsewhere in British Guiana, where there were Brazilian deserters. Fr. José provided a rather fuller and different account of what had happened. In October 1843 it was Evaristo who had been killed with a shotgun by two

Indians who had then fled to Waraputa, seeking the missionary's protection. He had gone to Pirara at the time in order to ascertain what had happened and the facts had been well known to Captain Coelho, then still commandant of the fort, who had reported the matter to his superiors in December 1843. Coelho had declined to send men to arrest the murderers because Pirara lay in neutral territory and his detachment was much reduced in strength through illness. Furthermore, he was not certain that Evaristo did not deserve his death given that he had murdered his commanding officer. Otherwise all was quiet at Pirara except for the fact that deserters from Waraputa were ascending the Rupununi and stealing Brazilian cattle. Thus the incident fizzled out with the Brazilian minister of foreign affairs replying to the British protest that there was no truth in its claims and countering with the accusation of the continued harbouring of Brazilian criminals and deserters in British Guiana (AHI/308/4/2).

With that typically indecisive exchange Pirara's brief appearance on the stage of international affairs more or less came to an end. Fr. José left the region in 1846 and, as we have already noted, was met on the Rio Negro by Wallace in 1850. Fr. José's successor died in 1851, and although a further priest was appointed the mission closed down in 1852 (de Mattos, J.W. 1856: 125). John Lohrer of the Church Missionary Society paid a visit to the Rupununi in 1851 and the Macushi invited him to stay and offered to build a house and cut a field for him. He dismissed the offer on the grounds that a mission in the region was untenable until such time as the boundary issue was settled. He noted that the memory of Mr Youd was still alive among the Indians, and an 18-year-old woman said to him 'How do you do, Mr Youd', the only English she knew. In 1857 there were reports that the Brazilians were still making incursions with the aim of carrying off Indians (CW/O/55: 6, 9).

The mission at Waraputa did not survive long either. After Youd left, and subsequently died in 1842, James Pollitt was appointed to the place. This was a curious appointment to have been made because Pollitt had already served a number of years for the Society in Jamaica, and had suffered so severely from ill-health that he had been advised in 1841 not to return to a tropical climate. Even so he was appointed to Waraputa in November 1842, and arrived there in April the following year to find the place entirely run down and virtually deserted. Richard Schomburgk saw him there at the end of June and described the misery in which he and his family were living; indeed his sister-in-law took the opportunity to escape and accompanied the Boundary Commission's canoes to Georgetown. Pollitt himself did not last there much longer and was back in Georgetown by September. To all intents and purposes, that was the end of the mission. In 1844 there was brief interest in reviving it. For various reasons a relocation to Omai, below Potaro mouth and below the second set of the Essequibo falls, was proposed and although the governor approved the proposal nothing came of it because the intended incumbent, Bernau's assistant Edmund Christian, retired ill to Britain (CW/O/9b: 4; CW/O/24: 7; CW/O/67: 22; CW/O/68: 18, 19; CW/L/3: 103, 169, 172; RS, II: 320–3).

In 1868, Charles Barrington Brown travelled through the region in the course of conducting a geological survey. Of Pirara he writes that 'the charred hardwood upright posts of Mr. Youd's church still remain' and of Fort New Guinea he found 'an almost circular earthwork, four feet in height, and some thirty yards in diameter, surrounded by a shallow ditch, within which were the shattered remains of many beer and wine bottles' (1876: 135–6). He also visited Fort São Joaquim, where nothing much had changed. The place was barely manned and in a state of dilapidation, but the commandant was daily expecting stores and reinforcements to put the fort in thorough repair (1876: 297–8). Expectations identical to those of fifty-six years earlier, as expressed to Waterton by the then commandant.

The diplomatic negotiations continued for a while, but with relatively little success. In the autumn of 1843, the Brazilians sent an envoy, José de Araújo Ribeiro, to London to negotiate a new commercial treaty. Negotiations on this matter were already complicated enough given that they involved the cessation of the slave trade. Ribeiro, however, had orders to include in the discussions a settlement of the boundary question and brought forward some proposals to this effect. The Foreign Office referred the proposals to the Colonial Office on 17 October, but the latter declined to offer an opinion on them until Light had been consulted.

On 3 November Ribeiro sent the Foreign Office the draft treaties, one concerning commerce, the other the boundary. It appeared as though the acceptance of one was dependent on the acceptance of the other, although the nature of this dependency was to give rise to later misunderstanding. The following day the Foreign Office forwarded the draft boundary treaty to the Colonial Office, saying that there was some urgency attached to the matter and asking whether it would agree to dispense with consulting Light. The Colonial Office assented to this on condition that immediate settlement was desirable because of its bearing on other important interests, presumably referring to the commercial treaty. At the same time it recommended a different frontier line from that proposed by Ribeiro. The Brazilians proposed that the Rupununi River form the boundary line, whereas the British wanted the boundary to run along the Mahu and Takutu rivers.

The British Foreign Secretary, Lord Aberdeen, and Ribeiro met on 15 November and the former put forward the alternative boundary line, insisting that the British were not interested in territorial gain but merely concerned with the welfare of the Indians to whom they had given their word. Ribeiro then countered with the suggestion that those Macushi who wished to become British citizens would be given safe passage to British Guiana and that Brazil would give its word not to molest the Indians. Aberdeen contemptuously dismissed the value of the Brazilian word and proposed that the Brazilian line stand but that a bulge be made in it so that Pirara fell in British territory. Ribeiro, in response, demonstrated that he had some knowledge of Amerindians. He pointed out that it was quite likely that by now the area around Pirara had been deserted by all the Indians. He continued that:

> as for the protection [of the Indians] to which so much importance was attached, it was in fact meaningless; that in Brazil the alleged circumstance had been considered as the pretext and not the true reason for the invasion; that I could prove to him with documents that these same Indians or those from the same region went more than once to Fort São Joaquim requesting protection from and friendship with the Brazilian government or its authorities, which was the means that they practised in order to obtain the presents which they were normally given on these occasions.

Negotiations continued on 18 November when Aberdeen reiterated the demand that Pirara be included in British territory. His fallback position from this was that if the treaty had an additional article dealing with the Macushi then it should include a clause stating that the Brazilians would protect the Indians who remained at Pirara. Ribeiro was unable to accept this on the grounds that this would be an intrusion into Brazilian internal affairs, as the Indians who remained there would be Brazilian citizens. No agreement was reached, but on 22 November Ribeiro presented a treaty amended by the addition of an article which stated that Brazil would provide assistance and protection in order to facilitate the passage to British territory of those Macushi Indians who wished to become British subjects. This, however, the Colonial Office declined to accept without first consulting Light on conditions at Pirara and the circumstances of the Indians in the neighbourhood.

At a further meeting, on 24 November, Aberdeen pointed out that the problem was that Ribeiro was empowered to sign both the treaties or neither. Ribeiro denied this by saying that whereas he was not in a position to conclude the commercial treaty without concluding the frontier question, the other way round was possible. However, an impasse had been reached and the following day Ribeiro wrote requesting an audience in order to take his leave. Even so some further diplomatic sniping continued into December. Early that month Aberdeen repeated that the breakdown in negotiations resulted from the condition that the two treaties were inseparable despite the fact that the boundary 'has no connection whatever with the question of commercial relations'. Ribeiro replied a week later complaining that the British government's insistence that agreement over sugar imports depended on the emancipation of the slaves did not seem to be to any more closely connected with commerce than the boundary question (Braz 2nd Mem, Ann I: 207–15; Brit C, Ann II, ii: 13–14; CO111/206: 1943, 2083, 2209; CO112/25: 156, 164, 173).[4]

Light's response to the Colonial Office's request for comments on Ribeiro's proposals, when it arrived the following year, was far too late to have any bearing on the matter. Even so his position, as advised by Schomburgk, was predictable and would have done nothing to help reach an agreement if it had been in time. It was that no ground should be yielded to the Brazilians as they had no right to it, and as for the additional article concerning the Brazilians' assurance of safe passage to the Indians, it could not be put into effect (CO111/208: 324).[5]

The question of the boundary re-emerged in 1845 in conjunction with a further attempt to agree a commercial treaty, but once again the negotiations got nowhere. After that the item more or less dropped off the agenda until the final decade of the century and then, when there was still no agreement in sight, both countries agreed to send the matter to arbitration in 1901. The arbitrator, the King of Italy, gave his decision on 6 June 1904. Unable to accept that either country had established unquestioned right over the disputed territory and finding it impossible to divide it into equal portions, the king drew the boundary along geographical features, the Rivers Mahu and Takutu. This gave the larger area to Great Britain but these rivers remain the frontier between Brazil and Guyana.

Notes

1. This voyage was the first made by steamboat on the Amazon. The upstream voyage from Belém to Manaus took nine days, including towing a heavily laden canoe from Santarém onwards. The downstream journey took four and a half days. However, despite President Silva Pontes's pleas for the provision of a steamboat, the Guapiassú did not remain in the region, for in 1849 the then President of Pará renewed requests for a steamboat (AHI/308/4/2/; d'Azambuja 1961: 288; Santa Rosa 1926: 73.

2. It must have been later than July because we know that the expedition did not reach Manaus until the 28th of that month. I have not been able to trace the source of Rio Branco's statement. It is also noticeable that very little use was made of their report in the Brazilian memoir at the time of the frontier arbitration.

3. Official knowledge of the geography of the interior must have still been rather hazy. It is difficult to see how a missionary located at Waraputa could have had any influence on events at Pirara.

4. In fact both Aberdeen and Ribeiro were wrong when they denied these respective connections. From the perspective of the other country these things were closely associated. Thus Aberdeen failed to appreciate that for Brazil the questions of the boundary and commerce were related because in both cases it was a matter of national sovereignty and integrity. Likewise Ribeiro was wrong to assume that sugar and slavery had nothing to do with one another. Because of the abolition of slavery in the British Caribbean and the monopoly those colonies had in supplying sugar to the United Kingdom, the British were paying a much higher price for their sugar than anyone else in Europe.

5. For a full discussion of the negotiations between Great Britain and Brazil on the renewal of the 1827 commercial treaty and how the question of the boundary related to them, see Manchester 1933: 293–6 and Pryor 1965: 240–56.

CHAPTER 10

AFTERTHOUGHTS

Farage (1991) has argued that the frontier dispute of the nineteenth century was a legacy of the Amerindian policies pursued by the Dutch and Portuguese in the preceding centuries. As she observes, the Brazilian policy had been to form alliances with Amerindian groups, then declare them to be Brazilian subjects and, as a result, claim their territory as part of Brazil. The Dutch, while following a similar policy of Indian alliances, tended to be interested less in territorial rights than in trade, of goods or slaves. When it came to settling the question of the frontier, the British, claiming to be the legitimate heirs of the Dutch, mainly but not exclusively based their claims to territory on former alliances with groups of Amerindians. The Brazilians, on the other hand, tended to ignore their past policy of claiming rights to a territory through alliance to its inhabitants. Instead they based their argument on date of earliest permanent colonization.

Why, however, the frontier dispute should have erupted at this time is a different matter; one to which Governor Light had the answer when he wrote in January 1844 that 'had it not been for our successful, but now abandoned mission at Pirara there would have been no discussion as to the limits of territory' (CO111/208: 324). While it is obvious that the question of the limits between Brazil and British Guiana would have had to be settled at some point, it is unlikely that the matter would have arisen at that particular time if it had not been for the founding of the Pirara mission. We have seen that although the Church Missionary Society had for a number of years contemplated setting up a mission among the Indians of the interior, the Society as such never reached a decision on the matter and never gave permission for it. It was the sole initiative of Youd who, without permission, and indeed with directions to do no more in the interior than make exploratory trips, founded the Pirara mission. Indeed, one of the unexplained things from this work is why neither the Society nor the Committee made a determined effort to stop Youd from founding a mission against their instructions, for he never tried to hide what he intended to do. In this case the action of the Society contrasts greatly with the two severe reprimands it issued to Youd who, when still a catechist, had referred in his journal to preaching to the Indians and had thus usurped the duty and privilege of an ordained minister.

It is clear that Youd, at least when he first went to Pirara, was not the slightest bit interested in political matters. His expectation was that because he was only interested in saving souls and had no political motives the Brazilians would not mind his being at Pirara, even if it turned out to lie in Brazilian territory. This has all the hallmarks of innocence and naïvety rather than of cunning and political machination. Baron do Rio Branco later claimed that Youd was increasingly to suffer from imperialist greed, but it is difficult to see what evidence there is for this. It is true that Youd agreed to accompany the military expedition to Pirara, but his sole concern was with the spiritual and physical welfare of the Indians; he believed that the latter could only be ensured if they were under British protection and that they were British citizens. Territorial gain was a secondary consideration; it was merely a means to an end.

The notion of *civis Britannicus sum* was a value that carried some weight at the time. The incident at Pirara took place only four years before Palmerston was to order the bombardment of Piraeus in response to the maltreatment of Don Pacifico, a person with a rather flimsy claim to British citizenship. The years 1835 to 1860 have been described as the era marking the high tide of British gunboat diplomacy, and the frequent reference by those involved in the affair to how much easier it would be to settle the business by the dispatch of Royal Navy ships to blockade Brazilian ports is some indication of how deeply ingrained such a policy was. There is, however, another aspect to take into account: the humanitarianism that so strongly motivated the actions of those at the centre of the Pirara affair.

The British expressed their concern about the sovereignty over Pirara less in terms of disputed territory and more as a worry over the protection of British citizens who, it was feared, would be enslaved if Brazilians were left in control of the territory. Indeed, the agreement between the two countries to neutralise the disputed zone centred on the freedom and independence of the native population. That these things might be threatened by allowing the continued activities of Christian missionaries did not cross anyone's mind at that period. If territorial encroachment was the underlying motive for the whole expedition, and it seems unlikely that it was given the willingness with which the British withdrew their troops, then it made sense, given the values of the time, that it should be done in the cause of humanism and anti-slavery sentiment.

Britain had outlawed the slave trade in 1804 and abolished slavery in 1834, but Brazil had been unwilling to adopt similar measures despite the pressure that Britain brought to bear. The slave trade was still operating and did so until it was virtually put out of business by the Royal Navy in the 1860s. Brazil did not abolish slavery itself until 1888. The subject of slavery was a touchy one as far as Anglo-Brazilian relationships were concerned and even more so when it was a matter of Amerindians, the enslaving of whom was forbidden under Brazilian law. Towards the end of the century Baron do Rio Branco dismissed Schomburgk's account of slavery as an exaggeration aimed to exploit the philanthropic feelings of the British public. In fact the purpose of the expedition Schomburgk had seen had been to recruit men for the army and to arrest criminals. The enslaving of Amerindians, claimed Rio Branco, had been suppressed following Pombal's laws of the mid-eighteenth century (1897: 45). At the time, however, the Brazilian authorities, while strongly denying that Amerindians were enslaved, were perfectly aware that their treatment was not what it might be. We have noted that, in 1838, the Amazonian authorities, while claiming that there was nothing wrong with the employment of Indians, accepted that the manner of their recruitment left much to be desired. Ponte Ribeiro, in 1844, discussing the advantage of founding settlements in the disputed territory in order to support claims to it, noted that various Indian villages might form the base for these but that this would only be possible if the present dreadful system used against the Indians was changed. In the meantime the far better treatment they received at the hands of the English would induce them to desert to British Guiana (1895: 3–4).

Humanitarianism has been identified by Hyam as one of the powerful influences that directed British imperial policy during the early part of the nineteenth century. Certainly it is not difficult to identify this position among both those immediately involved and those in London. Among the latter we have already noted that two members of the Colonial Office, Lord Glenelg (colonial secretary 1835–39) and James Stephen (permanent under-secretary from 1836) were closely associated with the Church Missionary Society. At the same time, in this incident one can observe the change that Hyam has registered. 'Humanitarian influence declined after 1842. Its heyday was over. ... A humanitarian policy required strong imperial control and this was expensive; the treasury had no desire to finance moral crusades. ... increasingly arguments of humanity proved not to be enough' (1976: 45–6). The hard-nosed attitude of the Treasury to spending money on the boundary survey and the horror expressed when the actual cost of the military expedition became apparent have been amply documented.

The other impression one is left with is the relative lack of interest in and indecisiveness about the whole affair. As we have seen, Governor Light certainly could not interest the colonists in the question of their distant frontiers. Their minds were firmly concentrated on more immediate concerns, such as where they were going to find a labour force to work their plantations. Governor Light himself oscillated. At one point he was decidedly against sending troops into the interior, but within a year he had changed his mind and it was his recommendation on the occupation of Pirara that spurred the British government to take such an action. Even so there is an air of half-heartedness about this decision. There were almost immediately questions about the cost of the military expedition, which became more acute as it became apparent just how expensive it was. The Colonial Office was looking for ways to backtrack and when the chance of a agreement was announced it was quickly seized. By the time the troops were withdrawn almost everyone involved thought it was a poor, if not disastrous, idea. Nor was this half-heartedness confined to the military expedition. Worries were expressed as soon as it became apparent that the boundary survey could not be completed as some sort of spin-off from Schomburgk's geographical explorations and that there would be costs involved. These became more troublesome when it was discovered that the colony refused to contribute to the cost of the survey, and the point was even reached where scrapping the survey was seriously proposed. In fact it was only completed because of the length of time it took for a decision to be reached on the matter.

Governor Light on various occasions alluded to the commercial possibilities that holding the Pirara portage would open up. Even so he admitted to the present barrenness of the area and saw the securing of the region merely as an investment in future development. Light, however, never went near the interior, and, more often than not, he seems simply to be echoing Schomburgk's voice. It was rare for officials in London to put forward commerce as any reason for claiming the region round Pirara. Nor had they any obvious grand design of imperial gain, or if they had it certainly does not reveal itself in their comments and minutes. However, they, like everyone else involved, put forward again and again the welfare of the Indians and Britain's moral obligation to provide protection for them as the reasons why Britain should lay claim to the disputed territory. Even when there was almost a negotiated agreement on the frontier as part of a wider commercial treaty, it foundered on the question of the British promise to protect the Indians' welfare.

If there was a hidden agenda and territorial acquisition was the real aim, it was either cunningly dressed up in terms of a pseudo-humanitarianism or people were being used as a metaphor for territory. There is, however, no real reason to suppose that the concern for the Indians was not genuine, and that claims to territory were anything other than the means to an end, i.e. the protection of the Indians. The idea of persuading the Indians to settle nearer to the coast where more adequate protection could be afforded them and where they could provide labour in return for the benefits of civilization failed, because, it was said, that the Indians would not leave their homes. It is far more likely that the Indians' refusal to move was based on an awareness of the dangers from disease, bad enough in the interior, that arose from close contact with the coastal population. The decision to occupy Pirara followed from the fact that this was the only way in which British protection could be extended to these people.

The factor that we have not yet taken into account is the presence of Robert Schomburgk in the interior of British Guiana throughout the whole affair. His determination and actions, alongside those of Youd, were crucial to what happened. To some extent their motivations overlapped. There is no doubt that Schomburgk applauded and supported Youd's efforts to bring Christianity and civilization to the Indians and strongly disapproved of the Brazilians' treatment of them. Schomburgk's position on this is interesting. We have observed that he changed his mind between 1837 and 1840 on the best policy to adopt concerning the Indians and that his view influenced official policy. In the former year, he had argued in favour of persuading the Indians to settle near the coast; in the latter he declared such a policy to be impracticable and stated that protection ought to be extended to Indians in their own territories. This change of heart was in line with a coincidental adjustment to his view of where the British Guiana boundary lay. This is a topic at which we have looked only in passing and it is something to which a separate work might be devoted. Briefly, however, during his early years in British Guiana, Schomburgk was relatively vague about, even uninterested in, the southwestern boundary of the colony. In his first visit to the interior, he referred to the boundary, as marked on maps, as striking the Rupununi River at Annai and then running south down that river. Even in August 1838, at the time he witnessed the abduction of the Wapishiana Indians, he was still referring to the Rupununi as the boundary. It would, however, appear to have been this incident that made him rethink the question of where the frontier lay. That same month he remarked that the safety of the Indians could only be assured by a survey to settle the line of the frontier. By November 1838, he was proposing for the first time a boundary that lay much further west, along the Takutu and the Surumu Rivers. Nothing else seems to have happened at this time that could account for Schomburgk's sudden interest in the boundary question.

It must be added that, without abandoning his humanitarian feelings concerning the fate of the Indians (and there is no reason to believe these were anything but genuine and sincere), Schomburgk was able to square them with his imperialist ambitions. If the Indians were unwilling to move from their territory and the proper thing to do was to protect them, then the answer was to exert a claim to that territory. The alternative to this is that Schomburgk saw in the slave-raiding incident a morally impeccable justification for drawing the boundary to Britain's commercial advantage.

Schomburgk had appreciated from the outset the great commercial potential the Pirara region offered. He had a grandiose vision of the possibilities. In 1837 he foresaw no difficulty in connecting the Rupununi with the Mahu via Pirara, and whereas he was uncertain about feasibility of a canal he saw nothing to prevent the construction of a railway. He wrote that he thought that:

> The object of opening a communication between the Essequibo and the Amazon, is of such importance, that it ought to form one of the first considerations in the question of Colonizing the Interior of British Guiana (CO111/150: 2977).

He saw this as opening up a vast area to trade. In his *Description of British Guiana* he went further and stated that 'during the rainy season, the river Amazon and the upper Orinoco may be reached from Demarara entirely by inland navigation ... [and this] with a little trouble ... might be extended ... to the Pacific on the west, and to Buenos Ayres on the south' (1840: 150). Even so it is difficult to accept that, with his wide geographical knowledge and his great local experience, he believed quite so unreservedly in the commercial advantages that would arise from holding the Pirara portage as he had expressed in his writing. He must have realised the difficulties of transport in a country in which the water level in the rivers might fall so low that it was necessary to dig channels in their beds in order to move the canoes. Nor can he have been so shortsighted as not to have appreciated what impact the advent of steamships on the Amazon would have on travel and transport in Pará. If it is worth questioning whether Schomburgk's overt humanitarian concern was a cover for imperialist designs, it is equally right to ask whether the reverse might not be the case. In other words there is the possibility that Schomburgk used the lure of commercial advantages to interest the British government, realising that the humanitarian bait was not in itself enough.

Whichever may be right, not even Schomburgk had the imperialist dreams of extending the boundaries of the British Empire to the north bank of the Amazon that many Brazilians, then and since, have attributed to him. He had not been in favour of sending a military force to Pirara, proposing instead a few policemen. There is no evidence of an imperial conspiracy of the sort that the Brazilians suspected and which had the effect of freezing them into inactivity, fearful that anything they did would be taken by the British as a pretext for further advances. Indeed the lack of any planned strategy becomes only too obvious when we look at the British government's actions and reactions in the whole affair. It would be wrong, however, to dismiss the Brazilians' fears as complete paranoia because in 1841, Palmerston wrote to the Board of Trade, noting that the main rivers of South America, including the Amazon had 'not been rendered available for commercial intercourse with the interior of the country' and that in due course 'the use of them may render these great water communications ... available for the purposes of commerce' (quoted in Hyam 1976: 23).

At the same time British attitudes and behaviour were almost invariably high-handed and arrogant. This was true at all levels, whether it was the Foreign Office informing foreign states that their boundaries were to be surveyed and they could object to the result if they wanted; or the offhand way in which the Earl of Aberdeen treated the Brazilian minister, Araújo Ribeiro, or the British Guiana inspector-general of police gave peremptory orders for the evacuation of Pirara with threats of force if they are not obeyed; or the way in which Richard Schomburgk mockingly describes the table manners of the Brazilians in the Upper Rio Branco. Indeed, when Hamilton in Rio de Janeiro complained that:

> The most inveterate prejudices, the most unbounded vanity and self confidence are to be combated here, and under such disadvantages candid argumentation has but little chance to obtain a fair hearing (CO111/197: 1116)

one wonders which side he was writing about.

The Brazilians have never lost the conviction, voiced at the time and frequently since, that the whole affair was a plot to further British imperialist interests and expand their frontiers to the Amazon. Duarte da Ponte Ribeiro, writing soon after the affair was over, referred to Fort São Joaquim as 'the single floodgate that prevented the ambitious torrent of Great Britain reaching the Amazon' (1895: 4). Another writer of the same period, Luiz Augusto May, claimed that Youd had been sent by the English authorities, who had their eyes on the Rivers Amazon and Negro and were demonstrating in these regions the same greed for trade that they had practised all over the world. Nor does this theme go away. Ernesto Mattoso, sometime Brazilian consul in Georgetown, was convinced that Youd had been instructed to invade Brazilian terrritory and to persuade Indians to desert (1898: 130). As recently as 1968, the eminent Brazilian historian, Arthur Ferreira Reis, repeated the view that it was a British imperial plot to extend markets for manufactured goods and secure new sources of raw materials, although he gives due recognition to the part played by Schomburgk's personal ambitions in the affair (1968: 117–29).

A French commentator, shortly after the arbitration made by the King of Italy, accepted that neither of the first two expeditions were political; the first, that of Schomburgk, was purely scientific, and the second, that of Youd, exclusively religious. However, he continues, success and ambition gradually went to Schomburgk's and Youd's heads so that the idea grew of their becoming the founders of an empire (Fauchille 1905: 3–5). Whereas there may be some truth in these remarks in so far as they apply to Schomburgk, there is no evidence at all to suggest that Youd had any imperial vision that was not driven by the desire to spread the protestant faith.

On the other hand I do not finding it too surprising that Brazilians had difficulty in understanding the British motives. Early on in the whole affair, a president of Pará remarked that the British, friends of humanity in the abolition of black slavery, were now showing themselves attentive to the salvation of souls, occupying territory in order to save the souls of the inhabitants. But, on the whole, one may expect a certain scepticism on the part of the Brazilians about British humanitarianism, especially given the dispute about the slave trade and slavery that gave rise to accusations of meddling with Brazil's internal affairs. The present international worries about the fate of the Amazon region represent a similar example. Many Brazilians today, like those from other developing countries, feel that the developed nations have got rich on the exploitation of their own environments, and are now trying to prevent them from getting rich on theirs.

The Pirara affair is a small and relatively insignificant incident in British imperial history. It does, however, illustrate that at least parts of an empire may be the result not of any grand design, but rather of the unintended outcome of a number of individuals going about their own lives with Britain absent-mindedly looking on. Hyam has written about the problem of getting 'public support at home for the effective maintenance of the empire, for it was the public, not the policy-makers, who behaved with a 'fit of absence of mind' about the empire for much of the century' (1976: 16). In the case of Pirara it was not the absent-minded public at home, almost totally unaware of the incident, that was involved, but the actions of a few individuals who forced on the policy-makers steps they were loath to take. If this cannot be accurately described as 'absent-mindedness', it certainly suggests a loss of attention. Policy became, like a sticking plaster, first-aid to be applied after the event.

APPENDIX

CHRONOLOGY OF MAIN EVENTS

1831

March/April — Armstrong founds mission at Bartica Point.

1832

December — Youd arrives at Bartica Point.

1833

February/May — Armstrong visits Pirara.

1835

October — Robert Schomburgk sets out on first expedition to the interior.

1836

March — Schomburgk returns from first expedition.
November — Youd ordained as deacon and marries Rachel Adamson.

1837

January — Bernau arrives at Bartica Grove.
September — Schomburgk sets out on third expedition.
December — Youd receives permission from Corresponding Committee to undertake exploratory trip into the interior.

1838

January — Mrs Youd seriously ill.
February — Youd takes his wife to Barbados to recuperate and is ordained a priest while there. Returns to British Guiana.
March — Mrs Youd dies.

CHRONOLOGY OF EVENTS

April 5	Youd leaves to set up mission at Pirara.
May 15	Youd arrives at Pirara.
June 30	Schomburgk and Youd arrive at Fort São Joaquim, where they are greeted by Pedro Ayres. Schomburgk spends the rainy season there and Youd returns to Pirara, arriving there on 7 July.
August	Brazilian pressgang arrives at Fort São Joaquim. Ambrosio Ayres, Commander of the Upper Amazon receives news of Youd's mission. He sends Captain Leal to investigate.
August 8	Ambrosio Ayres killed.
August	News of Brazilian pressgang reaches Pirara.
August 25	Brazilian pressgang departs downstream with Wapishiana Indians.
September	Youd reconnoitres alternative site for mission at Urwa.
September	Schomburgk returns to Pirara.
October	Schomburgk leaves for journey to Esmeralda on the Orinoco River.
October 8	Ambrosio Ayres's report received in Santarém.
November 3	Leal arrives at Pirara and departs in search of boundary marker at Siparuni Mouth on 5 November.
November 11	Pedro Ayres in Santarém. Commander at Santarém writes to Youd.
November 22	President of Pará receives news of Youd's mission.
November 25	Leal returns from Siparuni and departs downstream.
November/ December	Youd visits Indians of the Upper Rupununi.

1839

January	Youd at Bartica Grove.
March	Youd in Georgetown.
	Leal's report on his reconnaissance reaches Santarém.
March 13	Youd marries Jane Ross and leaves to found mission at Urwa.
April	Leal's report reaches president of Pará.
May 1	Schomburgk arrives back at Pirara from his journey to Esmeralda and finds Brazilian detachment under command of Pedro Ayres in occupation.
May 17	Youd arrives at Pirara and receives letter from commander at Santarém.

May 23	Youd arrives at Urwa.
June	Ayres abandons Pirara and flees to Venezuela.
June 20	Schomburgk arrives back in Georgetown at end of his 3rd expedition.
September	Schomburgk arrives in London.

1840

January 1	Mrs Youd dies.
January 30	Leal and Fr. José arrive at Pirara.
February 1	Youd receives letter from Fr. José inviting him to Pirara.
February 6	Youd arrives at Pirara.
February 11	Youd returns to Urwa having been warned that he must leave Brazilian territory.
February 29	Leal visits Urwa with written instruction for Youd to leave.
March	Youd evacuates Urwa.
	British government decide to proceed with boundary demarcation.
April	Youd visits Georgetown with deputation of Indians protesting at Brazilian action.
	Schomburgk appointed boundary commissioner.
May	Youd founds mission at Waraputa.
	President of Pará receives Fr. José's report of meeting with Youd.
November	Foreign Office informs Brazilians of proposed boundary survey.

1841

January	Schomburgk arrives in Georgetown to begin boundary survey.
February	Brazilians learn of boundary survey and propose sending their own commission.
February 4	Light sends Crichton with message to Brazilians at Pirara that they must retire.
March 30	Crichton back in Georgetown having completed his mission.
May 21	Light proposes that Pirara should be occupied by troops.
June	Fr. José in Belém with news of Crichton's mission.
August	Decision taken to send troops to Pirara.

CHRONOLOGY OF EVENTS 181

September	de Mattos appointed Brazilian boundary commissioner.
December 10	Brazilian government informed of British intention to send troops to Pirara.
December 23	Boundary commission leaves Georgetown for Pirara.

1842

January 8	Brazilians propose that Pirara be declared neutral territory until boundary question settled.
January 11	Military expedition leaves Georgetown.
February 9	Boundary commission arrives Pirara Landing.
February 12	Military expedition arrives Pirara Landing.
February 14	Pirara, virtually abandoned by the Brazilians, occupied by British forces and Youd re-installed. de Mattos sets out from Belém.
February 28	Meeting between British and Brazilians (Leal and Fr. José) who have been summoned to Pirara. Brazilians given orders to leave.
March 2(?)	Brazilians evacuate Pirara.
March 10–12	Troops construct and occupy Fort New Guinea.
March–May	Survey of the Takutu and erection of boundary markers.
April	News of occupation of Pirara reaches Belém.
May	Brazilian neutrality proposals agreed by British government.
June	News of occupation of Pirara reaches Rio. News of erection of boundary markers reaches Belém. Brazilian military force ordered to the frontier, but order cancelled in July.
June 3	Youd leaves Pirara.
June 15	Orders issued for troops to withdraw from Pirara.
August	Youd dies at sea.
August 4	President of Pará orders Brigadier d'Oliveira to reconnoitre Upper Rio Branco.
August 22	Orders to withdraw reach Pirara.
September	News of erection of boundary markers reaches Rio.
September 1	Troops leave Pirara.
September 11	Survey of northwestern frontier begins.
September 14	Troops arrive back in Georgetown.

Oct/Nov	Discussions in London concerning removal of boundary markers. It is agreed to remove them.
November	Brazilian boundary commissioners (Seweloh and Pederneiras) arrive in Belém from Rio.
December 12	d'Oliveira's expedition reaches São Joaquim.
December 16	de Mattos dismissed from boundary commission.

1843

January	d'Oliveira's expedition retires.
March 24	Schomburgk arrives back at Pirara.
April	Boundary markers removed.
	de Mattos reaches São Joaquim.
April 30	Boundary commission sets off on Courantyne survey.
May	Brazilian boundary commissioners leave Belém for Rio Branco. Seweloh recalled and dismissed.
June	de Mattos hears of his dismissal.
	Last of boundary commission abandon Pirara.
July	Two new Brazilian boundary commissioners (Carneiro de Campos and Taulois) arrive in Belém and depart for the Rio Branco.
August (?)	Brazilian boundary commissioners in Upper Rio Branco.
October 3	de Mattos back in Belém.
October 13	British boundary commission returns to Georgetown after survey of the Courantyne.
Oct/Nov	Araújo mission to London. Negotiations fail.

BIBLIOGRAPHY

Abbreviations

AHI	Arquivo Histórico do Itamaratí.
ANB	Arquivo Nacional, Rio de Janeiro.
Braz M	The Brazilian case in the boundary dispute with Great Britain.
Brit C	The British case in the boundary dispute with Brazil.
Brit C-C	The British counter-case in the boundary dispute with Brazil.
Brit A.	The British argument in the boundary dispute with Brazil.
CW	Church Missionary Society Archives.
CO	Colonial Office Papers, Public Record Office.
FO	Foreign Office Papers, Public Record Office.
JRGS	Journal of the Royal Geographical Society.
NAG	National Archives, Guyana.
RGS	Royal Geographical Society.
RHS	Robert H. Schomburgk.
RS	Richard Schomburgk.
WO	War Office Papers, Public Record Office.

Primary Sources

Manuscripts

Arquivo Histórico do Itamaratí, Rio de Janeiro

AHI/308/4/1 Governo do Pará: Officios 1825–41.
AHI/308/4/2 Governo do Pará: Officios 1842–43.
AHI/308/4/11 Governo Estaduais do Pará: Avisos Expedidos.
AHI/SP Arquivo particular de Rodrigo de Sousa da Silva Pontes.

Arquivo Nacional, Rio de Janeiro

ANB/IG[1]10 Ministério da Guerra – Pará, Correspondencia do Presidente da Provincia 1835–40.
ANB/IG[1]11 Ministério da Guerra – Pará, Correspondencia do Presidente da Provincia 1841–43.
ANB/IJJ[9]110 Presidentes do Pará: Correspondencia com o Ministério do Império, Vol. 29, 1834–40.
ANB/IJJ[9]111 Presidentes do Pará: Correspondencia com o Ministério do Império, Vol. 30, 1841–52.

Church Missionary Society Archives, University of Birmingham

CW/L1 & L2 Letter-books, outgoing.
CW/M1, M2 & M3 Letter-books, incoming.

CW/O/1–100 Original incoming documents.

National Archives, Guyana
NAG/MBD Miscellaneous Boundary Documents.
NAG/MCP Minutes, Court of Policy.
NAG/GSO Letter-Book, 1839–41, Government Secretary's Office.

Public Record Office, Kew
CO111 Original Correspondence – Guiana, British.
CO112 Correspondence, etc., Entry Books of – Guiana, British.
FO13 General Correspondence – Brazil.
FO128 Embassy and Consular Archives – Brazil.
WO1 War Office in-letters.
WO6 War Office out-letters.

Royal Geographical Society, London
RGS/RHS/Corr: Letters from RHS to RGS.
RGS/RHS/MS: RHS's journal manuscripts.

Printed documents

Baena, Antônio Ladislau Monteiro, 1841a, Letter to Januário da Cunha Barbosa, Biblioteca Nacional, Rio de Janeiro (I-3, 11, 42).

Braz M1, The Brazilian case in the boundary dispute with Great Britain, First Memoir (1903), Annexes 1–5.

Braz M2, The Brazilian case in the boundary dispute with Great Britain, Second Memoir (1903), Vols 1–3, Annexes 1–3.

Braz M3, The Brazilian case in the boundary dispute with Great Britain, Third Memoir (1903), Vols 1–4.

Brit C., The British case in the boundary dispute with Brazil (1903), Annexes 1–4.

Brit C-C., The British counter-case in the boundary dispute with Brazil (1903), Annexes 1–3.

Brit A., The British argument in the boundary dispute with Brazil (1903).

Ponte Ribeiro, Duarte de, 1842, *Memoria sôbre os limites do Império do Brasil come a Guiana Inglêsa*, Biblioteca Nacional (8, 1, 10).

Relatórios dos Presidentes do Pará. Arquivo Nacional (040/0/79), Rio de Janeiro.

Contemporary published works

Alexander, J.E., 1833, *Transatlantic sketches, comprising visits to the most interesting scenes in North and South America and the West Indies with notes on Negro slavery and Canadian emigration*, London: Richard Bentley.

Araujo e Amazonas, Lourenço da Silva, 1852, *Diccionario topographico, historico, descriptivo da Comarca do Alto-Amazonas*, Recife: Typographia Commercial de Meira Henriques.

d'Azambuja, Joaquim Maria Nascentes, 1961 'Amazonia – Limites', *Revista do Instituto Histórico e Geográfico Brasileiro*, 250: 286–93.

Baena, Antônio Ladislau Monteiro, 1841b, 'Memoria sobre o intento, que tem os Inglezes de Demerari de usurpar as terras ao oeste de Rio Repunuri adjacentes a face austral da cordilheria do Rio Branco para amplificar a sua colonia', *Revista do Instituto Histórico e Geográfico Brasileiro*, III: 322–32.

Barrington Brown, C., 1876, *Canoe and camp life in British Guiana*, London: Edward Stanford.

Bernau, J.H., 1847, *Missionary Labours in British Guiana*, London: John Farquhar Shaw.

Brett, W.H., 1851, *Indian missions in Guiana*, London: George Bell.

— 1868, *The Indian tribes of Guiana; their condition and habits*, London: Bell and Daldy.

Goodall, Edward A., 1962a, 'Diary during his sojourn in Georgetown from 28th July to 11th December 1841', *Journal of the British Guiana Museum and Zoo*, 35: 39–53.

— 1962b, 'Diary 23rd December 1841–13th June 1842 (on the Essequibo & Rupununi Rivers)', *Journal of the British Guiana Museum and Zoo*, 36: 47–64.

— 1977, *Sketches of Amerindian Tribes 1841–1843*, London: British Museum Publications.

Hilhouse, William, 1896, 'Up the Cuyuni in 1837', *Timehri*, 10 (n.s.): 310–34.

de Mattos, João Henrique, 1844, *Exposição analitica do Forte de São Joaquim do Rio Branco, de Missão do Macuxi no Rio Pirará, e do Forte de S. Joxé da Barra do Rio Negro*, Biblioteca Nacional (I–32, 19, 3).

— 1979 [1845], 'Relatório do estado de decadência em que se acha o Alto Amazonas', *Revista do Instituto Histórico e Geográfico Brasileiro*, 325: 140–80.

May, Luiz Augusto, 1845, Observações sobre a navegação do Amazonas por occasião de baixarem por elle varios Peruanos en 1844, e outros pontos de politica externa que tem relação com of Brazil, Biblioteca Nacional (4, 3, 11).

Schomburgk, Richard, 1922, *Travels in British Guiana 1840–1844*, Vols I & II (trans. W.E. Roth), Georgetown: Daily Chronicle.

Schomburgk, Robert H., 1836, 'Report of an expedition into the interior of British Guiana', *JRGS*, VI: 224–84.

— 1840, *A description of British Guiana, geographical and statistical: exhibiting its resources and capabilities, together with the present and future condition and prospects of the Colony*, London: Simpkin, Marshall & Co.

— 1841a, 'Report of the third expedition into the interior of Guayana, comprising the journey to the sources of the Essequibo, to the Carumá Mountains, and to Fort San Joaquim, on the Rio Branco, in 1837–8', *JRGS*, X: 159–90.

— 1841b, 'Journey from Fort San Joaquim, on the Rio Branco to Roraima, and thence by the River Parima and Merewari to Esmeralda, on the Orinoco, in 1838–9, *JRGS*, X: 191–247.

— 1841c, 'Journey from Esmeralda, on the Orinoco, to San Carlos and Moura on the Rio Negro, and thence by Fort San Joaquim, to Demerara, in the spring of 1839', *JRGS*, X: 248–67.

— 1843, 'Visit to the sources of the Takutu, in British Guiana, in the year 1842', *JRGS*, XIII: 18–75.

— 1845, 'Journal of an expedition from Pirara to the Upper Corentyne, and from thence to Demarara', *JRGS*, XV: 1–104.

Wallace, A.R., 1889, *A narrative of travels on the Amazon and Rio Negro*, London: Ward, Lock & Co.

Waterton, Charles, 1973 [1825], *Wanderings in South America*, London: Oxford University Press.

Secondary Sources

Barata, Manoel, 1973, *Formação histórica do Pará*, Obras reunidas, Universidade Federal do Pará: Coleção Amazônica, Série José Veríssimo.

Bethell, Leslie, 1970, *The abolition of the Brazilian slave trade*, Cambridge: University Press.

Bittencourt, A, 1973, *Dicionário Amazonense de biografias vultos do passado*, Rio de Janeiro: Conquista.

Bos, G., n.d., Some notes on the history of the Pirara portage, unpublished MS.

Farage, N., 1991, *As muralhas dos sertões. Os povos indígenas no rio Branco e a colonização*, São Paulo: Editora Paz e Terra.

Fauchille, Paul, 1905, *Le conflit de limites entre le Brésil et la Grande-Bretagne et la sentence arbitrale du Roi d'Italie*, Paris: A. Pedone.

Hemming, J., 1987, *Amazon frontier. The defeat of the Brazilian Indians*, London: Macmillan.

— 1990a, 'How Brazil acquired Roraima', *Hispanic American Historical Review*, 70: 295–325.

— 1990b, *Roraima: Brazil's northernmost frontier*, University of London, Institute of Latin American Studies.

Hurley, J., 1936, 'Traços Cabanos', *Revista do Instituto Histórico e Geográfico do Pará*, 10: 3–284

Hyam, Ronald, 1976, *Britain's Imperial Century 1815–1914, A Study of Empire and Expansion*, London: B.T. Batsford.

Lloyd, C.A., 1895, 'Stray notes from Pirara', *Timehri*, 9 (n.s.): 220–32.

Manchester, Alan K., 1933, *British preëminence in Brazil, its rise and decline. A study in European expansion*, Chapel Hill: University of North Carolina Press.

de Mattos, João Wilkens, 1856, 'Alguns esclarecimentos sobre as missões da Provincia do Amazonas', *Revista do Instituto Histórico e Geográfico Brasileiro*, 19: 124–31.

Mattoso, Ernesto, 1898, *Estado do Amazonas. Limites da República com a Guyana Inglesa. Memoria justificativa dos direitos do Brasil*, Rio de Janeiro: Typographia Leuzinger.

BIBLIOGRAPHY

Menezes, M.N., 1977a, *British policy towards the Amerindians in British Guiana 1803–1873*, Oxford: Clarendon Press.

— 1977b, Introduction and Notes to *Sketches of Amerindian Tribes 1841–1843* by Edward A. Goodall, London: British Museum Publications.

Moore, Brian L., 1987, *Race, power and social segmentation in colonial society. Guyana after slavery 1838–1891*, New York: Gordon & Breach Science Publishers.

Ojer, Pablo, 1969, *Robert H. Schomburgk. Explorador de Guayana y sus líneas de frontera*, Caracas: Universidad Central de Venezuela.

Ponte Ribeiro, Duarte de, 1876, *Commissões scientificas nomeadas pelo Governo Imperial desde 1843 para exames de limites e demarcações da fronteira do Brazil com as Colonias e Estados confinantes*, Rio de Janeiro: Typographia Universal de E. & H. Laemmert.

— 1895, *Apontamentos sobre estado da fronteira do Brasil em 1844*, Rio de Janeiro: Imprensa Nacional.

Pryor, A.J., 1965, *Anglo-Brazilian commercial relations and the evolution of Brazilian tariff policy (1822–50)*, Unpub. Ph.D. thesis, University of Cambridge.

Reis, Arthur Cézar Ferreira, 1931, *Historia do Amazonas*. Manáos: Instituto Geográfico e Histórico do Amazonas.

— 1932, 'A explosão cívica de 1832', *Revista do Instituto Geográfico e Histórico do Amazonas*, 2: 45–63.

— 1935, *Manáos e outras villas*, Manáos.

— 1968, *A Amazônia e a cobiça internacional*, Rio de Janeiro: Gráfica Record Editôra.

Rio Branco, Barão de, 1897, *Mémoire sur la question des limites entre les États-Unis du Brésil et la Guyane Britannique*, Brussels: Imprimerie des Travaux Publics.

Rivière, P.G., 1972, *The forgotten frontier. Ranchers of Northern Brazil*, New York: Holt, Rinehart & Winston.

Rodway, James, 1889, 'The "Schomburgks" in Guiana', *Timehri*, 3 (n.s.), 1–29.

— 1896, 'Schomburgkiana', *Timehri*, 10 (n.s.): 132–50.

Santa Rosa, Renato B., 1926, 'Vias de communicação', *Revista do Instituto Histórico e Geográfico do Pará*, V, 57–83.

Schomburgk, O.A. (ed.), 1931 [1841], *Robert Hermann Schomburgk's travels in Guiana and on the Orinoco during the years 1835–1839* (trans. W.E. Roth), Georgetown: Argosy Company [Leipzig: George Wigand].

Souza, F.B. de, 1873, *Lembranças e curiosidades do Valle do Amazonas*, Pará: Typ. do – Futuro.

Stevenson, Canon, 1908, 'Ten years of mission life in Guiana', *The Guiana Diocesan Magazine and Diocesan Gazette*, 138: 122–5; 139: 142–3; 140: 158–60.

Swan, Michael, 1958, *The marches of El Dorado*, London: Jonathan Cape.

Whitehead, Neil L., 1988, *Lords of the Tiger Spirit. A history of the Caribs in Colonial Venezuela and Guyana 1498–1820*, Dordrecht & Providence: Foris Publications.

INDEX

Aberdeen, Lord, 123, 124, 144, 145, 166, 167, 168(n.4), 176.
Aborigines' Protection Society, 18, 40, 48(n.5).
Adamson, Rachel, *see under* Youd.
Alfred (Youd's Macushi interpreter), 21–2, 24, 30, 31–2, 47(n.1), 56, 76.
Amapa, 7, 77.
Amazonas, 4, 58, 114, 157.
Amazon River, 1, 2, 7, 55, 82, 100, 113, 126, 127, 132, 133, 156, 174, 175, 176.
Amerindians, 1, 2, 3, 4, 5, 6, 7, 8(n.2), 8(n.4), 10, 12, 14, 15, 16, 19, 21, 16, 18(n.5), 31, 34, 35, 35, 36, 37, 39, 40, 41, 42, 43, 44, 45, 46, 50, 51, 52, 53, 54, 55, 56, 57, 60, 62, 63, 65, 67, 70, 71, 75, 76, 77, 82, 89, 93, 94, 95, 96, 97–8, 100–1, 107, 108, 113, 114, 117–8, 120(n.14), 123, 132, 136, 137(n.5), 140, 146, 147, 160(n.12), 166, 169, 170, 171; British protection of, 62, 65, 66, 67, 69, 72–3, 79, 86, 95, 141, 145, 147, 148, 166, 173, *see also* Macushi *or* Wapishiana.
Amucu, Lake, 1.
Annai (Amerindian village), 17, 30, 44, 150, 174.
Armstrong, John (missionary), 10–2, 13, 14, 15–17, 18, 19, 20, 21, 22, 27(n.1), 28(n.2), 178.
Awarikuru Creek, 1, 94, 99, 100.
Ayres, Ambrosio Pedro (Military Commander of Upper Amazon), 32, 33, 35–6, 39, 40, 42, 47(n.3), 48(n.9), 53–4, 73(n.3), 82, 133, 179.
Ayres, Pedro Joaquim, 32, 33–4, 35, 38–9, 40, 43, 44, 48(n.5), 52,
53–4, 56, 73(n.3), 73(n.4), 81, 82, 127, 129, 133, 138(n.7), 144, 147, 149, 154, 157, 159(n.6), 179, 180.

Barbados, 20, 23, 24, 25, 30, 46, 50, 57, 100, 117, 120(n.16), 178; Bishop of, 18, 19, 20, 52.
Barrington Brown, Charles, 165.
Bartica Grove, 11, 12, 14–15, 16, 18, 19, 20, 21, 23, 29(n.10), 30, 31, 42, 44, 50, 51, 52, 57, 91(n.8), 94, 97, 115, 160(n.14), 178, 179.
Bartica Point, 10, 11, 12, 14, 15, 16, 27(n.1), 28(n.3), 30, 178.
Basiko (Macushi chief), 22, 44, 70, 150, 155, 163.
Belém, 2, 7, 45, 71, 84, 90, 123, 127, 129, 133, 134, 146, 147, 156, 161, 162, 168(n.1), 180, 181, 182.
Bernau, John (missionary), 15, 20, 23, 24, 27, 29(n.9), 29(n.10), 31, 42, 48(n.9), 51, 54, 57, 87, 88, 91(n.8), 91(n.9), 117, 118, 119(n.5), 120(n.16), 120(n.17), 132, 162, 163, 165, 178.
Bingham, Lt. Edmund Hayter (commander, British military expedition), 95, 96, 97, 98, 99, 100, 101, 102, 103, 104, 105, 106, 107, 108, 110, 111, 112, 114, 120(n.10), 120(n.11), 126, 131, 137(n.4), 137(n.5), 139, 140.
Booker Tate, x.
boundary between Brazil and British Guiana, markers, 104, 113, 125, 132–3, 135, 145, 146–7, 149, 150, 151, 152, 181, 182; negotiations concerning, 95, 104, 115–16, 122–3, 126, 130–1, 135, 144, 165–8, 168(n.4), 168(n.5); question of, vii, 8, 25, 27, 32, 35, 36, 39, 40, 41, 43, 45, 48(n.9), 53,

188

INDEX

54, 60, 61, 65, 66, 68, 77, 144, 169, 181; survey, cost of, 68, 141, 150–1, 172.
boundary commission, Brazilian, 89–90, 102, 104, 112, 126, 133, 134, 142, 149, 150, 152–3, 161–2, 180, 181, 182.
boundary commission, British, 67, 68, 72, 78, 85–7, 89, 90, 92, 93–4, 95, 98, 101, 104, 113, 114, 118(n.1), 118(n.2), 118(n.3), 119(n.8), 120(n.12), 127, 128, 139, 140, 141, 145, 147, 149, 150, 154, 155, 157, 158, 159(n.12), 161, 165, 180, 181, 182.
Bowlby, John George (assistant surgeon, British military expedition), 112, 132, 137(n.6).
Brazilian, Foreign Affairs, minister of, 44, 46, 76, 77, 84, 90, 91(n.2), 91(n.4), 122, 123, 125, 134, 135, 144; Foreign Affairs, Ministry of, ix, 70, 85, 89, 124, 126, 129, 135, 163; Minister in London (Marques Lisboa), 90, 95, 123, 144, 145, 153, 159(n.6); War, Ministry of, 136, 161.
Brett, William (missionary), 20, 27(n.1), 73(n.4).
British Academy, x.
British chargé-d'affaires in Rio de Janeiro (W.G. Ouseley), 76, 77, 78, 82, 83, 86, 90(n1), 91(n.4), 91(n.11), 122.
British Guiana, Bishop of, 162–3; Combined Court of, 7, 86, 89, 141; governor of, see Light or Smyth; plantocrats of, 7, 48(n.8).
British minister in Rio de Janeiro (H. Hamilton), 41, 53, 90, 91(n.11), 122, 123, 124, 125, 144, 145, 152, 159(n.5), 176).
Bush, Lt. Seddon William Settor (Adjutant, 1st West India Regiment), 95, 98, 102, 105, 132, 137(n.6).
Bush, Lt.-Col. William (commander, military forces in British Guiana), 85, 88, 99, 106.

cabanagem, 6–7, 33, 36, 38, 81, 82, 89, 128, 133.
Capadose, Lt.-C. Henry (commander, military forces in British Guiana), 124, 144.
Carneiro de Campos, Frederico (Brazilian boundary commission), 162, 182.
cattle, Brazilian, 4, 31, 35, 45, 64, 80–1, 82, 94, 105, 111, 127, 128, 139–40, 147, 149, 156, 157, 159(n.9), 164.
Church Missionary Society, see Society, the.
Coelho, Major Hygino José (commandant, Fort São Joaquim), 133, 146, 148, 149, 150, 152, 155, 156, 159(n.5), 164.
Colonial Office, the, ix, 40, 41, 55, 66, 67, 68, 72, 79, 82, 83, 84, 85–6, 87, 89, 104, 106, 115, 116, 120(n.15), 123, 124, 131, 141, 148, 150, 151, 158, 159(n.5), 165, 166, 167, 171, 172.
Committee, the, 10, 14, 15, 16, 23, 25, 26, 27, 27(n.2), 30, 32, 45, 46, 62, 71, 73(n.6), 73(n.8), 87, 88, 115, 116, 120(n.16), 132, 162, 169, 178.
Cordeiro, Capt. José Valente (commandant, Fort São Joaquim), 17–18, 28(n.7).
Corrêa de Araujo, Lt. Felisberto Antonio (commandant, Fort São Joaquim), 156, 159(n.8), 163.
Correa de Faria, Major Raimundo (Commander of Upper Amazon), 125, 126, 127.
Corresponding Committee of Church Missionary Society, see Committee, the.
Costa Pereira, Capt. José da (troop commander, Fort São Joaquim), 146, 156.
Courantyne River, 43, 150, 151, 152, 154, 182.
Crichton, William (Inspector-General of Police), 75, 79, 80–1, 82, 83, 84, 85, 88, 89, 90, 91(n.2), 95, 96,

97, 98, 99, 100, 101, 102, 103, 105, 106, 107, 108, 119(n.6), 119(n.8), 122, 123, 131, 136(n.2), 137(n.5), 176, 180.
Curtis, Mr (commissariat issuer, British military expedition), 95.

Davies, Ann, *see under* Youd.
descimentos, see Labour, recruitment of Indian.
Dowse, Richard Robert (assistant surgeon, British military expedition), 95, 97, 100, 105.
Doyce, John (Youd's assistant), 12, 20, 31, 51, 56, 57, 75, 76, 87, 91(n.8).
Dutch, the, 3, 4, 5, 8(n.4), 28(n.2), 169.
Dutch Guiana, 141, 151.
Dutch trade, 2–3, 169.

Esmeralda, 40, 52, 179.
Essequibo River, 1, 3, 6, 10, 17, 35, 40, 41, 42, 43, 51, 54, 61, 87, 150, 162, 165, 174.
Evaristo, 22, 29(n.11), 44, 53, 54, 63, 70, 76, 100, 105, 111, 112, 163, 164.

Farage, N., 169.
Foreign Office, the, 32, 67–8, 69, 70, 71, 72, 76, 83, 89, 90, 123, 124, 129, 145, 153, 159(n.5), 165, 175, 180.
Fort New Guinea, 109, 111, 120(n.12), 131, 165, 181.
Fort São Joaquim, 3, 5, 9(n.5), 9(n.6), 11, 17, 28(n.7), 32, 33, 34, 36, 37, 38, 39, 40, 42, 43, 44, 45, 47, 47(n.2), 47(n.4), 48(n.5), 51, 53, 54, 58, 59, 69, 73(n.3), 76, 79, 80, 81, 82, 84, 94, 101, 104, 112, 114, 120(n.11), 125, 126, 127, 128, 129, 131, 133, 135, 136, 136(n.2), 142, 144, 146, 147, 148, 149, 150, 152, 153, 154, 156, 157, 159(n.1), 163, 165, 166, 276, 179, 182.
French, the, 6–7, 61.
French Guiana, 7.
Fryer, William John (British boundary commission), 49(n.11), 92, 93, 94, 101, 111, 147, 148, 152, 155, 158.

Gatto, Manoel Affonço (commandant, Fort São Joaquim), 32, 40.
Georgetown, 2, 5, 10, 12, 13, 17, 25, 26–7, 28(n.2), 45, 47, 50, 52, 55, 56, 57, 60, 63, 65, 66, 73(n.5), 74(n.14), 75, 79, 81, 82, 83, 85, 86, 88, 89, 91(n.9), 92, 96, 97, 103, 105, 106, 107, 112, 116, 117, 118(n.2), 130, 132, 137(n.4), 140, 143, 150, 157, 158, 159(n.11), 160(n.12), 160(n.14), 165, 176, 179, 180, 181, 182.
Goodall, Edward (draughtsman, British boundary commission), x, 49(n.11), 59, 92–3, 94, 99, 100, 104, 108, 109, 111, 114, 118(n.1), 118(n.4), 119(n.6), 119(n.7), 120(n.9), 120(n.10), 120(n.12), 120(n.13), 141, 158.

Hackett, Lt. John (70th Regiment), 79–80, 81, 82, 89.
Hamilton, H., *see* British minister in Rio de Janeiro.
Hill, Lord (General Commander-in-Chief), 83.
Hilhouse, William, 15.
humanitarianism, 170, 171, 172, 173, 177.
Humboldt, Alexander von, 18.
Hyam, Ronald, 171, 172, 175, 177.

Indians, *see* Amerindians.
Ireng River, *see* Mahu River.
Italy, King of, 167–8, 176.

José, Fr., 58, 59–60, 61, 62, 63, 64, 70, 73(n.7), 74(n.10), 76, 80, 81, 82, 84, 85, 94, 100, 101, 102, 103, 104, 105, 107, 108, 110, 112, 113, 114, 119(n.8), 125, 126, 127, 132, 134–5, 136, 136(n.3), 137(n.8), 141, 143, 144, 146, 148, 149, 152, 153, 154, 155, 156–7, 158,

159(n.1), 159(n.11), 160(n.12), 163–4, 180, 181.

labour, 3, 36, 45; recruitment of Indian, 37–9, 43, 44, 47, 52, 62, 79, 148, 155, 171, see also slavery.
Leal, Capt. Antonio dos Barros (commandant, Fort São Joaquim), 36, 40, 41–2, 44–5, 48(n.9), 49(n.13), 51, 57–8, 61, 62, 63, 64, 73(n.7), 74(n.10), 76, 77, 80, 81, 82, 84, 85, 101, 102, 103, 104, 105, 111, 112, 113, 114, 126, 132, 133, 136, 139, 140, 142, 146, 147, 148, 149, 150, 152, 155, 156, 157, 160(n.11), 160(n.12), 179, 180, 181.
Liberadiña, Senhora, 103, 142.
Light, Sir Henry (Governor, British Guiana 1838–48), 28(n.6), 29(n.13), 37, 39, 40, 41, 42, 48(n.5), 48(n.8), 50, 53, 55, 59, 60, 62, 64, 65, 66, 67, 70, 74(n.12), 74(n.14), 75, 76, 77, 78, 79, 81, 82, 83, 84, 85, 86, 87, 88, 89, 93, 94, 95, 98, 100, 101, 102, 104, 106, 107, 108, 109, 110, 111, 113, 115, 119(n.5), 124, 126, 127, 129, 130, 131, 137(n.4), 140, 141, 144, 145, 148, 149, 150, 151, 158, 159(n.5), 160(n.14), 163, 165, 166, 167, 169, 172, 180.
Lisboa, Marques, see Brazilian, minister in London.
Lohrer, John (missionary), 164.
Lowe, Mr (Assistant Commissariat General, British military expedition), 95, 97, 111.

Macushi Indians, 5, 6, 8, 10, 18, 19, 20, 21, 22, 23, 24, 26, 30, 31, 37, 38, 39, 42, 44, 45, 58, 64, 67, 75, 76, 81, 93, 94, 99, 109, 114–5, 120(n.12), 120(n.13), 121(n.17), 145, 148, 152, 162, 163, 164, 166, 167.
Mahu river, 1, 35, 104, 113, 137(n.4), 141, 142, 152, 166, 168, 174.
Maister, Lt.-Gen. John (Military commander, the Caribbean), 83, 84, 89, 110, 123–4.
Manaus, 2, 32, 33, 53, 58, 60, 69, 73(n.5), 80, 125, 133, 134, 136(n.2), 137(n.3), 139, 153, 162, 168(n.1), 168(n.2).
Manchester, A.K., 91(n.2), 168(n.5).
Mattos, Colonel João Henrique de (Brazilian boundary commission), 89–90, 91(n.10), 126, 133, 134, 139, 142, 149, 150, 152, 153–4, 154–7, 159(n.8), 159(n.10), 160(n.12), 181, 182.
Mattoso, E., 176.
military expedition, Brazilian, 128–30, 133–4, 146–7, 148, 181.
military expedition, British, 83, 84, 87–8, 95–100, 101, 106–7, 108–9, 110–11, 113, 115, 116, 119(n.5), 119(n.6), 122, 123–4, 127, 128, 130, 131, 132, 135, 136, 137(n.4), 139, 141, 144, 145, 152, 157, 160(n.12), 170, 172, 175, 181; officers of, 49(n.11), 97, 98, 99, 100, 102, 104, 106, 119(n.6), 120(n.14), see also Bingham, Bush, Wieberg.

Ojer, P. 19.
Oliveira, Brigadier Francisco Sergio d' (military commander of Pará), 128, 133, 134, 146, 147, 148, 149, 150, 152, 156, 159(n.7), 181, 182.
Orinoco River, 4, 40, 43, 47(n.2), 137(n.7), 159(n.2), 175, 179.
Ouseley, W.G., see British chargé d'affaires in Rio de Janeiro.

Palmerston, Lord, 68, 72, 76, 83, 122, 170, 175.
Pará, 2, 7, 17, 33, 58, 59, 70, 71, 76, 81, 83, 85, 87, 89, 112, 122, 124, 132, 145, 152, 153, 160(n.12).
Pará, British consul at, 61, 69, 70, 85, 91(n.7), 125, 126, 127, 129, 133–4, 152, 153, 154, 161.
Pará, president of, 33, 42, 43, 44, 45, 46, 47, 52, 59, 60, 61, 62, 63, 69, 70, 71, 74(n.10), 77, 78, 84, 85,

90, 91(n.10), 103, 124, 125, 126, 127, 128, 129, 130, 131, 133, 134, 135, 136, 136(n.2), 136(n.3), 137(n.8), 139, 144, 145, 146, 147, 149, 152, 153, 161, 163, 168(n.1), 177, 179, 180, 181.

Pederneiras, Lt. Innocencio Veloso (Brazilian boundary commission), 161, 162, 182.

Pirara, vii, 1, 2, 5, 6, 8, 10–11, 17, 18, 26, 27, 18(n.7), 29(n.8), 29(n.12), 30–1, 35, 36, 38, 39, 40, 41, 42, 43, 47, 48(n.9), 49(n.11), 50, 51, 52, 53, 55–6, 58, 59, 60 61, 62, 63, 64, 66, 67, 68, 69, 70, 71, 72, 73, 76, 77, 78, 79, 80, 81, 82, 83, 84, 86, 87, 88, 89, 90 91(n.2), 91(n.11), 92, 94, 95, 96, 98, 99, 100, 101, 102, 103, 104, 105, 106, 107, 108, 109, 110, 111, 113, 114, 115, 116, 120(n.12), 122, 123, 124, 125, 126, 127, 128, 129, 130, 131, 134, 135, 136, 136(n.3), 137(n.4), 137(n.5), 137(n.6), 139, 140, 144, 146, 147, 148, 149, 150, 151, 152, 153, 154, 155, 157–8, 160(n.13), 162, 163, 164, 165, 166, 167, 168(n.3), 170, 172, 173, 174, 175, 176, 177, 178, 179, 180, 181, 182; mission, 30–32, 37, 38, 43, 44, 45, 46, 50, 74(n.10), 94, 107, 114, 115, 116, 117, 169, 179; mission, plans for, 10, 11, 18–19, 20–1, 22–3, 24, 25–7; territorial location of, 25, 27, 32, 35, 37, 39, 44, 45, 48(n.9), 53, 84, 146, 170.

Pirara Creek, 1, 109, 110.

Pirara Landing, 1, 18, 28(n.7), 39, 40, 58, 81, 94, 100, 103, 106, 181.

Pirara Mouth, 1, 102, 127.

Pirara Portage, 1, 2, 8(n.1), 66, 172, 175.

Pollard, William (Secretary, Corresponding Committee), 87, 116, 132, 162,

Pollit, James (missionary), 162, 164–5.

Ponte Ribeiro, Duarte de, 171, 176.

Portuguese, the, 3–4, 7, 8(n.2), 169.

Quatata Creek, 1.

Ranches, Brazilian, 4, 35, 36, 58, 80, 133, 148, 149.

Reis, Arthur Ferreira, 176.

Ribeiro, José de Araújo (Brazilian envoy), 165, 166, 167, 168(n.4), 176, 182.

Rio Branco, 1, 2, 3, 4, 5, 6, 8(n.2), 18, 35, 36, 42, 45, 47, 48(n.9), 52, 58, 59, 64, 71, 78, 84, 112, 113, 123, 125, 126, 127, 131, 133, 134, 139, 142, 154, 159(n.4), 161, 176, 181, 182.

Rio Branco, Baron do, 162, 168(n.2), 170, 171.

Rio Negro, 3, 6, 9(n.5), 40, 52, 58, 59, 89, 112, 113, 129, 144, 149, 164, 176.

Roraima, Mount, 40, 141, 142, 143.

Roraima, state of, 103.

Ross, Jane Ann, *see under* Youd.

Rouillon, Mon., 55, 70, 73(n.5).

Royal Navy, 8, 81, 87, 100, 132, 170, 171.

Rupununi River, 1, 5, 10, 17, 18, 28(n.2), 35, 39, 40, 43, 45, 47, 54, 56, 57, 60, 61, 62, 66, 76, 94, 98, 127, 135, 164, 166, 174, 179.

Russell, Lord John, 72, 83.

Santarém, 36, 43, 47, 52, 53, 162, 168(n.1), 179.

Santos Innocentes, José dos, *see* José, Fr.

Schomburgk, Richard, viii–ix, 9(n.5), 19, 27, 36, 42, 49(n.11), 59, 93, 94, 99, 100, 101, 102, 103, 104, 105, 109, 111, 112, 114, 116, 117, 118, 118(n.4), 119(n.5), 119(n.8), 120(n.12), 120(n.13), 125, 131, 132, 137(n.6), 142, 147, 148, 152, 154, 155, 156, 158, 159(n.4), 159(n.7), 160(n.11), 160(n.13), 160(n.14), 164, 176.

Schomburgk, Robert, 4, 15, 17, 18–19, 27, 18(n.6), 28(n.7), 29(n.8), 29(n.12), 30, 32, 33, 34, 36, 38, 39, 40, 41, 43, 44, 47(n.2),

INDEX

47(n.4), 48(n.5), 48(n.9), 49(n.12), 52, 53, 58, 59, 60, 66, 67, 68, 69, 72, 73(n.2), 74(n.16), 76, 77, 78, 79, 80, 81, 82, 85, 86, 87, 89, 92, 93, 98, 99, 100, 101, 102, 104, 108, 109, 113, 114, 119(n.6), 119(n.7), 119(n.8), 120(n.14), 127, 131, 132, 135, 139, 140, 141, 142, 143, 144, 145, 146, 147, 149, 150, 151, 152, 154, 157, 158, 159, 159(n.9), 160(n.14), 161, 167, 171, 172, 173, 174, 175, 176, 178, 179, 180, 182.
Seweloh, Lt.-Col. Adolfo Antonio Frederico (Brazilian boundary commission), 161, 182.
Siparuni river, 40, 41, 42, 75, 150, 179.
Slavery, 7–8, 11, 37–9, 44, 48(n.5), 48(n.9), 50, 52, 54, 61–2, 73(n.3), 76, 77, 78, 94, 113, 170, 171, 174, 177, *see also* labour, recruitment of Indian.
slaves, 3, 4, 5, 11, 39, 69, 169.
slave trade, 7–8, 9(n.8), 171, 177.
Smyth, Major-General Sir James Carmichael (Governor, British Guiana, 1833–8), 29(n.13).
Society, the, viii, x, 10, 13, 14, 16, 19, 20, 23, 25, 26, 27, 28(n.2), 31, 42, 48(n.10), 53, 54, 55, 62, 65, 73,(n.6), 75, 87, 88, 107, 114, 115, 116, 120, 164, 169, 170, 171.
Souza, Lt.-Col. Joaquim José Luis de (Military commander of Lower and Upper Amazon), 35, 42, 43, 44, 45, 47, 52, 53.
Spencer, James (British adventurer), 40–1, 42, 45, 48(n.11), 69–70, 73(n.5), 74(n.14).
Strong, Leonard (Secretary, Corresponding Committee), 10, 14, 16, 17, 26, 32, 87.
Stanley, Lord, 115, 159.
Surumu River, 40, 174.

Takutu Rivier, 1, 3, 38, 40, 104, 112, 113, 114, 120(n.12), 141, 142, 146, 152, 156, 159(n.1), 166, 168, 174, 181.

Taulois, Pedro (Brazilian boundary commission), 162, 182.
Tavares, Lt.-Col. Manoel Muniz (Commander of Lower and Upper Amazon), 125, 126–7, 136(n.2).
Teixera, Evaristo José, *see* Evaristo.
Treasury, the, 93, 150–1, 172.

Uraricoera River, *see* Rio Branco.
Urwa (mission station), 39, 42, 50, 51, 52, 53, 54, 55, 56, 57, 60, 61, 62, 63, 64, 66, 69, 73(n.7), 75, 179, 180.

Venezuela, vii, 53, 68, 73(n.4), 85, 127, 130, 133, 147, 151, 154, 159(n.6), 180.

Wallace, Alfred Russell, 59–60, 164.
Wapishiana Indians, 6, 19, 37, 38, 67, 147, 152, 174, 179.
Waraputa (mission station), 54, 75, 76, 81, 87, 88, 94, 97, 114, 115, 116, 117, 118(n.4), 150, 159(n.11), 162, 163, 164–5, 168(n.3), 180.
Waterton, Charles, 5, 9(n.6), 23, 29(n.12), 165.
West India Regiment, *see* military expedition, British.
Wieberg, Lt. John Andrew (officer, British military expedition), 95, 101, 131, 136.

Youd, Thomas (missionary), viii, ix, 10, 11, 12, 14, 15, 16, 17, 18, 19, 20, 21, 22, 23, 24, 25, 26, 27, 28(n.5), 30–2, 33, 34–5, 36, 37, 38, 39, 40, 41, 42, 43, 44, 45, 46, 47(n.1), 47(n.4), 48(n.5), 48(n.9), 48(n.10), 48(n.11), 49(n.13), 50, 51, 52, 53, 54, 55, 56, 57, 58, 59, 60, 61, 62, 63, 64, 65, 66, 69, 70, 71, 72, 73(n.1), 73(n.3), 73(n.6), 73(n.7), 74(n.10), 75, 76, 79, 81, 87, 88, 94, 96, 97–8, 100, 101, 102, 103, 104, 105, 107, 108, 109, 111, 114–15, 116, 118(n.4), 119(n.6), 119(n.8), 120(n.11),

120(n.13), 121(n.17), 127, 136, 140, 144, 145, 155, 157, 158, 159(n.11), 162, 163, 164, 165, 169, 170, 173, 176, 178, 179, 180, 181; Adamson, Rachel, Youd's first wife, 20, 23–4, 25, 26, 30, 46, 48(n.10), 178; character of, 12–13, 16–17, 32, 51, 54, 94, 118; Davies, Ann, proposal of marriage to, 13–14; death of, 116–18, 121(n.17), 137(n.6), 149, 181; Ross, Jane Ann, Youd's second wife, 50, 51, 52, 57, 117, 121(n.17), 179, 180.

Young, H.E.F. (Secretary, British Guiana government), 17, 28(n.6), 140, 160(n.14).

Yupukarri inlet, *see* Pirara Landing.